PLAYS BY RICHARD NELSON, EARLY PLAYS VOLUME THREE

BROADWAY PLAY PUBLISHING INC
56 E 81st St., NY NY 10028-0202
212 772-8334 fax: 212 772-8358
http://www.BroadwayPlayPubl.com

PLAYS BY RICHARD NELSON, EARLY PLAYS VOLUME THREE

First printing: May 1999
ISBN: 0-88145-152-5

Book design: Marie Donovan
Word processing: Microsoft Word for Windows
Typographic controls: Xerox Ventura Publisher 2.0 P E
Typeface: Palatino
Copy-editing: Elizabeth Whitaker
Printed on recycled acid-free paper and bound in the U S A

CONTENTS

PLAYS BY RICHARD NELSON

ACCIDENTAL DEATH OF AN ANARCHIST, *adaptation of Dario Fo*
BAL*
BETWEEN EAST AND WEST*
CHESS, *libretto*
COLUMBUS AND THE DISCOVERY OF JAPAN
CONJURING AN EVENT*
DON JUAN, *adaptation of Molière**
THE FATHER, *adaptation of Strindberg**
IL CAMPIELLO, *adaptation of Carlo Goldoni**
THE GENERAL FROM AMERICA
GOODNIGHT CHILDREN EVERYWHERE
JUNGLE COUP*
THE KILLING OF YABLONSKI*
LIFE SENTENCES
THE MARRIAGE OF FIGARO, *adaptation of Beaumarchais**
MISHA'S PARTY, *written with Alexander Gelman*
NEW ENGLAND
PRINCIPIA SCRIPTORIAE
THE RETURN OF PINOCCHIO*
ROOTS IN WATER*
SCOOPING*
SENSIBILITY AND SENSE
SOME AMERICANS ABROAD
THREE SISTERS, *adaptation of Anton Chekhov**
TWO SHAKESPEAREAN ACTORS
THE VIENNA NOTES*

**Published by Broadway Play Publishing Inc*

INTRODUCTION

The plays in this volume were written by Richard Nelson between 1981 and 1983—years in which he struggled to balance alienation and hope. His productive, but difficult early career ends with this work. His mature career as an American playwright of international acclaim would soon begin.

The intersection of politics and morality is central to Richard's plays. From the start, he has been a socially conscious and provocative writer whose values were defined largely by the anti-war and counter-culture experiences of 1960s America. With the election of the Reagan Administration in 1980, most of us who saw the world through the political prism of our 1960s youth felt despondent. The fragile center-left alliance of the post-Vietnam years had been defeated. The values of the 1960s were mocked. Reagan's slogan, "It's morning in America" suggested to us the ascendancy of simplistic and dangerous nationalism.

But in the theatre there seemed to be renewed possibilities. The field had undergone a nation-wide decentralization over the previous decade, establishing not-for-profit companies in cities across the U S A. An alliance of private foundation and public arts initiatives sustained major funding devoted largely to the production of new American plays. Experimental theatre thrived. Grants were available and new theaters opened. For a time, America's regional theaters were a safe harbor for those in opposition.

Richard was prominent in this new theatre movement, and not just as a free-lance playwright who followed the trail of his produced plays from city to city. He was also an insider; one of the few playwrights to work as a production advisor and dramaturg for major companies. RIP VAN WINKLE, AN AMERICAN COMEDY, and JITTERBUGGING were all written under the influence of these affiliations. Between the pages of these plays are the ghosts of abandoned repertory companies.

Of all the American theaters founded in the 1970s, the most audacious was the BAM Theater Company, based at New York's Brooklyn Academy of Music. Inspired by England's Royal Shakespeare Company (which often toured to BAM), the Theater Company lasted only four seasons. After the first two years, there was a reorganization and David Jones of the R S C was engaged as the new artistic director. Richard Nelson (at that time a Brooklyn resident) was hired to be the company literary manager. Their work together became a long-term partnership, with numerous stage productions in the United States and England, as well as a revealing book on the subject of collaboration.

Richard immersed himself in the BAM Company's needs, finding lost American plays for production, editing anthologies of American drama, and translating plays for production. His expertise blossomed in the best possible environment for a theatrical apprenticeship. RIP VAN WINKLE, with its large cast and epic style, was written specifically for BAM's expansive stage and large resident ensemble. Sadly, the Company's fifth season (which would have included RIP) was canceled. Debts were mounting and the Brooklyn Academy could not sustain the loss. The repertory company whose founding was front-page news in the *New York Times* ended without a trace. No public announcement was made, and the press let the closing pass in silence. The theater just disappeared, like Rip Van Winkle into the Catskill Mountains.

With the BAM Company closed, Richard and David Jones took RIP VAN WINKLE to Connecticut's Yale Repertory Theater, where it stretched the resources of that smaller organization almost to the breaking point. Many actors from the BAM troupe took the parts they would have played with their old company.

The script is spectacularly ambitious. Like Nelson's earlier BAL, he uses a play from the past as a base from which his own work may grow. This time, the older play is not an influential modern work, but the long-forgotten stage adaptation of RIP VAN WINKLE created by 19th-century American actor Joseph Jefferson. Parts of Nelson's first act quote generously from Jefferson's version of the Washington Irving short story, but these scenes soon dissolve into a blistering contemporary saga of lost American values.

At a time when most playwrights were writing small-cast and scenically minimal works, here came a play that defied the odds, requiring a considerable scale of production. Like Arthur Miller's THE CRUCIBLE, Nelson used American myth and history as a potent metaphor against a rapacious contemporary society. What McCarthyism was to THE CRUCIBLE, Reaganism is to RIP VAN WINKLE.

The bleak fury of Nelson's BAL and PINOCCHIO is pushed here to epic ends. Rip becomes an American King Lear, defying the storms of a new industrial nation. At this point in his development as a writer, Richard may not have had the technical skill to fulfill his vision. RIP VAN WINKLE has wayward passages, but its fearsome image of crushed American idealism is volcanic and heartfelt.

With AN AMERICAN COMEDY and JITTERBUGGING Nelson moved to gentler terrain. AN AMERICAN COMEDY was first staged at the Mark Taper Forum in Los Angeles, the theater that gave Richard his first professional recognition with a 1975 workshop of THE KILLING OF YABLONSKI. The play is an homage to the screwball American comedies of

George Abbott, Hecht & MacArthur and Kaufman & Hart, with a bit of Italy's Dario Fo brought into the mix. An outright farce about Broadway playwrights meeting a deadline, Nelson juggles an absurd mix of American art, politics and theatrical commerce with more than a little self-parody and respect for the humor of survival.

Although it was not produced until 1989, JITTERBUGGING was written in 1983. It is an independent project that grew out of Richard's work as dramaturg for the Guthrie Theatre in Minneapolis. Once the BAM Theater Company closed, Richard left New York and forged a close relationship with Liviu Ciulei, the Romanian stage director who was then head of the Guthrie. Ciulei's wife Helga is a respected German drama critic. She prepared the translation of Schnitzler's LA RONDE, a cynical turn-of-the-century romance that Nelson reinvented as a rueful American tale. Set in 1947, this cycle of brief sexual encounters in a seaside New England town contrasts the sadness of each manipulative liaison with the surface optimism of period songs. The World War has burned out; its passions are gone, too. What's left is a reflection of the play's subtitle: "Scenes of Sex in a New Society." Once again, Nelson is not far from the war of his own youth and its shallow aftermath.

RIP VAN WINKLE is a thundering American epic. AN AMERICAN COMEDY celebrates loud Broadway farce. But JITTERBUGGING is mostly tender. It has an interior quality that suggests how ready Richard was in 1983 for a fresh approach. An opportunity for change occured soon afterwards, when Liviu Ciulei commissioned him to write a new version of THE THREE SISTERS for the Guthrie. That encounter with Chekhov proved to be a turning point for Richard's own style and led to the plays that established his strong reputation in England (BETWEEN EAST AND WEST and PRINCIPIA SCRIPTORIAE).

Richard has written eloquently about how the events of 1983-84 changed his life and career: Within a matter of months his mother died of cancer and his first child was born. He struggled to balance the simultaneous needs of being a responsible son and a new father. AN AMERICAN COMEDY had just opened at the Taper. I was dramaturg on the production, and we were pleased with the results. But the reviews were poor.

I remember watching Richard backstage with our actors after the notices came out. His wife Cindy was seven months pregnant and exhausted after traveling to Los Angeles for the opening; his mother had received a diagnosis of terminal cancer; and here was yet another set of bad reviews for a play we all believed in. Richard showed no sign of hurt or weakness before the company. His role as the playwright was to be selflessly encouraging and grateful towards a hard-working ensemble. Here was a man who knew how to command the troops of the theater. Not until

Richard, Cindy and I were on the plane going home to New York, did any tension or anger show.

I often think of that sad trip back from California. Richard had been hit hard so many times in his persistent, faithful struggle to write for the theater. By now there had been almost a decade of productions, but none truly caught fire. He had his champions, but had no desire to level off as a cult writer for the profession alone. Between grants and royalties he had managed to sustain himself as a playwright—no mean feat under any circumstances—but could this continue? His marriage was strong, but could a family be supported? The questions were overwhelming.

I began these introductions by saying that Richard's faith is inspiring. Perhaps it was never more so than in those weeks immediately after the opening of AN AMERICAN COMEDY. He was soon at work on a new play. By 1986 he had his first production (directed by David Jones) at the Royal Shakespeare Company. Since then, the R S C has commissioned and presented ten more of his plays. That's not bad for an American writer who lives modestly in the rural Hudson Valley north of New York City. There have been productions in the U S A, too, both on Broadway and Off, and in many regional theatres. As I write this, Richard's most recent script is playing in repertory as part of the R S C's Stratford season, and there are plans for a transfer to London and New York. Richard has built a thriving, ironic and fundamentally optimistic career in America and abroad. The vital early plays presented in these three volumes are the foundation for that work.

Robert Marx is Executive Director of the New York Public Library for the Performing Arts.

AN AMERICAN COMEDY

for Cynthia

ORIGINAL PRODUCTION

AN AMERICAN COMEDY was first produced by the Mark Taper Forum in Los Angeles (Gordon Davidson, Artistic Director; Kenneth Brecher, Associate Artistic Director) on 13 October 1983, with the following cast and creative contributors:

GEORGE REILLY .... Bob Gunton
MAX WHITCOMB .... Mark Blum
JOE WILLIAMS .... Bill Macy
JULIE JACKSON .... Melora Marshall
TONY RICARDO .... Jack Hallett
FREDDY HART .... David Downing
COLONEL FACE .... Robert Ellenstein
SAMUEL CONKLIN .... Lester C Fletcher
EVA ROSE .... Demetra Arliss

Director .... John Madden
Set designer .... Andrew Jackness
Costume designer .... Julie Weiss
Lighting designer .... James F Ingalls
Dramaturgs .... Russell Vandenbroucke, Robert Marx

"Remember, there's nothing like liberty. That is, there's nothing like it in this country. Be free. Now and forever, one and indivisible, one for all, and all for me and me for you, and tea for two."

George S Kaufman, *from* COCONUTS

CHARACTERS

GEORGE REILLY, *playwright, late thirties*
MAX WHITCOMB, *playwright, thirties*
JOE WILLIAMS, *their agent, forties*
JULIE JACKSON, MAX'*s girlfriend, twenties, attractive*
TONY RICARDO, *a steward, twenties*
FREDDY HART, *another steward, black*
COLONEL FACE, *a wealthy producer*
SAMUEL CONKLIN, *the* COLONEL'*s secretary*
EVA ROSE, *critic for* The Daily Worker, *forties*

ACT ONE

(1936)

(A first-class cabin of an ocean liner. Bed, desk, victrola, chairs, a porthole through which we see the sky. Three doors—to a closet, the bathroom, and the hallway.)

(In the dark, the Internationale *plays in the house. As the lights come up, we hear a loud boat horn, and the music switches to the victrola.)*

*(*MAX WHITCOMB *sits at the desk, before a typewriter. He reads* Das Kapital. *Around the desk are crumpled pages from the typewriter. On the wall behind him is a photo of Lenin.* MAX *wears wirerimmed glasses, a bolshevik-type hat, pressed suit pants, white buck shoes—a picture of a man whose wardrobe is in political transition.)*

(The Internationale *ends.* MAX *reads from the book.)*

MAX: *(Reading)* "If capital grows, the mass of wage labor grows, the number of wage-workers grows; in a word, the domination of capital extends over a greater number of individuals. *(He nods in agreement.)* To say that the worker has an interest in the rapid growth of capital is only to say that the more rapidly the worker increases the wealth of others, the richer will be the crumbs that fall to him." *(He closes the book. Short pause.)* "Crumbs." Just "crumbs!" In one word, Mr Karl Marx, you say it all. *(Gets up)*

(The door to the hallway opens, and GEORGE REILLY *enters.)*

GEORGE: Good morning Max. What's for breakfast?

MAX: *(To himself, shaking his head)* Now he doesn't even knock.

GEORGE: Oh. *(Beat)* Sorry. *(He backs out and closes the door, knocks, and enters again.)* Morning. And what a glorious morning it is!

MAX: Now that you know where the door is, why don't you just get out.

GEORGE: Max! If I didn't know you better, I'd feel hurt.

MAX: Feel hurt. *(Beat)* I'm not kidding, George. What do I have to do, call the captain?

GEORGE: Call the captain what? *(Beat. He laughs.)* Come on, I only dropped by because I was worried about you. I understand you didn't even get off the ship. To come all the way from New York and never get off—

MAX: You hid my passport, George.

GEORGE: Oh. *(Beat)* Right. Well, take it from me, you didn't miss much, England's a lot like New Jersey really. *(He starts to pick up the crumpled pieces of paper.)* And in five days we'll be back in New York and you can see all you want of Jersey then—depending, of course, on visibility—

MAX: Get your hands off those! *(Grabs the papers away and pushes* GEORGE*)* We are through, George, can't you understand that?!!

GEORGE: And we've been through many times before, Max.

MAX: Not like this!! *(Short pause)* Sorry. *(Beat)* Okay— I won't lie and say I'm not going to miss us working together, but people change. And now I need some time to be on my own and to start understanding what is happening to me. And to figure out where I belong.

GEORGE: Ask me. I know where you belong. *(Beat)* With me, Max.

MAX: There has to be more to life than writing plays—or at least the kind of plays we've written together.

GEORGE: Not much. Trust me.

*(*MAX *turns away.)*

GEORGE: I'm serious. *(Beat)* Please, Max, I just don't want to see you get hurt. It's a cruel world out there.

MAX: *(Turns back)* And that is just my point! Haven't you seen the breadlines? Grown men selling apples and pencils on the sidewalk! How does one deal with that?

(Beat)

GEORGE & MAX: You learn to take cabs.

MAX: I'm sorry I asked.

GEORGE: You're always great with the straight lines.

MAX: I've stopped writing straight lines for you, George.

GEORGE: Maybe, but you haven't stopped saying them. *(Short pause)*

MAX: Excuse me, but I was on my way to the bathroom. I wish to take a shower. And I do not want to be disturbed. *(Starts to go)*

GEORGE: Don't worry, Max. No one's going to bother you. Not with me here. I'll be standing guard at your door. I'll keep the crowds away. You have nothing to fear—

(A knock on the hallway door)

GEORGE: Come in.

MAX: *(Screams)* George!!!!!

*(*JOE WILLIAMS *enters from the hallway.)*

JOE: *(With open arms)* Max!

MAX: Joe?? What are you doing here?

JOE: Hello boys, how's everything going?

GEORGE: Max doesn't want to be disturbed, Joe sit down.

MAX: When did you come on board? I thought you were in New York.

JOE: Just now in Southampton. I've been flying for two and a half days—didn't George show you my cable?

MAX: George and I haven't been talking much lately.

JOE: *(To* GEORGE*)* I ask you, is that any way for collaborators to act? You fellas are pros, you going to let some silly little spat that we'll all be laughing about in the morning throw everything we've done down the toilet?

GEORGE: To say nothing about your ten percent.

JOE: You've got me wrong, George. To hell with my ten percent.

GEORGE: Lie down, Joe, you're not feeling well.

JOE: I'm talking art now. I'm talking about the contribution you two have made to the culture of our great country. I'm talking patriotism. I'm talking genius. I'm talking Broadway! *(He goes to hug both of them.)* Now come on, you two, tell Joe what happened. *(Pinches* GEORGE*'s cheek)* What'd you do, George, beat him at cards again?

GEORGE: Don't look at me. *I've tried* to talk with him.

MAX: He's right. It's just his idea of talking and mine are very different now, Joe.

GEORGE: That's because I speak out of my mouth and he speaks out of his—

JOE: *(Grabs them again)* Hey! I've told you fellas this before, but let me tell you again. I have worked with the best. I mean, the best of the best. But—and I wouldn't repeat this to anyone—those guys couldn't hold a candle to you two. You two have something special. Call it chemistry, if you want. Call it fate. That's it! You two were fated for each other. Like Astaire and Rogers.

GEORGE: Like Sacco and Vanzetti.

JOE: Right! *(Beat)* Who are they?

GEORGE: A vaudeville team on the Albee circuit.

JOE: Are they good?

GEORGE: They were hot once, but they've cooled off.

JOE: Oh.

MAX: That's not funny, George.

JOE: And as long as I'm your agent I'm not going to stand by and let you throw away what God—and I mean God in red white and blue letters—has Himself brought together. You can call me any name you want—

GEORGE: *(To* MAX*)* And we have, haven't we?

MAX: Leave me out of this.

JOE: But don't ever call me a nonbeliever. When I believe in something, my belief is unshakable. And I believe in you boys! I believe in you with all my heart. Now tell me, you're not so cruel as to shake an old man's belief, are you? *(Moves away, nearly in "tears")*

GEORGE: *(To* MAX*)* Come on, it's got to be easier to write the play than listen to this.

MAX: *(Cleaning off his desk)* Who's listening?

JOE: *(Suddenly turns back to them)* Max, look at me. Do you see the tears?

MAX: *(Looks up, then goes back to cleaning)* No.

*(*JOE *checks his face for tears, finds one, turns to* GEORGE.*)*

JOE: George, do you see the hurt on my face?

GEORGE: Uh... Stand a little closer to the light.

JOE: I'm a drowning man! Throw me a life preserver! I have three ex-wives to feed. And God, do they eat.

GEORGE: We've seen them, Joe. They could start a fat farm and harvest three times a year.

JOE: My seventeen-year-old has holes in her shoes!

GEORGE: He's talking about his fiancée, Max.

JOE: I've stopped accepting new clients—

GEORGE: You want the address of Sacco and Vanzetti?

JOE: So I could concentrate on the two of you! So I could mold you two into the best playwriting team on The Great White Way!

MAX: I thought he said God did that.

JOE: *(Grabs* MAX*)* I've given you the best years of my life! You can't do this to me!! *(Suddenly pulls away, calm)* Forgive me. I didn't know what I was saying. Who do I think I am? You're the artists. The creators. You should be able to do anything you want. What am I, but some hanger-on. Believe me, I'd probably be acting the same way if I were in your shoes. I'd kick the old guy in the teeth too. What good is he? There are plenty of other agents in the ocean.

(GEORGE *looks out the porthole.)*

JOE: But there's only one team of Whitcomb and Reilly. I understand. It's the American Way, after all. You should have just told me you didn't want me, I'd have left quietly. *(He starts to go. Then bursts out crying.)* You were like my sons!! Forgive me.

(He goes out. GEORGE *begins to silently count out: one, two, then on "three"* JOE *enters again.)*

JOE: *(Matter-of-factly)* Okay, what do you want? You want a bigger advance? I'll get it. I'll get on my knees in front of Colonel Face and beg. When have I been proud? You want women? I'll find you some even if I have to row them out here. You want the Pulitzer Prize? We can buy you one. I know five playwrights who will sell you theirs for a hot lunch. Anything, Max. I'll do anything you want. Please!

(Pause. MAX *looks away.)*

MAX: There is one thing you can do for me.

JOE: Name it, Max!

MAX: I want another cabin.

JOE: Is that all? Why didn't you say so? *(Looks around the cabin)* I see what you mean. This place is a dump. Is this what they call first class? They ought to be ashamed of themselves. But this is what you get for taking an English ship. The moment those limeys hear you talk American, they're right there to take as much advantage of you as they can. It makes me sick.

GEORGE: This is an American ship, Joe.

JOE: I find the cabin sort of cozy. Maybe a little small, but you can't blame the ship's owner for wanting to make an honest buck.

MAX: You don't understand.

JOE: Of course I understand! Creativity needs rooms! It needs space! It needs a top of a mountain! I'll have them knock out that wall. Who's in that cabin?

GEORGE: I am.

JOE: We'll knock out that wall. *(Different wall)* And we'll paint the whole cabin white. Like the womb. So the roll of the waves will feel like your mother's heart. We'll get rid of some of this broken-down furniture—

GEORGE: Antiques, some people call them.

JOE: And—oh my God—that picture! What a face. He looks like a Bible salesman I worked for in Des Moines. *(He goes to the picture of Lenin.)*

MAX: Don't touch that!

GEORGE: He's right! Who knows where that picture's been!

MAX: Joe, it's not the room. It's what's under it.

JOE: *(To* GEORGE*)* What's under it?

GEORGE: *(Shrugs)* Water.

JOE: That might be a problem, Max. I doubt if there are too many cabins without water under them. This is, after all, a ship.

MAX: I don't mean the water.

JOE: Then what else is under—?

MAX: Injustice!! I'm talking about the *people* down there. Those in second class. And below them in third class. They're down there right now—hordes of them. Masses. Workers. Eating our crumbs! It's obscene, Joe.

JOE: I don't think we can kick them off the ship. That wouldn't be right, Max. Even a Broadway hit isn't worth drowning— *(Turns to* GEORGE*)* What? A couple hundred people?

GEORGE: Even more.

JOE: No. *(Beat)* No. That would not be right, Max.

MAX: I don't want to kick them off. Don't you understand, I want to join them, to become a part of them.

JOE: *(To* GEORGE*)* I don't get it.

*(*GEORGE *shrugs.)*

MAX: I wouldn't expect you would. *(He moves toward the bathroom.)*

JOE: Wait! I get it! You want to go down there for material. You have an idea for an immigrant play—another *Abie's Irish Rose*! What do you think, George?

GEORGE: *(Perking up)* I heard there was a big group of Italians down there. A new Italian comedy might not be a bad idea.

MAX: I'm not talking about plays now! I'm talking about a passion. The biggest passion I've ever had!

JOE: *(To* GEORGE*)* What's this? Some Italian skirt got Max wrapped around her little finger?

GEORGE: First I've heard about it. I guess you better get out your checkbook, Joe. We know from experience, she isn't going to let go for nothing—

MAX: Will you two shut up for a second! *(Beat)* This isn't about a woman. And this isn't about going down there to write a play. I don't care a damn about hits anymore.

JOE: Careful, Max, I got a weak heart.

MAX: My life's changed! Or maybe my blindfold's been taken off. Don't you know what is happening in the world? What's happening in America?!

JOE: I know the Shuberts are opening a new comedy this week.

MAX: Don't you understand, that it is those people down there who are *the* people, who are the future.... We, you and I, are the decadent past. We are dying, while they are only beginning to live. I have wasted the last ten years of my life—doing what? Writing stupid comedies. Spineless entertainments to please the fancy of the bourgeoisie!

JOE: *(To* GEORGE*)* Bourgeoisie, what's that?

GEORGE: It's Russian, for honest and hardworking.

MAX: Yet during this same time, what have *they*, the people down there, been doing?

GEORGE: *(Shrugs)* Trying to write movies?

MAX: They have been struggling and sacrificing themselves to achieve justice! Universal justice. That's all I'm talking about. A justice where every man, woman, and child has the right to eat, the right to a job, the right to a roof over their heads! They have started with nothing and are trying to achieve everything. And I have everything and what have I done with it? Wasted it on cheap bourgeois material possessions.

JOE: Not cheap, you've got good taste.

MAX: What do I have? A house in the Poconos. An apartment on Fifth Avenue. I have a closet full of clothes that could feed a thousand hungry people!

JOE: *(To* GEORGE*)* They'd have to be real hungry to eat clothes. *(Beat)* Wouldn't they?

MAX: It just isn't fair! And it doesn't take a genius to figure out that everything I own has in fact been stolen from them!

GEORGE: And everything you've written has been stolen from Kaufman and Hart. But so what?!

MAX: That is just the kind of wise-crack I now expect from you, and you wonder why we're through.

JOE: But you boys have been through lots of times.

MAX: *(Almost screams)* Not like this!!! *(Pause. He paces around, trying to calm himself.)* Joe, you were poor once.

GEORGE: *(Whispers to* JOE*)* And maybe soon again.

MAX: Try to understand what I'm saying. *(Beat)* Maybe I can't convince you that I'm right, but at least listen.

(JOE *cocks his ear so he can listen. He concentrates hard now on listening.)*

MAX: You see, I can't stay in this room anymore for the simple reason that every time I take a step I feel like I am walking on their heads. *(Short pause)* Now, excuse me. *(He goes into the bathroom and closes the door.)*

GEORGE: He should try slippers.

(JOE *hurries to the bathroom door.)*

JOE: I'll see what I can do, Max!

(JOE *turns to* GEORGE. *They move away from the bathroom door.)*

JOE: How long has he been like this?

GEORGE: For weeks. *(He gets himself a drink.)* I don't know how it happened. I left him alone so he could get a start on the play and when I finally go to his apartment he hands me *The Communist Manifesto.*

JOE: Uh-huh.

GEORGE: So that's when I figured I better get him out of New York. I pretty much had to kidnap him and Julie to get them on this ship.

JOE: You did right. This is serious. He handed you what?

GEORGE: *The Communist Manifesto.*

JOE: What's that?

GEORGE: It's not box office, Joe. Trust me.

JOE: Maybe we should get an option on it just the same. Who's the agent, do you know?

GEORGE: I believe it has many agents, Joe.

JOE: They've already cut up the pie, have they? Sounds hot to me. I'll cable William Morris and see if they have a piece. *(Takes out a notepad)* What was the title of that play again?

GEORGE: *The Communist Manifesto*. But it's not really a play, Joe.

JOE: Not a play? What is it, more like a treatment?

(Beat)

GEORGE: Yes. I guess you could say that.

JOE: *(Writing down the title)* Dollars to donuts Sam Harris has already got it sewn up. George, are you sure there isn't something you could write on your own?

GEORGE: You know how we work. Max does the draft and I rewrite. I've never written a play on my own in my life. I wouldn't even know how to start.

JOE: And you're positive that this *(Reads from his pad) Communist Manifesto* isn't something you'd like to work on?

GEORGE: I'll be curious to know what you hear about the rights.

JOE: Fair enough. But that could take a day or so. So we still have our problem. Colonel Face hasn't been paying you fellas a grand a week to watch waves. He still expects a play.

GEORGE: We still have the trip back, and if I know Max he'll pull out of this—

JOE: You have one day.

GEORGE: What are you talking about? What do you mean we have one day?!

JOE: Colonel Face is on this ship, George. I ran into him getting on in Southampton just now and he asked me to arrange a reading for tomorrow night.

GEORGE: But tomorrow night's impossible! Tell him we can't do it! *(Beat)* Who does he think he is, that he can just snap his fingers and— Joe, you can't rush art.

JOE: Who said anything about art, I'm talking a hit Broadway play!

GEORGE: Tomorrow?

*(*JOE *nods;* GEORGE *begins to pace.)*

GEORGE: Then you're just going to have to tell the Colonel the truth.

JOE: What's that?

GEORGE: That Max and I finished the script a week early and we were walking along the deck reading it for the last time before giving it to the typist when a gust of wind blew it out of our hands into the sea. Then I tried to hold Max back from jumping when we both slipped and fell overboard. And after a two-day rescue operation involving ships from seven countries we were found by an Icelandic fishing boat whose crew fed us lard and homemade schnapps until making contact by chance with the outside world through a makeshift telegraph system that I put together; at such time we were brought back on board the ocean liner, and have been in our beds ever since, clinging to life, battling a rare form of pneumonia.

(Short pause. JOE *thinks.)*

JOE: Nah. Sounds too much like the plot of your last play.

GEORGE: Now you see why I need Max!! *(Beat)* Wait a minute! There's no reason to panic. *(Beat)* In fact, I don't know what we're really worried about. What can the Colonel do to us? We're on a ship.

*(*JOE *looks at him, then looks toward the porthole, then goes back to thinking.)*

GEORGE: He wouldn't throw us off! We're on the ocean! *(Beat)* He'd never get away with it.

JOE: He's been paying a grand a week.

GEORGE: *(Panicking)* So damnit, we'll pay him back!

JOE: With what?

GEORGE: We've had three hits in the last five years.

JOE: And you've had five wives in the last three. Six kids in the last five. Nine racehorses in the last seven, six of which went lame, two are impotent, and one you gave as a birthday present to your oldest daughter.

GEORGE: Who would have guessed that would be the horse that would win!

JOE: She's the richest ten-year-old on Central Park West.

GEORGE: Fine. So you're telling me we're broke?

JOE: It depends on how you define the term.

GEORGE: We have no money.

JOE: If that's how you define it, then we're broke. *(Suddenly stands)* George, what are we going to do?!

GEORGE: Calm down. Calm down. This is not the time for panicking. *(Beat)* There's still a chance, in fact, a damn good chance that we could get lucky and come across a play I could fix up by tomorrow night.

JOE: In the middle of the ocean? I'll go on deck and watch for bottles floating by.

GEORGE: I'm serious. I didn't tell you this before, because I didn't want to worry you, but for the past three days now I've been starting to think that maybe Max just might not pull out of this state he's in. In time, I mean. Give him a couple of weeks—then sure.

JOE: Sure.

GEORGE: So—to protect myself—I figured I'd better take some steps of my own to come up with a play.

JOE: What kind of steps?

GEORGE: I've put the word out among the crew that I'll pay fifty dollars for the best idea for a play.

JOE: You know that's not a bad idea—though I would have offered forty. You get anything yet?

GEORGE: The maid came up with the idea of doing a play about a maid on an ocean liner. The ship's lieutenant suggested a play about a ship's lieutenant who becomes a captain. And the steward—

JOE: Don't tell me. A play about a steward on an ocean liner.

GEORGE: Close. His idea was about a steward who writes a hit play and becomes the toast of Broadway.

JOE: Doesn't sound too bad. At least that idea has some depth to it.

*(*JULIE JACKSON*, enters from the hallway. As with* MAX*'s, her wardrobe is also in political transition—hair pulled back, glasses, gray dress, nail polish—you get the idea. She enters, carrying a large pile of newspapers.)*

JULIE: *(To* JOE*)* What are you doing here? *(To* GEORGE*)* And you. I thought Max said his cabin was off-limits.

JOE: Julie, you sweet girl, just the person I wanted to see.

JULIE: Well, you've seen me so you can get out.

GEORGE: What's with the newspapers, Julie?

JULIE: None of your business. *(She puts them on the bed.)*

JOE: *(To* GEORGE*)* What's with her?

GEORGE: One can only conclude that decent manners and good breeding are not top priorities in the revolution.

JOE: The rev—? Not Julie too? This *is* serious. That last time I saw her she was a shoe-in for the triple crown for clothes horses.

JULIE: Mr Williams, if you are here because of why I think you are, then you have wasted your time. George should have told you that before dragging you out here.

JOE: George didn't drag me here.

GEORGE: No, he was in the neighborhood. You know how it is—there's the Upper East Side, then Murray Hill, then Southampton, England. What's a few more blocks to see a friend.

JULIE: Sure. Where's Max?

JOE: He's in the shower, Julie.

JULIE: Then I better come back later.

GEORGE: There's a door between you and him. I think you can still stay and keep your modesty.

JULIE: It's not my modesty that I am concerned about. It's just—Max only takes a shower when he's thinking out a new idea and I wouldn't want to disturb him when he comes out.

GEORGE: For your sake then, as the future Mrs Max Whitcomb, let's hope he continues to have new ideas.

JOE: George, maybe he's got an idea for a play!

GEORGE: As we speak, he's probably working out the second-act finale for *Das Kapital.*

JOE: What's that?

GEORGE: *(Is about to answer, then changes his mind)* Never mind. You just keep working on *The Communist Manifesto.*

JULIE: And for your information, I haven't the slightest interest in becoming Max's wife. Marriage only stands in the way of a relationship. It is simply an archaic middle-class crutch which has no meaning for us today.

GEORGE: I wish she had defended me in my last alimony suit.

JULIE: Now I do think we better go before Max comes out.

JOE: We'll go. I promise. But first I have to talk to you.

JULIE: If it's about Max, just forget it. I've already told George not only do I stand *behind* Max and what he believes in, but I stand *beside* him as well as his equal partner.

GEORGE: *Behind* and *beside* him, Joe. I think you have to be bow-legged to do that.

*(*GEORGE *has begun to look through the pile of newspapers.)*

JULIE: I told you those were none of your business! *(She tries to pull the papers away from him.)* Put that down!

GEORGE: Look what's handwritten on the back.

JULIE: If you don't put—

*(*GEORGE *grabs her and covers her mouth with his hand; she fights.)*

GEORGE: *(Reading)* "The proletarians have nothing to lose but their chains. They have a world to win. Workers of the world, unite!" Check out the other ones.

JOE: They're the same. George, why would anyone write that on the sports page of a pile of *Herald Tribunes*?

*(*JULIE *bites* GEORGE'*s hand.)*

GEORGE: Ow!

JULIE: Don't ever touch me again, George. I am not one of your wives.

GEORGE: They didn't like me to touch them either. *(Beat)* We should go. You had something you wanted to do, Joe.

JOE: I did?? Do you remember what it was?

GEORGE: You wanted to cable William Morris about the rights for *The Communist Manifesto.*

JOE: You're right. I almost forgot. *(He moves toward the door, stops.)* What about you?

GEORGE: I'll meet you at the cable office in a few minutes. I want one minute with Julie.

*(*JOE *starts out, stops.)*

JOE: Miss Jackson, it's always good to see you.

(He goes. GEORGE *turns to* JULIE*, who steps back.)*

GEORGE: I'm not going to hurt you. *(Beat)* I would appreciate it if you'd pass along a little message to your boyfriend.

JULIE: Mr Reilly, I don't think you understand how Max and I have changed.

GEORGE: I don't give a damn if you want to be revolutionaries! In fact, if you remember, I have always been the first to say: "Never begrudge a man his hobby". But that is not my message. You ask him: "Just what kind of a sucker does he think I am?"

*(*MAX *comes out of the bathroom, drying his hair with a towel; he is unseen by both* GEORGE *and* JULIE*.)*

GEORGE: What does he think, I'm deaf and couldn't hear the little clack-clack-clack of his typewriter through that wall? He's been writing that play for Colonel Face for a week now, hasn't he?! *(Beat)* Of course I haven't said anything. Assuming, naive human being that I am, that Max was once again at work on our first draft and it would be only a matter of time before I'd be asked to take it over and fix it. *(Beat)* As I have been asked so many many times in the past. And this is what I would have continued to think except for an ugly thought that has crept into my brain. And here is that thought, Julie: Max is writing this play on his own. He has no intention of collaborating with me; in fact, he is cutting me out completely.

JULIE: I've heard him tell you to your face—

GEORGE: Max says a lot of stuff! Who listens to him?! *(Beat)* Now should this be the case. Then what I am saying now is my message. You tell Judas this: Doesn't he know he needs me?! I am going to get my hands on that play whether he gives it to me or not! I make an oath! Anything Max writes, I am going to rewrite!!

(He leaves. Pause.)

MAX: He just doesn't understand, does he?

JULIE: Max, you—

MAX: I heard. Poor George. I'm beginning to feel sorry for him.

JULIE: I wouldn't do that.

MAX: If he can't come up with a play, think what Colonel Face will do to him.

JULIE: I see your point.

MAX: *(Picks up the phone)* Stewards' cabin, please.

JULIE: I finished with the papers. I suppose I should start sliding them under the doors of all the first-class cabins like you said you wanted me to.

MAX: There's no rush. *(Into the phone)* Hello, this is Max Whitcomb in 805. I gave Tony a message to deliver for me this morning. Do you know if he has? I see. Thank you. *(Hangs up)* Did anyone come by looking for me when I was in the shower?

JULIE: I didn't see anyone. Are you expecting—?

MAX: Sort of... *(He goes into the hallway and looks down the hall.)* There's this critic on board....

JULIE: A critic? Why in the world would you be expecting a critic? You've always said that critics were scum.

MAX: *(Back in the room)* I may have said something like that once in passing, but—

JULIE: In passing?! You said it all night at your last opening. No one could talk to you because that's all you kept shouting while you and George were trying to choose what quotes to use in the advertisements.

MAX: *(Picks up the phone again; to* JULIE*)* I'm not trying to meet one of *those* critics. *(Into the phone)* Maids' quarters please. *(To* JULIE*)* This one writes for a paper called *The Daily Worker*. I found out—that this critic happened to be on board and sent a note through the steward. I'm hoping this—critic could help me place my play with one of the leftist theaters in New York.

JULIE: Your play?

MAX: I finished it this morning.

JULIE: But that's wonderful! Why didn't you tell me, I would have ordered champagne to celebrate.

MAX: With this kind of play you don't drink champagne when you've finished it.

JULIE: What do you do?

MAX: You act. The time for patience is over. *(Into phone)* No, I don't mind waiting. *(To* JULIE*)* This play is a call for action. And the call I'm speaking about is not one to the steward to bring champagne. *(He laughs to himself. He opens the desk drawer and takes the script out.)* Take a look if you like.

JULIE: If I like? There's nothing in the world I'd rather do. *(She takes the script.)*

MAX: I only pray that it's good enough.

JULIE: I'm sure it's good enough, Max.

MAX: How do you know, you haven't read it.

JULIE: I know how much you've struggled over this play, and struggling makes things good.

MAX: If it only were that easy.

(She has started to read.)

MAX: *(Into the phone)* Yes, this is 805, have you seen a steward named Tony around this morning? Who's Ingrid? I see. Thank you. *(He hangs up, shakes his head.)*

JULIE: Then the play is not for Colonel Face?

MAX: This play attacks everything that a Colonel Face stands for. He'd have a heart attack if he read one page of it. No, this is one play he wouldn't touch with a ten-foot pole, and don't think I didn't plan it that way. My work's taken a whole new direction— and that direction is—*left*!!

*(*JULIE *continues to read.* MAX *goes to the hallway door again.* JULIE *laughs to herself.)*

MAX: What's funny?

JULIE: This line you put x's through. It's very funny.

MAX: Those x's mean I've cut the line. Because I don't want this play to be funny.

(She nods. Short pause)

MAX: I'm going on deck for a minute, maybe I'll find the steward there. *(Grabs his jacket and starts to leave)*

JULIE: Max? Do you know what would make this perfect?

MAX: What would?

JULIE: Snow.

MAX: Snow?? But the play's set in the middle of August. It says so right on the first page.

JULIE: I don't mean the play. I mean us. Together like this. You, with a wonderful new play. Me, the first to read it. I wish there were a fire in the fireplace.

MAX: What fireplace? This is a ship.

JULIE: Don't be so literal. Come on, close your eyes and imagine. *(Beat)* Just try it.

(He closes his eyes.)

JULIE: Good. Now do you hear the wind howling across the meadow? And there, that's the old rustic windows banging.

MAX: I feel silly.

JULIE: Keep them closed. *(Beat)* See that over there? It's the white picket fence. And just around the other side of the barn are the chickens in their pen.

MAX: *(Still with eyes closed)* Huh. *(Short pause)* And crickets? The sound of crickets has always helped me work.

JULIE: Why not? *(Beat)* Though not too many because it's snowing. Fresh eggs in the morning. Sunsets over golden fields.

MAX: The chatter of crickets. And tree frogs.

JULIE: Yes. And sometimes just quiet, Max. *(Beat)* Absolute quiet.

(Pause)

MAX: I always do get a lot of work done in the country. Maybe I shouldn't sell my house in the Poconos after all.

JULIE: We could at least use it on the weekends.

MAX: *(Suddenly breaking out of the picture)* What are we talking about, we can't live in the country. It is very important that we live in the city.

JULIE: It's awfully noisy. But I gather that doesn't bother you.

MAX: We'll find someplace near the Bowery. In one of those immigrant sections. That's where the people are.

JULIE: Oh. *(Beat)* Fine. *(Beat)* We can talk about it later.

(Knock at the door)

MAX: Come in.

*(*TONY*, the steward, enters.)*

MAX: Oh it's you, Tony. How good of you to drop by.

TONY: I don't understand, Mr Whitcomb. Didn't you tell me you wanted me to come back?

MAX: But my friend, that was a mere three hours ago. I am flattered you found the time to visit within what must certainly be a very busy schedule.

*(*JULIE *goes back to reading the play.)*

TONY: Oh I haven't been so busy, Mr Whitcomb.

MAX: I've been looking all over this damn boat for you!!

TONY: But I've been in the stewards' cabin.

MAX: I called there. You haven't been seen there all morning.

TONY: Then uh—I may have dallied too long in the maids' quarters.

MAX: I called there too. They said the Latin lover hadn't punched in yet today.

TONY: Latin lover? Is that what Ingrid calls me behind my back? *(Laughs)* To my face she calls me other things. *(Laughs)* Women! But I'm sure I don't have to tell you, Mr Whitcomb, about women.

JULIE: *(Under her breath)* Don't tell him, Tony. *(She goes back to reading.)*

TONY: But to answer your question truthfully, I was on the deck, where the wind blows and the salt water sprays, thinking out my idea for a play for Mr Reilly.

JULIE: *(Looks up)* A play for George?

MAX: Him and everyone else on board, or so I've heard. I told you, poor George.

TONY: If you have a moment I would very much like to tell you my—

MAX: I don't have a minute.

(JULIE giggles. MAX turns to her.)

JULIE: It's not the play, Max—I was thinking of something else. *(She is lying.)*

MAX: *(Turns back to TONY)* All I want to know is if you've found the odd second to deliver my note?

TONY: Oh yes, Sir.

MAX: And?

TONY: And?

MAX: And was there a reply?

TONY: Oh yes, Sir.

MAX: May I ask what the reply was?

TONY: Sure you can ask, Mr Whitcomb.

MAX: I'm asking, damnit!

TONY: Miss Eva Rose replies that she would gladly meet with you.

JULIE: Who??

TONY: Miss Eva Rose.

JULIE: Who's that?

MAX: The critic I told you about. *(Turns to TONY)* Did she—?

JULIE: A woman?

MAX: Yes, I guess she is a woman.

JULIE: You didn't tell me this critic was a woman.

MAX: A woman, a man, what's the difference?

TONY: If you want to step into the hall, I think I can answer that question.

MAX: Shut up. Just tell me what she said.

TONY: She will meet you anytime you wish. But if you wish to speak to her now she would be on the deck, though that was two hours ago.

MAX: Two hours ago?!! *(He lunges at* TONY, *hesitates, lets him go.)* Keep that face just as it is, because if Miss Rose is gone, I've got a few thoughts about how to change it. *(He hurries to the door.)*

JULIE: *(Getting up)* Maybe you'd like company?

MAX: Why?

JULIE: I—I wouldn't mind getting some air.

MAX: If you do, lock that script in the desk. Here's a spare key. *(Hands her a key)* Oh and don't forget to deliver those newspapers—when you have the chance. *(He hurries out the door.)*

JULIE: But—!

(He hurries back in and goes to the mirror; he rumples up his clothes and messes his hair.)

MAX: There, how do I look?

JULIE: Like a mess.

MAX: Good. I wouldn't want Miss Rose to think I was so bourgeois that I cared about my appearance. *(He hurries out.)*

JULIE: *(Calling)* Max! *(Short pause; she sits down. Turns to* TONY*)* I wonder if he messes himself up as much before going to see me.

(Short pause)

TONY: Would you like to hear my idea for a play for Mr Reilly?

JULIE: No, I wouldn't. *(She is distracted.)*

TONY: Yesterday I had an idea but I don't think he liked it very much. But today I have a whole other idea. You want me to tell it to you?

JULIE: No, I wouldn't.

TONY: My old idea was about a steward, but my new idea is about an orphan from Boston who becomes very rich.

(He takes out a piece of paper and tries to show her. She ignores him.)

JULIE: *(Turning away from him)* Please, Tony.

TONY: A definite improvement, don't you think?

JULIE: No, I wouldn't.

TONY: Also I think I figured out an important reason why Mr Reilly didn't like my first idea. *(Beat)* You want to know why?

JULIE: Please, Tony.

TONY: Because it wasn't typed. *(He goes to* MAX*'s typewriter and looks it over.)*

JULIE: *(Suddenly seeing him)* I don't think you should—

TONY: Trust me, he'll never know I touched it. *(He sits down, starts to type; it is clear he doesn't know how. Short pause.)*

JULIE: Tony? This critic—

TONY: *(Typing)* You mean the woman?

JULIE: *(Yelling)* Yes, I mean the woman!! *(Calms herself)* What was her name? Eva. Eva something.

TONY: Eva Rose.

JULIE: That's right. Eva Rose. Would you call her—

TONY: Pretty?

JULIE: I wasn't going to say that!! I was going to say— "interesting". Why would I want to know if she's pretty or not? We should be beyond judging people by their appearances. True beauty is in the heart, it's in the mind, in the soul. But since you brought it up.

TONY: *(Stops typing)* Let me see. *(Beat)* She wears glasses. And her hair's all pulled back behind her head. And her clothes—she was wearing this gray dress.

JULIE: *(Not realizing the similarity of the description)* Oh. The poor woman has no taste. And her teeth, I suppose, they're not straight.

TONY: No. *(Thinking)* Her teeth were straight.

JULIE: *(Opens her mouth and shows her teeth)* As straight as mine?

TONY: I didn't get this good of a look at her teeth.

JULIE: *(Turning away)* So she doesn't smile. I knew it.

TONY: Oh no, she smiles. *(*JULIE *turns back.)* When I told her Mr Whitcomb, the Broadway playwright, wanted to see her, she didn't stop smiling.

JULIE: When you said Max—? Oh, that is interesting. Very very interesting. *(Beat)* And I suppose her eyes got all aglow.

TONY: I just noticed the—

JULIE: And then she blushed. And wet her lips. Women like that always wet their lips. *(She wets her lips.)* And then became a little breathless, am I right?

TONY: I only noticed the—

JULIE: Excuse me, Tony.

(JULIE has gone to the desk with the script and puts it in the drawer and locks it.)

TONY: Are you going somewhere?

JULIE: I have this sudden urge to go on deck myself. And get some air. *(She heads for the door. Turns back)* Just be careful with that. Max is very finicky about his typewriter. *(She goes.)*

TONY: *(Calls)* As any writer must be! *(He goes back to typing, jams the keys, pulls them apart. He reads off his paper.) From Rags to Riches* a new play by Tony Ricardo. *(Types one or two letters, stops)* No. *(Pulls out the paper, throws it away, finds more paper, puts in another piece) From Rags to Riches,* a new play by Anthony Ricardo. *(Types a few letters, pulls out the paper, throws it away, puts in another piece)* A new play by...Anthony Richards. That's it. *(Beat)* No. *(Doesn't type, but rips out the blank paper and throws it away. Another piece; thinks.)* No. *(Pulls out the paper, etc.)*

(FREDDY HART enters from the hallway.)

FREDDY: Tony?? Is that you?

TONY: Jesus Christ, can't a man create without being constantly interrupted?!!

FREDDY: What are you doing in here alone?

TONY: Typing. *(He types a couple of letters, and the keys get stuck.)* Damnit. *(He forces them apart, bending the keys, of course.)* What do you want, there's nobody here. *(To himself)* A new play by—????

FREDDY: I heard Mr Reilly was in here, and I wanted to give him this outline for the play I'm writing.

TONY: *(Almost chokes)* You're writing a play too? *(Forces a laugh)*

FREDDY: Why is that so funny?

TONY: Freddy, don't you know it takes a lot of experience to say nothing of time to write a play? There is a big big difference between being a playwright and being a—a steward.

FREDDY: *(Putting him on)* Oh. I hadn't realized that.

TONY: Well now you know. So if you'll excuse me—

FREDDY: What is the difference between being a playwright and being a steward?

TONY: It's— *(Beat)* It's too complicated to go into now. Freddy, Freddy, Freddy, why does everyone think he can write a play? *(Laughs to himself)* Why does the whole human race want to be something that they are not?

Do you think I want to become a Negro steward? Of course not. So why should you want to become a playwright?

FREDDY: I don't understand the logic of that.

TONY: Freddy, what do you know about the theater? To be a playwright you must have experienced the theater.

FREDDY: If you mean the American theater, really very little. The two plays I've had produced have been in French.

TONY: *(Chokes)* In French?? *(Beat)* Let me tell you something, there's a difference between French and English. A big, very, very, very, big difference.

FREDDY: What is the—?

TONY: Don't ask me!! I'm busy!! *(Puts in another piece of paper)*

FREDDY: The writer I was secretary to in Paris felt I had an excellent chance of making my mark on the American theater.

TONY: To make your mark on the American theater you'll have to know a lot more than French. *(Laughs)* A lot more. *(Laughs)* You'll have to know how to.... How to... Type. Now if you'll excuse me. *(He types, jams the keys, bangs on the typewriter.)*

FREDDY: I'll just leave this on the desk for Mr Reilly. I should be getting back to work.

(He leaves the outline, which has a red cover, and starts to go. TONY *opens the manuscript.)*

TONY: *(Reading)* "A sharecropper's hut in Mississippi."

*(*FREDDY *stops.)*

TONY: Freddy, is this a Negro play? *(Laughs to himself)*

FREDDY: *(At the door)* It's about my childhood. About my father in particular.

TONY: But Freddy, Negro plays don't sell.

FREDDY: I didn't know there were many Negro plays to sell.

TONY: Perhaps there's a reason for that, Freddy. Think about it.

FREDDY: Believe me, I have. *(He goes.)*

TONY: *(Calling after him)* I hope you can handle rejection! *(Turns back to the typewriter) From Rags to Riches* a new play by... *(Snaps his fingers)* Richard Anthony!!! *(Starts to type, stops)* The Third!!!!! *(Types, then picks up the phone. Into phone)* Maids' quarters please. *(Looks down at the paper, and writes on it)* I dedicate this play to—Ingrid. *(Into phone)* Hello, is Ingrid there? It's her Latin lover calling. *(Laughs)* She's not? What room? That's just two rooms from here. Thank you. *(Hangs up. Grabs up the paper and begins to leave; he stops at the mirror, checks himself out, but realizes something is missing. He looks around, then gets the idea. He goes back to the desk, grabs a pipe—and now, feeling very much the writer, looks one last time in the mirror and leaves.)*

(A tap on the porthole)

GEORGE: *(Off)* Max? Max? *(*GEORGE *struggles through the porthole into the room.)* Max, are you here? *(Slaps his hand)* Okay, creep, where'd you hide the new play? *(He goes to one of the bedside tables.)*

MAX: *(In the hallway, yelling)* She wasn't there!!!

*(*GEORGE *freezes for a second, then hurries into the closet.)*

MAX: *(Entering)* When I get my hands on that steward— *(Phone rings. Into the phone, angry.)* Who is it?!! Oh, Miss Rose. Now? Sure, now's fine. In the lounge? I'll be right there. *(Hangs up)* Oh boy.

(He hurries out. GEORGE *comes out of the closet.)*

GEORGE: That was close.

(Begins to look again; opens a drawer. The door opens and TONY *runs in, holding his face, which has just been slapped. He goes to the desk and picks up a pencil.)*

TONY: Why didn't she tell me "Ingrid" has only one "n"?!

(Crosses out an "n" and runs out, never seeing GEORGE, *who shakes his head and shrugs and continues looking. He moves toward the bathroom. A knock at the door.* GEORGE *freezes, begins to move back toward the closet.)*

JOE: *(Off, knocking)* It's Joe. Can I come in?

GEORGE: Oh, it's you. Come on in. *(He relaxes, and goes to check out the bathroom.)*

JOE: *(Entering as* GEORGE *goes, so doesn't see him)* We've got ourselves a problem, don't we? *(He sits.)*

GEORGE: *(From the bathroom)* You can say that again. What a jerk he's become. And you saw what he's like. You can't even talk to him.

JOE: And you know something—you never really could. He never could listen. That's George for you.

GEORGE: *(Sticks his head out)* George?

JOE: *(Without looking up)* You're right, he's a real jerk. *(Beat)* But you, Max—you're different. You've got class.

(It has dawned on GEORGE *what* JOE *is saying. He goes back into the bathroom.)*

JOE: Max, how long have I been your agent? Let me tell you, it's been almost eight years. Eight glorious years, if I do say so myself. I wouldn't trade those years for anything. *(Beat)* In all that time, Max—I'm going to confess something to you now. In all that time, I have come to feel very,

very close to you. Did you know that? As a rule, Max, I try to keep my feelings to myself.

GEORGE: *(Entering with a towel over his head, pretending to dry his hair)* Though not your hands—according to my oldest daughter.

JOE: What? You don't even have a daughter, Max. I get it. *(Laughs)* Always with the jokes. Boy are you a funny man. *(Laughs)* Look, let's get to the point, okay. So tell me the truth—it's George, isn't it? *(Beat)* He's gotten on your nerves or something. Let me tell you, this comes as no surprise to me, Max. To be honest, I don't know how you stood him this long.

GEORGE: As you say, he's a jerk.

JOE: One of the biggest. And you don't need him, that should be painfully obvious to you by now. Of course, I understand, he's your friend—

GEORGE: And your friend.

JOE: Don't put words in my mouth, Max. What I've had with George has been strictly business. *(Beat)* So now that you know where I stand.

GEORGE: You're standing about eight feet over there. *(He makes a fist, which* JOE *does not see.)*

JOE: I'm asking you to come clean with me, Max. I'm not blind, you know. I'm not stupid. Max Whitcomb does not sit in a room for a week to look at the wallpaper. *(Beat)* Where's the new play, Max? Where is it? *(Beat)* Don't be so surprised. I know you must be writing something. The joy of creation is written all over your face. Come on, Max. *(Beat)* Give it to me.

GEORGE: Don't tempt me.

JOE: I know why you're hesitating

GEORGE: Why?

JOE: Because you still are afraid that I'll pressure you to work with George. Because I am his agent, too.

GEORGE: But you won't.

JOE: Max, you've written a wonderful work—a masterpiece, all by yourself. Who needs George?

GEORGE: But what'll he do? Doesn't he need the money?

JOE: This is art, not charity. *(Beat)* Of course we'll continue paying his way back to New York, though perhaps he should move to second class.

GEORGE: But you'll let him know, Joe? I couldn't face him myself.

JOE: Sure I'll let him know. I'll write him a note and get the steward to change the lock on his cabin.

GEORGE: Sounds fair. But why don't you write him now. Just to get it over with. I'll type while you dictate.

(GEORGE goes to the desk.)

JOE: You're right, the sooner this is settled the better.

GEORGE: *(Types and reads)* "Dear George."

JOE: No, no, too personal. I've only known George for—

GEORGE: Eight years.

(He lets the towel fall off, but JOE doesn't at first notice.)

JOE: And how close can you really get to a person in just eight years? Write: "Dear Mr Reilly."

(GEORGE types.)

JOE: "This is to inform you—" *(He turns, sees GEORGE, but it doesn't at first register.)* Got that? "That your services as a collaborator to Mr Whitcomb are..." *(It registers. He freezes.)* Uh. Uh. Uh. Uh.

GEORGE: "Are—" what?

(JOE suddenly bolts for the bathroom door and flings it open.)

JOE: Max?!!

GEORGE: *(Without looking up)* He's not in there. We are alone. Now you were saying: "That your services are—"?

(Pause. JOE is frozen, then suddenly he tries to laugh.)

JOE: Ha ha ha! I bet I had you going, George.

GEORGE: I'm only getting started.

JOE: Ha ha ha! I guess now we're even.

GEORGE: That would not be my opinion.

JOE: Don't tell me you've forgotten all those wonderful practical jokes you've pulled on me over the years. I guess now we're even. *(Beat)* I remember one. *(He laughs.)*

GEORGE: I don't remember that one.

JOE: If you could only have seen your face. *(Laughs)*

GEORGE: Come here.

(JOE hesitates and forces more laughter.)

GEORGE: Come here.

(JOE slowly moves to GEORGE. GEORGE forces a laugh, then as JOE gets close, he grabs him around the throat.)

JOE: Ah! Ah!

(From the hall we hear shouting in Swedish.)

GEORGE: I'll finish with you later. Someone's coming.

(Lets go of him. JOE *gasps for breath.* GEORGE *looks around.)*

GEORGE: *(Continued)* Get in the closet.

JOE: *(Gasping)* Why are we hiding?

GEORGE: If Max finds us sneaking around his room, he'll make sure we never see his play.

JOE: Wait a minute, you knew he'd written a new play and you didn't tell me? I'm offended by your lack of trust, George.

*(*GEORGE *grabs him and pulls him into the closet. In the hall we hear a big slap.* TONY *hurries in; his clothes are a bit dishevelled.)*

TONY: *(Screaming back down the hall)* And you call yourself Swedish!!!!! *(He slams the door. The closet door opens.)*

GEORGE: *(Whispers)* It's only Tony, the steward.

JOE: What's he doing in here?

*(*GEORGE *shrugs. They approach* TONY *from behind; he doesn't see them.* TONY *goes to the desk, takes out his piece of paper, and crosses something out, then writes something new. He reads.)*

TONY: "I dedicate this play to Mother!" *(He begins to type.)*

JOE: What sentiment.

TONY: Mr Williams! Mr Reilly!

GEORGE: It makes you remember why we're in this business. *(Beat)* I'll bet his mother dedicates all her plays to him. *(To* JOE*)* Check under the bed.

(They look for the manuscript.)

TONY: My mother doesn't write plays.

GEORGE: *(Looking through the closet)* No? What is she then, an actress?

JOE: Nothing under the bed.

TONY: No. She's never even been inside a theater.

GEORGE: Ah. She's an agent. *(To* JOE*)* Look inside the pillow cases.

TONY: May I ask what you two are doing in here?

GEORGE: We were swimming by, saw the light in the window, and thought we'd drop in.

TONY: You were swimming? But your clothes aren't wet.

JOE: *(While he's looking)* We weren't really swimming, Tony.

TONY: But Mr Reilly just said—

JOE: Mr Reilly says many things, Tony.

TONY: Oh, you mean it was like a joke, then?

GEORGE: It once was, Tony, many many moments ago. *(To* JOE*)* It's not in the closet.

JOE: Tony, what are you doing in Mr Whitcomb's room?

TONY: Mr Whitcomb has sort of let me use his typewriter.

*(*GEORGE *looks at the typewriter, with the bent keys, etc.)*

GEORGE: And I can see you're taking very good care of it.

TONY: There's a problem with the keys, though, they seem to be too close together.

GEORGE: But you're fixing that.

*(*GEORGE *and* JOE *have started to go through the drawers of the desk.)*

JOE: Do you know where Mr Whitcomb is, Tony?

TONY: He's not here.

JOE: Oh really? Thank you. George, this drawer's locked.

GEORGE: Hand me that paper clip. *(Pushes* TONY *out of the way)*

TONY: Mr Reilly, I wanted to tell you I have a new idea for a play. It came to me this morning in a flash.

GEORGE: Take a laxative, it'll pass.

(A knock at the door. Everyone looks up, freezing. Another knock)

VOICE: Mr Whitcomb, are you there?

JOE: Who can that be?

*(*GEORGE *shrugs.)*

VOICE: Mr Whitcomb, my name is Samuel Conklin, Colonel Face's secretary. Can I see you for a minute, please?

JOE: What do we do? Let's not answer the door, he doesn't know anyone is in here.

CONKLIN: I know you're in there, I hear voices.

GEORGE: Quick, put this robe on.

JOE: What for?

GEORGE: Just do as I say.

(JOE *puts on* MAX's *robe.)*

GEORGE: Tony, answer the door, tell him... Say you're our secretary or something and we can't be disturbed because we're in the middle of inspiration.

*(*GEORGE *sits* JOE *at the desk. He leans over him.* TONY *goes and opens the door.)*

*(*CONKLIN, *an older man in a business suit, enters.)*

CONKLIN: *(To* TONY*)* Mr Whitcomb??

GEORGE: Sh-sh!!!

TONY: *(To* CONKLIN*)* Sh-sh!!!

CONKLIN: *(Whispers)* Is anything the matter?

TONY: I am the secretary. As you see, the writers are in the middle of inspiration.

CONKLIN: Oh, I see.

*(*GEORGE *groans in pain.* JOE *then groans.)*

CONKLIN: Is something wrong—they appear to be groaning. Ah, but I understand—art is pain. I'll be brief—Colonel Face has asked you all to dine with him at the captain's table tonight. Do you think that is possible?

*(*GEORGE *nods.)*

TONY: Yes. That is possible.

CONKLIN: *(Still whispering)* Shall we say eightish?

TONY: *(Taking cue from* GEORGE*)* We shall say eightish.

CONKLIN: Forgive me, but when I made the reservation, I did not realize their secretary was with them. I assume you will be dining with us as well?

*(*GEORGE *shakes his head "No".)*

TONY: Oh sure, I'd love to.

CONKLIN: Then with the Colonel and myself, and Mr Whitcomb, Mr Reilly, Mr Williams, and Mr Whitcomb's friend, Miss Jackson, that was six, so with you it will be seven. I better call the dining room to see if the captain's table is large enough.

TONY: It's large enough.

CONKLIN: I see you've been to his table before.

TONY: Four times a meal. Five if anyone wants soup.

CONKLIN: I don't understand.

*(*GEORGE *suddenly stands and screams a primal scream; feels better and goes back to the huddle with* JOE.*)*

CONKLIN: *(Taken aback)* I never realized writing a play was like this.... I'm sorry, I don't think I caught your name.

TONY: Tony. I mean Anthony. I mean Richard Anthony.

CONKLIN: You seem to be confused about your name.

TONY: You know us writers, we use a lot of names, you can't help but get yourself confused sometimes.

CONKLIN: Then you are a writer as well.

*(*GEORGE *gestures to get rid of him.)*

TONY: Then we'll see you tonight. *(Leads* CONKLIN *to the door)*

JOE: *(Suddenly stands up, rips a piece of paper, and screams)* It's no good!!!!

*(*GEORGE *is shocked and just stares at him.)*

JOE: *(Whispers, embarrassed)* Sorry. I got carried away.

CONKLIN: No, this is certainly not how I imagined it. *(To* TONY*)* What sort of writing do you do, Mr Anthony?

TONY: Uh—the menu.

CONKLIN: Excuse me?

GEORGE: *(Turns to* CONKLIN*)* He means for the *Menu*. It's a small poetry magazine. *(Goes back to "work")*

CONKLIN: You know I fancy myself a poet—amateur of course. Do you think I could see a copy?

TONY: Tonight. Around meal time.

CONKLIN: Around meal time? *(Suddenly laughs)* The *Menu* around meal time! That's very witty! *(Beat)* Oh, by the way, the Colonel has had to make other plans for tomorrow evening, and he's asked if after dinner tonight he could read the play he's been paying for. I'm sure that won't be a problem. Until tonight then. *(He goes.)*

*(*GEORGE *and* JOE *scream.)*

JOE: Tonight, George!!

GEORGE: I heard!

JOE: *(Yells)* What are we going to do?!! *(He rips up the paper he has in his hand.)*

TONY: You can stop that now, he's gone.

JOE: *(Bangs on the desk drawer)* We need a wedge of some kind. I'll look in the bathroom. *(He goes.)*

GEORGE: I'll open this drawer if I have to chew up from the leg.

TONY: You want to get into that desk drawer?

*(*GEORGE *takes off his shoes and begins to pound the desk drawer.)*

TONY: You know they don't like passengers to do that to the furniture.

JOE: *(Coming out of the bathroom)* The only thing I could find was Max's toothbrush. *(Tries to use it as a wedge)* It won't work.

GEORGE: Give it to me. *(He takes the toothbrush and rubs it around in the wastepaper basket.)*

JOE: What are you doing?

GEORGE: Max is going to suffer for what he's done, so he might as well start tonight when he brushes his teeth. Put it back. *(Hands the toothbrush back to* JOE*)* Give me your lighter.

JOE: My lighter??

GEORGE: I'm going to burn the lock off.

JOE: Careful you don't burn the play.

GEORGE: Get some water ready.

*(*JOE *runs into the bathroom.* GEORGE *sprinkles lighter fluid around the lock.)*

TONY: You know passengers aren't allowed to start fires in their rooms. They're not even supposed to have hot plates.

JOE: *(Coming out)* I got the water.

GEORGE: I've sprinkled a little lighter fluid around the drawer. I need a fuse. *(Looks around, grabs paper out of the typewriter)*

TONY: That's the idea for my play! *(He grabs it back.)*

GEORGE: Joe, give me your tie.

JOE: Use your own tie, this one comes from Saks.

GEORGE: *(Grabbing the tie, choking Joe, looking at the label)* Since when is Saks spelled "P-E-N-N-E-Y-S"?

JOE: I found it in the men's dressing room at Saks.

(Suddenly the door opens and CONKLIN *enters. They all freeze:* GEORGE *with his shoe in one hand, choking* JOE *by the tie with the other.)*

CONKLIN: *(Entering)* I'm sorry to bother you again, but— *(He notices them.)* I think I noticed some *Herald Tribunes*. There they are. The shop appears to be sold out. I wondered if—I think I'll just take one. *(He does.)* Thank you. *(He looks at them.)* If only the world knew what suffering goes into art. *(He goes.)*

JOE: *(Grabbing* FREDDY*'s manuscript off the desk)* What about using this, George?

TONY: Mr Williams, you can't, that's Freddy's outline for his play.

GEORGE: *(To* JOE*)* Who's Freddy??

JOE: *(Shrugs)* Look, if a playwright doesn't think it's worth his bother to hang around and protect his play, he can't expect us to. *(Hands* GEORGE *the manuscript)*

*(*GEORGE *pours more lighter fluid on it, shoves it into the lock.)*

GEORGE: There. Stand back. Get the water ready—

TONY: You know I have a key to that lock.

GEORGE: Quiet! One. Two. Three.

(He lights it. Suddenly, what TONY *has just said registers, and* GEORGE *and* JOE *start to pound the fire out and pour water on the desk.* FREDDY*'s manuscript is destroyed.)*

(Pause)

GEORGE: *(Standing up and going over to* TONY*)* Tony, when are you going to let me see that play idea of yours?

TONY: You really want to read it, Mr Reilly?

GEORGE: I'll have the time as soon as I get this drawer open.

TONY: That's no problem. I have a key.

GEORGE: Funny. I thought you might.

*(*TONY *takes out his keys and finds the right one.* GEORGE *grabs it and unlocks the drawer.)*

JOE: Is it in there?

GEORGE: *(Taking out the script)* Look. *(He sets it on the desk. Pause)*

JOE: What's wrong? Open it.

GEORGE: I just had a terrible thought. What if the play is so bad I can't even fix it.

JOE: And I thought you were an American.

GEORGE: What does that have to do with anything?

JOE: Americans don't think thoughts like that. They are optimistic. They have hope. They take a play like this and say: this is the best goddamn drama ever written! You could put Shakespeare's name on it and no one would know the difference.

GEORGE: Or care.

JOE: Right! Americans are the first to anticipate art—even before they've seen it. The quickest to call a man genius—whether he is or not. They have hope. They hunger for the chance to say something is: "Brilliant dot dot dot. Magical dot dot dot. Run don't walk dot dot dot". And they put these thoughts in big letters on marquees. They have no pride. Now open that script and let's start reading! *(He does.)* What is this crap?

GEORGE: It says that all proceeds from this play are donated to the Socialist Workers' Party of America.

*(*JOE *rips out the page, crumples it, and tosses it away.)*

JOE: Keep reading.

*(*TONY *puts his pages onto the script.)*

TONY: Mr Reilly, here's my idea. See, we first meet our hero in a small and rickety shack near Boston.

JOE: *(Pushing him away)* Oh, is that where he is, go meet him.

*(*TONY *grabs* MAX's *play away from them.)*

TONY: You don't understand, that's where my play begins.

GEORGE: And it'll end there too if you don't give that back to us.

TONY: But Mr Reilly, you promised!

JOE: Listen, Son. I'm his agent, and any promises he's made I can get him out of, understand?

TONY: No.

(They grab the script back, just as the door is opened. They look up and start to scramble to put the script back in the desk as JULIE *enters.* GEORGE, JOE, *and* TONY *freeze, as if they were caught; but* JULIE *has her mind on something else.)*

JULIE: *(After a pause)* Tony, you did say Max was to meet this woman on the deck?

TONY: Yes, Miss.

GEORGE: Julie!!

JOE: *(To* GEORGE*)* Woman? What woman?

*(*GEORGE *shrugs and gestures to* JOE *that they should get out with the script.)*

JULIE: Well they weren't there. *(She goes to the door and without thinking closes it, blocking* GEORGE *and* JOE's *escape.)*

TONY: Maybe they went to her room, Miss. Now why would Max go to a woman's room?

JOE: Bite your tongue, George.

GEORGE: *(Looking at his watch)* If you'll excuse me, we should be going.

JULIE: *(Stopping them)* George, Mr Williams, you've known Max for a long time. I'm really worried about him. You know, he doesn't have much experience with women. *(Beat)* I know, because he told me.

*(*JOE *looks at* GEORGE.*)*

GEORGE: I am biting, Joe.

JULIE: Max has such a big heart; he's always thinking the best of people. I just don't know how he would react to someone who isn't just interested in his mind. It could crush him.

TONY: She's not that heavy of a woman, Miss.

(She looks at TONY; GEORGE *pushes him away.* JOE *moves toward* JULIE *to comfort her.)*

JOE: Julie. Julie. *(He puts his arm around her.)*

JULIE: I don't know what to do. I feel so helpless.

JOE: Trust Uncle Joe, whatever trouble Max might be in, he can take care of himself.

(He tries to guide her away from the door. GEORGE, *with the script, is about to make his break.)*

JULIE: George?

GEORGE: *(Stops)* Yes, Julie?

JULIE: In the plays you and Max have written, there have been some love scenes.

GEORGE: A few.

JULIE: Max told me you wrote all of them yourself. Is that true?

GEORGE: If Max Whitcomb says something is true, you know it's true. Lassie's told more lies than Max has.

JOE: Well, George, I think it's nearly lunchtime.

JULIE: Then I won't keep you.

JOE & GEORGE: Good!

(They move to the door.)

JULIE: But before you go.

(They stop.)

JULIE: I know I haven't been too nice lately.

GEORGE: Don't say another word.

JULIE: I can hardly believe the way I've behaved.

GEORGE: She's saying another word.

JULIE: I just want to say—thanks for being here. It was really lucky for me that you happened to be in Max's room. There are times when one really needs someone to talk to.

GEORGE: But there also are times when it's best to leave someone alone. *(Looks at his watch)* What do you know—it seems to be one of those times right now. *(They break for the door.)*

JULIE: By the way—why are you in Max's room?

JOE: Us?

JULIE: And what is that smell?

GEORGE: Uh, what smell?

JULIE: It smells like lighter fluid.

GEORGE: I'll go tell the steward to check on it.

TONY: I'm the steward.

GEORGE: Check on it. *(He bolts for the door, with manuscript under his arm. He starts out, then hurries right back and closes the door.)* It's Max and some woman, they're coming down the hall!!

JULIE: It's her!!

(They scramble to hide. GEORGE *jams the script back into the desk, has trouble getting the drawer closed, then beats it closed.* JULIE *chooses to hide under the bed.* JOE *runs into the closet,* GEORGE *into the bathroom.* TONY *watches them—can't find anyplace to hide. Then, as the door opens, he hides behind that.)*

(Door opens—and is left open during the scene. Sudden calm)

*(*MAX *and* MISS ROSE *enter. She is rather attractive—dressed as* TONY *has described, though clearly not the femme fatale of* JULIE*'s imagination.)*

MAX: *(Entering)* I really do appreciate your offer to read my play.

MISS ROSE: My pleasure.

MAX: Make yourself comfortable, I'll just be a second. You don't mind if I call you Eva, do you? *(He goes to the desk.)*

JULIE: *(From under the bed)* I mind.

MAX: *(Turns to* MISS ROSE*)* Oh. Excuse me then. It's just that in the theater everyone always calls—

MISS ROSE: *(Who has turned to where the voice came from)* I didn't say anything. Mr Whitcomb, I think someone else—

MAX: *(At the desk)* Please, please, call me Max. *(Noticing)* What's happened to this desk?

JULIE: *(Hidden)* I'd like to call you something else.

MAX: *(Looking at the desk)* Something else? Oh—you mean like comrade? *(Looks up)* Please, feel free. That is what we are after all, isn't it? *(Back to the desk)* The drawer is stuck. *(He struggles with the drawer.)*

MISS ROSE: Are you sure this is the best time to give you that tour of the lower decks, Max?

JULIE: *(Picks her head up, to* MISS ROSE, *who now sees her) Mr Whitcomb*!

MAX: *(Struggling)* Really, "comrade" is fine. I promise this will just take a second. You don't mind if I take a notebook along with me, do you? I don't want to forget anything I see.

MISS ROSE: Is your notebook also in that drawer?

MAX: *(Struggling)* No. I keep that in the bathroom.

MISS ROSE: I'll get it if you wish.

MAX: Please, don't bother.

(She has moved toward the bathroom, but before she can open the door, GEORGE *opens it from the inside and hands her the notebook, then closes the door.)*

MISS ROSE: It was no bother.

MAX: *(Looks up)* That's it, thanks. *(Finally opening the drawer)* There. Here's the play. For some reason it's a little damp. Must be the humidity.

MISS ROSE: *(Taking the script, almost speechless now by what she's witnessed)* Thank you.

MAX: *(Getting up)* Oh, and I don't suppose I'll be needing a jacket down there, will I? *(Takes his jacket off)*

MISS ROSE: I—I don't know.

*(He opens the closet—*MISS ROSE *gasps.* MAX *turns to her and therefore does not see what she is seeing:* JOE *has covered himself with clothes and has stuck out his arm like a hook.* MAX, *without looking, hangs his coat on* JOE*'s arm.)*

MAX: What's wrong?

*(*MISS ROSE *can't talk.)*

MAX: Oh, I understand. I do. *(He closes the door—never seeing* JOE.*)* For someone like you—this sort of room, well, I guess it must be pretty upsetting.

*(*MISS ROSE *nods)*

MAX: Everything about it just reeks bourgeois. Believe me, I do understand.

(He goes; MISS ROSE *follows. As she goes out,* TONY *comes out and closes the door behind her. She sees this, and he waves. Short pause. The others come out of hiding.)*

*(*GEORGE *and* JOE *look at the empty drawer, and they are stunned.)*

JULIE: *(In front of the mirror)* I think I'm going to take another walk on the deck. Excuse me. *(She goes.)*

(Pause)

*(*TONY *has sat in front of the typewriter.)*

JOE: *(Finally)* He gave her the play, George. *(*GEORGE *nods.)* What do we do now?

*(*GEORGE *shrugs.)*

(Short pause)

*(*TONY *types a few letters.)*

GEORGE: There's still Tony's idea. We haven't heard that yet.

TONY: *(Looking at the paper in the typewriter)* I don't get it. How come all the letters now come out crooked?

BLACKOUT

ACT TWO

Scene One

(The same, a few hours later)

(GEORGE sits at the desk, his feet up, throwing darts at the picture of Lenin. The typewriter has been moved onto the bed, a towel has been put over it as its shroud.)

(TONY, glass in hand, paces the room. He is drunk.)

(Pause)

TONY: Wait, I got it!

(He goes to get himself another drink.)

GEORGE: Don't you think you should lay off that stuff?

TONY: Why? I'm a writer, aren't I?

GEORGE: I'm over here, Tony.

TONY: Right. *(Beat)* Where was I?

GEORGE: *(Reads off his pad)* "Wait, I got it!"

(GEORGE settles in to again write down what TONY says.)

TONY: Wait, I got it. It's night. The wind howls. *(He howls.)* The rain pours down like cats and.... And...

GEORGE: Dogs?

TONY: Yeh, dogs! Thunder. Crash. Lightning. The curtains blow in the wet damp watery rain. And our hero, yes, our hero, sneaks slowly out of bed—

GEORGE: Yes.

TONY: Climbs down the drainpipe—

GEORGE: Yes.

TONY: *(Trips and almost falls over)* And leaving that orphanage behind forever, heads with bag and baggage to Boston to make his fame and fortune. That's it. Curtain!

GEORGE: That's the end of the play?

TONY: No. That's the end of the first act. *(Beat)* What's wrong, you think it's too abrupt?

GEORGE: No. As a matter of fact, I've been waiting hours for that act to end. It's just that so far, Tony, we've covered eight years, had two hangings, one forced marriage, an attempted rape, a suicide, a drowning which may or may not have been accidental, and a suspicion of witches.

TONY: You don't think it's serious enough. Look, I want this to be serious. I want my work to upset people.

GEORGE: If it's any consolation, you've already upset my stomach.

TONY: Really? Thanks.

GEORGE: Tony, I was only wondering if you thought that might be a wee bit too much plot for one act.

*(*JOE *enters with a pile of books.)*

JOE: The only plays they have in the ship's library are these by Shakespeare.

GEORGE: *(To* JOE*)* I've got to talk to you.

TONY: *(Thinking)* Too much—? What was the word?

GEORGE: Plot.

*(*TONY *nods and drinks.)*

JOE: *(Setting the books down)* Maybe we can take one of Shakespeare's plays and jazz it up a little.

TONY: Shakespeare! Jazz up Shakespeare! I won't let you change one word of Shakespeare. Shakespeare is a genius! Shakespeare is immortal! Shakespeare is—

JOE: Dead.

GEORGE: Tony, why don't you go out and get us some coffee.

TONY: And leave the play, I couldn't do that, Mr Reilly.

GEORGE: You finished the first act, right? *(Beat)* And what always happens after the first act? *(Beat)*

TONY: The second act?

GEORGE: Between the first and second acts, Tony? The intermission is what happens. And what do you do during the intermission? You go out and get coffee.

TONY: Oh. So it's intermission.

GEORGE: That's right, Tony.

TONY: I'll be right back. *(He goes.)*

GEORGE: Joe, this isn't going to work.

JOE: *(Going through the books)* Here's one. *Much Ado About Nothing.* Nothing—that's a good subject for a play. That always sells.

GEORGE: Joe, I'm telling you we're going about this all the wrong way. That boy is sick. He's ghoulish. We can't put his sick ideas on stage, it wouldn't be fair to our audiences. The people who come to our plays are nice people, decent people, good people.

JOE: By and large pretty wealthy people.

GEORGE: Same thing.

JOE: Then what are we going to do?

GEORGE: There is only one thing we can do, Joe. And that's shake Max out of this. *(Beat)* I've started to think we've underestimated all his revolution talk. It's confusing him, Joe. Look at him. He doesn't even know who his friends are anymore.

JOE: We're his friends.

GEORGE: Politics, I know this from experience, can sometimes have a severe disorienting affect upon a person, especially a fella like Max, who's so impressionable. *(Beat)* It clouds the mind, Joe. A guy becomes lost. He loses his hold on reality. And that's what has happened to Max. That is why he's been acting this way to me, his best friend. *(Beat)* He's crazy, Joe. I wouldn't be surprised if one day he even tried to stick some of that politics into a play.

JOE: He would have to be crazy to do that. So what do we do?

GEORGE: We got to get him to see that all this politics is just a lot of bunk. *(Beat)* We got to get him to realize that as an artist his responsibility isn't to a political party or platform, but to society as a whole, to the truth, Joe. And the truth knows no party line.

JOE: So that's why you've never voted.

GEORGE: No, I didn't want to register, I was afraid I'd get stuck with jury duty. *(Beat)* He needs to see reason! People don't come to the theater to be lectured at. So what happens? I've seen it a thousand times. Max'll end up just preaching to the converted. He'll end up espousing the same beliefs play after play. He'll end up—

JOE: Broke.

GEORGE: Exactly. And so, Joe, we must get Max to see that his beliefs, which he calls responsible, are in fact irresponsible. That they can have a serious effect upon many others. *(Beat)* He must think about that. *(Beat)* He must ask himself what has been the single rallying cry of writers, the glue which binds us writers together, I dare say all artists in America, together? What one principle unites us all?

JOE: Money.

GEORGE: Right again. And yet, one single writer, willfully accepting poverty, could become that chink in the armor, could be that break in our solidarity, and what could transpire, is the destruction of Art in America as we know it today!

(Beat)

JOE: The Dramatists Guild must love you.

GEORGE: I don't belong. I'm not a joiner.

(Knock on the door.)

GEORGE: Come in.

(FREDDY enters.)

FREDDY: Mr Reilly?

GEORGE: Who are you?

FREDDY: Freddy Hart. I ran into Tony in the hall and he said you were in here.

JOE: He's busy, he can't be disturbed.

FREDDY: I only was wondering if Mr Reilly had a chance yet to read my outline.

JOE: Outline?

GEORGE: What outline?

FREDDY: For the play I want to write.

JOE: A play! Come in, come in! This could be it, George!

GEORGE: Joe, I don't remember receiving any outline from....

FREDDY: I left it on that desk this morning. *(Beat)* When Tony was here. He said to— *(Beat)* You have it, don't you? Please, it's the only copy I had. *(Beat)*

GEORGE: No, I don't think I—

FREDDY: It had a red cover!

GEORGE: *(Shrugs)* Red cover— *(Remembers)* Joe... *(Nods toward the waste paper basket)*

FREDDY: Then you do know what I'm talking about?

JOE: I think maybe we do. Yes.

FREDDY: Do you have it?

GEORGE: In a manner of speaking—

FREDDY: If what you're saying is that you're not interested, then you can give it back.

GEORGE: Give it back to the man, Joe.

JOE: You give it back to him.

GEORGE: *(Moving toward the basket)* But before we do, I think you should be aware that it got a little.... *(Beat)*

FREDDY: A little what?

GEORGE: Soiled. It got a little soiled, didn't it, Joe. *(Grabs the basket and shoves it into* JOE*'s hand)* Give it back to him! *(He moves away.)*

FREDDY: It's in there? You thought it was so bad that you threw it away?! *(He looks through the basket, pulls out a bunch of burned papers.)* Where? I don't see it.

GEORGE: I think that is it in your hand.

(Pause)

*(*FREDDY *looks at the burned pages.)*

FREDDY: I don't understand.

GEORGE: These things happen.

FREDDY: Why was my outline burned?

GEORGE: Believe me, this kind of thing happens to plays all the time.

FREDDY: It smells of lighter fluid. *(He turns to go.)*

GEORGE: If there's ever anything we can do to help.

JOE: Just call. *(Beat)* Though not before eleven, remember we're theater people.

*(*FREDDY *turns and looks back at them. Pause.* FREDDY *leaves.)*

JOE: Now what's the matter? George, that kid had to learn the cruel reality of this business sometime, and it's just lucky for him he learned it from his friends.

GEORGE: Joe, I have an idea. What's the closest thing to Max's heart in the whole world?

JOE: That's easy. His typewriter, but Tony's seen to that. *(Picks up the towel)* May it rest in peace.

GEORGE: I mean after his typewriter.

JOE: After his typewriter? That's a hard one. I don't know, what?

GEORGE: Julie.

JOE: Julie?

GEORGE: He's in love with her, isn't he?

JOE: Yeh. *(Beat)* Wait a minute, I hope you're not suggesting we get Julie to write the play. I've seen some of those plays written by women. They're always about men and women and they're always written from a woman's point of view. I find that very limited.

GEORGE: I'm not suggesting she write the play. I'm suggesting we use her for bait.

*(*TONY *rolls in a cart with coffee.)*

TONY: Funny thing I just saw, Mr Reilly.

GEORGE: With your sense of humor I'm afraid to hear. What happened, did someone get mangled?

TONY: Oh no, nothing like that. Remember Mr Conklin? *(Beat)* He was here a little while ago.

JOE: Conklin?

TONY: I just saw him being dragged away to the brig.

GEORGE: Arrested? Why?

TONY: The Captain was yelling something about him being a revolutionary, and he kept yelling something about just wanting to read the sports page.

JOE: Oh. *(Shrugs. Turns to* GEORGE*)* What do you mean by bait?

GEORGE: I'll explain it to you. *(Turns to* TONY*)* Tony, where are you going?

TONY: To the bathroom while it's still intermission.

GEORGE: You'll have time to do that later.

JOE: Why don't you wait until you start the second act, you may need to go in there then to get inspired.

TONY: But I'm already inspired, Mr Williams. I see the whole play right in front of me.

(Breathes on JOE*, who coughs and pushes him away.)*

GEORGE: Tony, the Negro who was just here....

TONY: Freddy?

GEORGE: I need to have a word with him.

TONY: What's he done now? Has he been fluffing off again?

GEORGE: He hasn't done anything. I just want you to get him.

TONY: Me?? But my play. You sure I have enough time?

GEORGE: The lights haven't blinked, have they?

TONY: The lights??

GEORGE: That's how you know intermission's over. When they blink the lights.

(TONY *looks up at the lights in the room. He nods to himself. Slowly he goes to the door, opens it, stops.)*

TONY: You promise you won't start thinking about the second act until I get back?

GEORGE: I have promised myself to put the whole thing right out of my mind.

(TONY *nods and leaves.)*

JOE: I don't understand what you want Freddy for?

GEORGE: It's a long shot, but what's left but long shots now?

JOE: You know I'm all for trying anything. That is, as long as no one gets hurt. I draw the line at hurting people.

GEORGE: Someone could get hurt.

JOE: So I'll draw another line. What's your idea?

GEORGE: I once had this friend. He was a writer. And like Max, he started thinking about everything that's wrong in the world.

JOE: For a writer that is death.

GEORGE: I know that. And just like Max, he began reading all those leftist books and newspapers, and he started going to meetings, then he was speaking at these meetings, and pretty soon he had all these ideas about society and poor people and things like that. And like Max, he wasn't content just to have these ideas, he would not stop until he had put these ideas into his writing.

JOE: Some people just don't know when to stop!

GEORGE: Suddenly the whole world was his cause. He was full of convictions, and prided himself on his social awareness. *(Beat)* But then, Joe, something happened. One day he and his wife were on the subway, and who should sit next to his wife but a colored man. Of course, he didn't think anything about it.

JOE: Why should he? Colored people are just people.

GEORGE: But then, Joe, he noticed this colored man winking at his wife.

JOE: Those animals.

GEORGE: And then it happened. Call it protecting one's loved one. Call it irrational fear. Call it whatever you want, but, my friend found himself standing in the middle of the car screaming at this man. *(Beat)* Pretty soon the rest of the car was screaming at him too. And a few minutes later, two cops came by, and my friend remembers watching this poor colored man being pulled off the train at 72nd Street, and he remembers thinking—wasn't this the very same kind of person he'd so much wanted to help? *(Beat)* He was shocked with himself. And it was then that he realized he was no social reformer. And not a day has gone by since then, Joe, that my friend has not thanked that colored man for opening his eyes and letting him see the errors of his ways.

(Short pause)

JOE: That's beautiful.

GEORGE: Of course, he had a slight relapse after hearing from the colored man's lawyer that the Negro had had a cinder in his eye. So that's why he was winking. *(Beat)* But my friend soon realized there was no going back.

JOE: Sure. It's important to stick to your convictions. Who was this friend, George? Do I know him?

(Short pause)

GEORGE: He was me.

JOE: You?! *(Beat)* You never told me that about yourself.

GEORGE: There are some events in one's life that are so special that you don't wish to share them with anyone but yourself. *(Beat)* So if my plan works, Max'll one day feel about today the way I feel about that day many years ago. First we have to find Julie.

JOE: She said she was going to take a walk on deck.

(They start to go.)

JOE: But George, what exactly is the plan?

(The door to the hall opens and MAX *enters.* GEORGE *and* JOE *freeze.* MAX *has a number of magazines and papers with him.)*

MAX: What are you two doing in my cabin?

JOE: Us??

GEORGE: I can explain, Max, we—

MAX: Oh forget it. Stay if you want, I'm moving out anyway.

(He goes to the bed and pulls out his suitcase, and begins to pack.)

*(*JOE *and* GEORGE *look at each other.)*

JOE: Moving out? Where are you going, Max?

GEORGE: He decided to take the train.

MAX: Eva Rose got me a cabin in third class.

GEORGE: God! Miss Rose must have an awful lot of pull to find you a place down there.

MAX: Leave Miss Rose out of this.

GEORGE: I'd love to. In fact, I'd love to drag Miss Rose out of this and throw her overboard.

MAX: *(Packing)* What I'm doing, George, you'll never understand.

JOE: You're wrong there. George was just saying he once had beliefs just like yours.

MAX: When was that? Before his mother went into labor? *(Goes to the photo on the wall)* Who's been sticking darts in my picture of Lenin?!!

GEORGE: Lenin?! Joe, you told me it was Sam Shubert!

(The door to the hall had been left open, and JULIE *now enters and stands in the doorway.)*

MAX: *(Taking down the photo; to the photo)* They have no respect for property. *(Packs the photo)*

GEORGE: Joe has respect for property.

JOE: It's certainly a better investment these days than stocks.

MAX: *(To himself)* I'll be rid of them soon.

JULIE: *(Very tense)* Going somewhere, Max?

MAX: Oh there you are, Julie. I've been wondering where you were. *(He packs.)*

JULIE: How hard did you wonder, Max?

JOE: He's moving to a new cabin, Julie.

GEORGE: Compliments of Miss Eva Rose.

MAX: *(Packing)* She found me a bunk in third class. I was looking for you to tell you, but I'll explain later. *(Beat)* Julie, could you get the shirts in the closet?

*(*JULIE *just stares at him.)*

GEORGE: *(To* JOE*)* Something tells me she's not going to get those shirts.

JULIE: Why don't you explain now. How hard did you look for me?

MAX: What? *(Looks up)* What's wrong? Where are the shirts?

JULIE: If you really wanted to find me, I was on the deck—plain as day.

MAX: Oh really? *(He goes back to packing.)*

JULIE: *(Cold as ice)* Really.

GEORGE: *(To* JOE*)* Really. *(As in "oh come now")*

JOE: He's playing dumb.

GEORGE: I once tried that tactic with my second wife. Here, see, I still have the scar.

MAX: You won't believe some of the things Eva Rose has told me, Julie.

JULIE: Though I'll bet you believe them.

MAX: What's that supposed to mean? What is the matter?

(Both GEORGE *and* JOE *lean forward to listen.)*

MAX: Do you mind?

JOE: Not at all. They don't move.

MAX: What I meant was—I couldn't wait to see you.

JULIE: *(Cold)* Why?

GEORGE: Why?

(Beat)

JOE: Why?

MAX: Because, Julie, I wanted to share with you everything I've learned from my tour down into the lower decks. It's changed my life.

JULIE: All I want to know is—will it change ours?

MAX: I sincerely hope so.

JULIE: Fine. Enough said. *(She moves away.)*

MAX: Where are you going?

JULIE: I'm taking back the sweater I gave you for Christmas. *(Takes it out of the closet. Holds it up to* GEORGE *and* JOE.*)* Handmade!

MAX: Julie, this isn't the time to be thinking about some sweater.

JULIE: Now this is just some sweater! That wasn't how he talked about it when I gave it to him.

MAX: Julie, I'm not finished yet!

JULIE: I think we are, Max.

MAX: Goddamnit, will you listen?!!! *(Beat)* Please?

(She turns back to him, begrudgingly.)

MAX: Thank you. Julie, if I hadn't seen it with my own eyes, I wouldn't have believed it. You can't imagine how inhumane people can be.

GEORGE: She could if she'd met my second wife.

JULIE: I'm just learning how cruel some people can be.

MAX: She showed me the records of when this boat carried thousands of people down in its bowels.

JOE: Please, watch your language, Max.

MAX: And did you know they didn't even keep records of the names. They only knew the weight. One record showed that for one trip there were fifty thousand pounds. And on this same trip—according to Eva—

JULIE: Eva, Max? Please, I don't want to hear anymore, I still have my pride.

GEORGE: Tell Joe, he has no pride.

MAX: What does pride have to do with anything?

JULIE: I guess maybe we were just brought up differently.

MAX: Please, will you be quiet for a second. *(Beat)* On this same trip, Julie, people like us sat here in the lap of this grotesque luxury, while they down there were sleeping on wet wooden planks. While our kind sat and shoveled food into our faces, they were given nothing, and had to eat only what they'd brought with them.

JULIE: Speaking of which, I hope she's a good cook, for your sake.

MAX: Who?? What are you talking about? Will you just sit down and listen?!

JULIE: I'll sit, but I won't promise I'll listen.

MAX: According to this one report, one could already begin to smell the stench of rotting meat, even though they were only one day out of England.

GEORGE: You sure it was stench and not just English cooking?

MAX: *(Trying to ignore him)* So you can imagine what it would be like in two or three days. If one walked down into that hold, Julie, you could hear this roaring—women yelling, men groaning—

GEORGE: Sounds like Sardi's.

MAX: Children crying, one could hardly hear oneself think down there.

JOE: No. Jack Dempsey's.

GEORGE: I didn't know you went to Dempsey's.

JOE: I go for the cucumber salad.

GEORGE: German or Irish?

JOE: I never asked. Let me see, there's vinegar, paprika, and a layer of sour cream.

JULIE: That's German. I know *my* way around a kitchen.

MAX: Will you three shut up?! *(Beat)* You don't know what you're saying.

GEORGE: Maybe, but you have to admit we know our cucumber salad.

(Short pause. MAX *is about to give up.)*

JOE: Go on, Max. I'm interested. I had an uncle who came over on a boat like that.

MAX: I didn't know that, Joe. *(Beat)* Then here's what he experienced: He had to have a physical at Ellis Island. Of course someone who might have been healthy at the start, might not be so fortunate a few days later. And yet—here are pictures—no matter how sick or hungry or in pain these people might have been, they were not immediately let off at Ellis; no, first this ship, surrounded by tugs and water cannon and confetti, cruised into the Hudson, docked on the West Side, let off those passengers who were not just pounds of flesh, and then in the middle of the night these human beings, Joe, were herded like animals, taken back into the harbor—marched through the dark into Ellis compound, where one third—that was the quota—one third learned that they were not desirable emigrants to our wonderful country.

*(*MAX *looks at* GEORGE, *who is staring at the floor.)*

MAX: And there they were kept in cells, until another ship with another hold could pick up their pounds. *(Beat)* You have something you want to say now, George?

GEORGE: What? I'm sorry, my mind was still on the cucumber salad.

MAX: Julie, will you just look at this picture? *(Holds up a picture from a magazine)*

JULIE: I suppose. *(Beat)* Just as long as she's not in it.

MAX: That young man there had his hand crushed—crushed because someone forgot to or didn't care to rope together some barrels. He was sent back—because he couldn't work. *(Beat)* That is, he couldn't do a slave's work at a slave's wage which is the only work and wage these people could even hope of doing, which is the only reason our great land let them in in the first place—so the rest of us wouldn't have to get our hands dirty. And we think of America as free!

(Beat)

GEORGE: *(Under his breath, to* JOE*)* I don't, my neighborhood's very expensive.

MAX: Joe, is this pretty true to how your uncle described his trip?

JOE: It's close. *(Beat)* Though mostly he told me about meeting Noel Coward in the lounge.

*(*MAX *turns away from* JOE *and goes back to* JULIE, *grabbing more papers and magazines.)*

MAX: Julie, just look at this material Eva gave me.

JULIE: If I hear that name again I am going to scream.

MAX: Do you know where these people are today?

GEORGE: Noel Coward? Isn't he playing the 47th Street Theater?

MAX: *(Showing her pictures)* That's them there. Hungry, out of work, helpless. *(He looks up.)* Oh, did you know Eva's husband has been in prison three times for trying to organize unions? Imagine going to jail for your beliefs. God, I envy him—they won't throw playwrights into jail for their beliefs.

GEORGE: How do we know?

JULIE: Max—? Miss Rose has a husband?

MAX: Of course. *(Opens more newspapers. Looks up)* Oh I see what you mean. "Rose" is her maiden name. She still uses it as a journalist.

JULIE: But Max, why didn't you just tell me she was married?

MAX: What does that have to do with anything? *(Shakes his head)* Here, just look at this—

JULIE: I'm terribly sorry.

MAX: I think every American should be.

JULIE: I feel so stupid. I just want to cry.

MAX: I can understand that. These pictures aren't easy to take. But Julie, no tears ever changed the world—don't cry, get angry.

GEORGE: My second wife had that same philosophy.

MAX: And look here. Did you know that in our wonderful country, unemployment is growing at the rate of four thousand a week? I knew it was bad, but four thousand?! That's four thousand faces. Four thousand mouths!

GEORGE: Eight thousand legs. Forty thousand toes.

*(*MAX *looks at* GEORGE.*)*

JULIE: I'm listening, Max.

MAX: Read this—even that four thousand figure doesn't tell the whole story, because millions of workers, millions have already given up the search for a job.

JOE: Quitters never win.

MAX: And this—bread lines stretched eighteen blocks in San Francisco last week, sixteen blocks in Chicago. In Detroit —they couldn't even form a line—there was a riot. *(Beat)* And yet—look at this—last year the president of General Motors paid himself a salary of more than three hundred and seventy thousand dollars. *(Beat)* And he paid his vice president more than three hundred and twenty thousand. *(Beat)* What does that tell us?

JOE: It's better to be president than vice president?

MAX: It tells us that in our great country all is not right! Some people are winning, but the rest are losing. And that is why I am moving out!! *(He begins to pack again. Short pause.)* I can't stand it here. I can't stand what this room represents, the kind of society it reflects, where things, possessions are more valued than human beings. *(Beat)* A room can't be called first class, unless there is also a second class. *(Beat)* Have you seen my green bag?

JULIE: It's in my room. I borrowed it to distribute the newspapers in.

MAX: Julie, you knew that was my favorite bag. You could have gotten newsprint all over it.

JULIE: I'm sorry, I'll—

MAX: My mother gave that to me when I went to college.

JULIE: I'll go get it, Max. *(She turns to go.)*

MAX: *(To himself)* Of all the bags... *(He packs.)*

*(*JULIE *turns back at the door.)*

JULIE: Max?? Just one question. *(Beat)* Miss Rose—I mean, Eva—she is a communist, correct?

MAX: That's right. Why?

JULIE: And she's married. Correct?

MAX: Yeh. So what?

JULIE: See, Max, more than once you have told me—communists do not get married.

MAX: Oh. I see what you mean. *(Beat)* Funny, that contradiction hadn't dawned on me. *(Laughs to himself)*

JULIE: I thought I'd just point it out to you. *(She goes.)*

(Short pause. MAX *packs.)*

JOE: You really believe all that stuff, Max?

MAX: What stuff are you referring to? *(Packs)*

JOE: About the social classes and big business and the poor being stepped on.

MAX: It's not a question of belief. You don't have to believe in the truth. You just have to have the courage to accept it.

GEORGE: Oh, it's the truth! I see. And the truth's written in those newspapers?

MAX: *(Packing)* I believe that.

JOE: *(Pointing to the papers)* Max, do you mind if I take a look?

MAX: *(Packing)* That's what they're there for. Maybe what's in them will open your eyes, as it's opened mine.

GEORGE: A strong cup of coffee—first thing in the morning. That too will get your eyes open.

MAX: *(Looking around)* Have you seen my typewriter?

(JOE and GEORGE look at each other.)

JOE: Which typewriter is that?

MAX: What do you mean which—? *(Looks at them suspiciously)* You two haven't done anything to damage that machine have you?

GEORGE: I doubt if we could damage that machine any more than that machine has damaged the American theater.

MAX: Everything I've ever written since I was fourteen has been on that typewriter.

GEORGE: There's no need to apologize.

MAX: Where is it?!

GEORGE: I don't know how to tell you this, but while you were out, Max, bounty hunters from the Pulitzer Prize Committee charged into the room and shot it right in the back space. *(Beat)* It didn't have a chance.

JOE: When I heard that little bell ring for the last time, I thought I'd die.

MAX: Go ahead and wisecrack, I don't have the time to deal with you two now, but when I come back for the rest of my things, that typewriter better be here, or you better not. *(He packs.)*

GEORGE: *(To JOE, scratches his head)* How far can a typewriter go on its own?

(MAX goes to the closet and packs furiously.)

GEORGE:He seems to be in a big hurry to leave this room.

MAX: I am!

GEORGE: *(Goes up to MAX)* Max, if Joe has done anything to offend you—

JOE: Me?!

GEORGE: Or if I have committed some small indiscretion—which for the life of me I can't imagine what it could have been—let me take this time to say: We are sorry.

(MAX comes out of the closet. GEORGE holds out his hand. MAX pauses, then shakes it and continues to pack.)

GEORGE: Now that is more like how it used to be. When someone's wrong they just have to be man enough to admit it. *(Beat)* Thanks, Joe, for admitting it. *(Beat)* Max, we've had fights before—I wouldn't want to think how many—but Max, someone has always been big enough to say he was sorry.

MAX: *(Packing)* I don't remember either of us ever apologizing for anything.

GEORGE: But we've always got someone else to apologize. That's why we're such a team. *(Puts his arm around* MAX*'s shoulder)* Come on and sit down. Let's have a drink together.

MAX: No, thank you.

GEORGE: Then let's sit down and talk for a while. We've hardly talked together for a week.

MAX: I can't now. *(Short pause)*

GEORGE: *(One more try)* Then how about just chatting while you pack and catching each other up on what we've been working on?

MAX: Sorry, George. *(He heads for the bathroom.)*

GEORGE: *(Yells)* And you claim to care about people! You don't care about me!

MAX: You care about yourself enough for the both of us.

GEORGE: Max, charity begins in the home.

MAX: This isn't my home.

GEORGE: Home is where you hang your hat, Max.

MAX: No, George. Home is where your heart is.

GEORGE: It's where you hang your hat!

MAX: It's where your heart is!

JOE: *(Who has been looking through the newspapers)* Now that you two have thoroughly discussed the nature of home, could one of you tell me where the sports page is in these papers?

GEORGE: *The Daily Worker* doesn't have a sports page, Joe.

JOE: You're kidding? That's un-American.

MAX: To be honest, it's not that I wouldn't like to sit around with you, it's just that right now I have other more important things to do.

GEORGE: Like what?

MAX: I want to get to work. After what I've seen this morning, I feel I have a thousand ideas for a new play.

GEORGE: *(Grabbing a pencil and paper)* You wouldn't mind mentioning just one of those ideas, would you?

*(*MAX *ignores him and goes into the bathroom.)*

GEORGE:You goddamn socialist, I thought the whole idea of you people was to share!

MAX: *(Storming out)* I call myself a communist! There's a difference!

GEORGE: Semantics! There's no more difference than between Gimbels and Klein's!

JOE: Wait a minute, George, I find that Klein's, especially in men's sportswear—

GEORGE & MAX: Shut up!

GEORGE: Communist, socialist, you both want to give everything away. Give, give, give. But where the hell will the money come from to give to all your poor people? *(Beat)* There's an awful lot of poor people. I mean, an awful lot, Max. *(Beat)* If you think it's going to come from the rich, well, let me tell you about that. From my experience, rich people are more than willing to give a little—if it's tax deductible—but there comes a point where they are going to say enough is enough!

MAX: I don't give a damn what rich people will say.

JOE: That's easy to say now, but wait until the commies become rich.

MAX: You can't be a rich communist, Joe. That's the point.

JOE: No ambition, huh?

GEORGE: And if you think you're going to achieve your goals by tearing down America, let me tell you about how I feel about our country. *(Beat)* It's the best country this world has ever seen. *(Beat)* We've got poor people, sure. So what? Who's perfect? *(Beat)* But we've got a lot of rich people. We've got more rich people than the rest of the world put together, I'll bet. *(Beat)* And that means to me—hope. Hope for all of us. Hope for Joe and you and me. *(Beat)* And it means freedom. The freedom to make the most of our lives.

MAX: And the most money we can?

GEORGE: That's right. And that is just what it says in the Declaration of Independence.

MAX: It says we can make the most money we can?

GEORGE: Not in so many words, but that's what everyone knows it means.

(Short pause. MAX *paces.)*

MAX: Why I bother I do not know. But— *(Turns to* GEORGE*)* Try to understand that I simply want to be able to live with myself. Look around, open your eyes, can't even you see that things aren't right?

GEORGE: No, looks all right to me.

JOE: The bed's a little messy. *(Covers up the typewriter a little more)*

MAX: That is because you have blinders on. You don't see the suffering, the pain, the poverty that is right in front of your face.

(Pause)

GEORGE: Next, Mr Communist here is going to tell us he wants to write plays that will help people!

MAX: That is exactly my hope. Yes. I'm glad you finally understand. *(Beat)* Now excuse me. *(He goes into the bathroom and closes the door.)*

GEORGE: *(Shouts)* Let me tell you something about the theater: A play has never gotten anyone to change their sheets let alone the world!

MAX: *(Opens the door)* Fine! Even if I don't change the world with my plays, I am damn well going to try to change it with my life! What can't be done in the theater, I'll do in the streets. *(Slams the door shut)*

JOE: In New York, no one will notice. *(Beat)* I don't think you're convincing him, George.

GEORGE: Shut up. *(Shouts toward the bathroom)* So what specifically, Max, are you going to write about that is going to help the goddamn world?!!

*(*FREDDY *appears in the doorway.)*

FREDDY: Tony said you want to see me. If it's about an apology I think you're a little late.

GEORGE: Sh-sh.

MAX: *(Off, from the bathroom)* Okay, George, let's take the Negro!!

(Beat)

(Everybody looks at everybody else, then FREDDY *looks at the bathroom door.)*

JOE: Take him, where, Max?

FREDDY: Who's—?

MAX: *(Off)* The Negro race is certainly something worth writing about!

GEORGE: *(Taking* FREDDY *by the arm)* Come with me. *(Starts to lead him across the room)*

JOE: *(Whispering)* What are you doing, George?

FREDDY: Get your hands off me!

MAX: *(Off)* It is a disgrace what our country has done to them.

GEORGE: He took the words right out of my mouth. *(To* FREDDY*)* Get in that closet. *(Opens the closet door for* FREDDY*)*

FREDDY: Are you crazy?

MAX: *(Off)* The incredible lies they've been told.

GEORGE: It's just for a minute. I'll explain everything later.

MAX: *(Off)* The selfishness with which they've been treated.

FREDDY: Why would I get in a—

*(*MAX *enters from the bathroom.* GEORGE, *before* MAX *can see, shoves* FREDDY *into the closet and closes the door.)*

(Beat)

*(*MAX *looks around.)*

MAX: Did someone just come in?

GEORGE: A draft.

*(*FREDDY *knocks on the closet door.)*

MAX: Is someone knocking?

GEORGE: That's me. My foot's asleep.

MAX: Huh. *(Beat)* Anyway, you, George, would rather keep your eyes shut to their misery! It's people like you who'd rather keep that part of history, that particular skeleton, in the closet.

JOE: Not a skeleton, he looks in good shape.

MAX: What?

*(*GEORGE *bangs his foot again.)*

MAX: George, you probably haven't noticed, but unemployment among Negroes is at fifty-three percent. And those who do have jobs are paid the lowest wages and are the first to be laid off. And they're not even allowed to live where they want! *(Beat)* We don't treat them as human beings, this great country of ours! *(Beat)* You know, if I were a Negro today, I don't know how I'd keep myself from burning the whole damn country down! *(Goes back into the bathroom)*

GEORGE: *(Opening the closet, at eye level)* Don't listen to this! *(He slams the door closed, and we hear a crash in the closet. The closing door has hit* FREDDY. GEORGE *slowly opens the closet door again, looks down at the floor and says, quietly and guiltily:)* Don't listen to this.

MAX: *(From the bathroom)* The treatment they have received at our hands! It just isn't fair. We should all feel guilty as hell. *(Beat; opens the bathroom door)* I know of no better subject to write about. *(Beat)* You asked for an idea. There it is. Take it, if you want.

GEORGE: I think I'll pass. But you got any more?

MAX: I don't think you'd be interested.

GEORGE: Something with a love interest maybe?

MAX: Sorry. *(Turns)*

GEORGE: *(It just bursts out)* Then how about giving me the play you've just written?!!!!

(Long pause. MAX *turns back to face* GEORGE.*)*

MAX: No, George. *(Beat)* Not ever again. *(Short pause, then throws him a little salute)* Good luck with Colonel Face. Sorry. *(He turns.)*

JOE: Max, why do you keep going into the bathroom?

MAX: I'm trying to take a shower before I move. *(He goes.)*

(Beat)

JOE: What's the matter with the shower in his new room?

GEORGE: *(Explaining)* You never know who's been in there before you, Joe. *(Beat. He sighs and shakes his head.)* The son of a bitch doesn't leave me much choice, does he?

JOE: Much choice for what? Why is the Negro in the closet, George?

GEORGE: *(Pacing)* I tried to convince him. I tried to use reason. If I'd had a gun I would have tried to use that. I don't want him hurt, Joe. But what choice does he leave me? I would have much preferred that he came to his senses on his own and save me the pain of having to break him, of having to shatter every belief he has, of having to see him crawl on his knees through broken glass and beg me to work with him again.

JOE: You can get him to do that? Is that why the Negro's in the closet?

GEORGE: Promise me, when Max is begging to be taken back, that we will be kind.

JOE: I promise, George. You can really get him back just like that?

GEORGE: According to my plan it'll take about—twenty minutes. Maybe twenty-five.

JOE: That's the plan you mentioned before? It must be incredible.

GEORGE: I don't know, Joe, maybe it's too drastic. Everyone has to draw a line somewhere—even someone in the theater. Maybe we should forget the whole idea.

JOE: No, no!

GEORGE: Who knows, maybe Tony will come up with an idea.

JOE: Tony?! George, we need that play! Do it! Whatever it is, do it!

GEORGE: You're sure, Joe?

JOE: Positive. What's your idea?

GEORGE: In that case—

JOE: Tell me!

GEORGE: Remember I talked about using Julie as the bait?

JOE: I remember.

GEORGE: Remember I talked about the time when that colored man winked at my wife?

JOE: The one with the cinder in his eye. I remember.

GEORGE: *(Whispers)* Remember how I felt about that?

JOE: You got the guy arrested, I remember.

GEORGE: Well, here's my idea. *(Beat)* In order to shake Max out of this great love he has for poor people, we get Max to walk in and find Julie and this Freddy Hart in a compromising situation.

JOE: George, that's really low. That's sick. How do we do it?

GEORGE: Of course, we just have to get it so it appears that—

JOE: —they're in a compromising situation. Of course. How do we do it?

GEORGE: I've thought it all out. The first thing we do is get Max out of the room.

JOE: How do we do that?

GEORGE: I don't know, we'll find some excuse. That'll be easy.

JOE: Sure. Then what?

GEORGE: Then we get Julie in here.

JOE: How do we do that?

GEORGE: I'll think of something.

JOE: Uh-huh.

GEORGE: Then we get Julie to take off some of her clothes.

JOE: How do you get her to do that, George?

GEORGE: I don't know yet. And then, we get Freddy to take off some of his clothes. *(Beat)* I don't know yet. *(Beat)* Then we get Max to come back into the room and he finds them alone without their clothes on and what can he think but—! *(Beat)* Well? It's foolproof! It's brilliant! It's perfect! It isn't going to work, is it?

*(*JOE *shakes his head.)*

GEORGE: I didn't think so. I told you I can't write plots.

JOE: If it's any consolation, you sold it well. Almost like an agent.

GEORGE: What are we going to do? In four hours we have to give the Colonel a play. And when my ex-wife finds out I can't pay the alimony, she'll have me in jail in no time.

JOE: Your second wife?

GEORGE: No, she's not so bad. *(Beat)* Now are we sure the Colonel is not an understanding—forget it. *(Short pause)*

JOE: I could always go back to selling Bibles.

GEORGE: Least that's already written.

*(*TONY *enters. He carries a large envelope.)*

TONY: *(Entering)* Is the intermission over?

GEORGE: Everything is over, Tony. *(He gets up and goes toward the porthole.)*

TONY: Why didn't you blink the lights then? I've had eight cigarettes out there waiting for you to blink the lights.

GEORGE: The intermission is over, the play is over, the curtain is down, the audience has gone home, and the magic has turned into cold reality. *(He begins to climb out the window.)*

TONY: What's he doing, Mr Williams?

JOE: He's going to throw himself into the sea, Tony.

TONY: He's going to have to bounce a lot, there's two decks below that porthole.

*(*GEORGE *smiles and climbs back down.)*

GEORGE: I have always said—it is the thought that counts.

TONY: Is Mr Whitcomb here? This envelope was left for him.

GEORGE: He's in the shower. Drowning, we hope.

JOE: Put it on the desk.

TONY: Are you ready to hear my new idea for the second act?

GEORGE: *(Holding* TONY*'s head)* Oh Tony, Tony, Tony, always a new idea. Remember, Joe, when we were young and enthusiastic?

TONY: I got inspired from reading Mr Whitcomb's play. You know, it's pretty good, though I don't understand why he crossed out all the funny lines.

GEORGE: Mr Whitcomb's play? *(Laughs to himself)* Now where would you get a hold of Mr Whitcomb's play?

TONY: This is it here. Miss Rose dropped it off. She'd have come in herself, but we heard all this shouting.

GEORGE: *(Grabbing the envelope)* Give me that!! *(Rips it open)* Joe, it's the play!

TONY: There's also this note. *(He gives* GEORGE *the note.)*

GEORGE: *(Reading)* "Dear Mr Whitcomb: I am sorry to have to say that I found your play naive and the beliefs espoused in it undigested. Though you are obviously a talented writer—the lines which you appear to have crossed out are very funny—sheer enthusiasm is no substitute for clear thinking. Should you wish to discuss the play further with me, I will be happy to accommodate you." *(Beat)* Signed, Eva Rose.

(Short pause)

JOE: Poor Max.

GEORGE: A communist being panned by *The Daily Worker*. *(Beat)* That must be as bad as a capitalist being panned by *The Times.*

(They look at each other.)

JOE & GEORGE: *(Shaking their heads)* No. *(Beat)*

JOE: *(Looking at his watch)* You've got three and a half hours until dinner. Is that enough time to rewrite?

GEORGE: I won't even be late for the soup!

JOE: You can use my room.

GEORGE: I'll need paper. *(Grabs some from the desk)*

JOE: And coffee. I'll order coffee.

GEORGE: Cigarettes.

JOE: And cigarettes.

GEORGE: Sweet rolls.

JOE: And sweet rolls to go!

(They start to go.)

TONY: Wait! To go where?!!

JOE: To Broadway, Tony!

GEORGE & JOE: Broadway!!

(They leave.)

TONY: Wait! That's where I've always wanted to go!!

(He runs out after them. Short pause. The closet door slowly opens. FREDDY *gets up from the floor, sticks his head out, and looks around. The bathroom door opens.* FREDDY, *frightened, hurries back into the closet.* MAX *comes out.)*

MAX: And there's one more thing I just thought of.... *(He looks around.)* They're gone. *(He goes to get his jacket on the chair and sees the note. He picks it up and reads it. Obviously pained)* Oh God. She didn't like it. *(He puts the note down. Pause)* I've got to talk to her. *(He grabs his jacket and hurries out.)*

*(*FREDDY *again opens the door, peeks out. The hallway door opens, he hides again, and* JULIE *enters.)*

JULIE: Max, I'm sorry I took so long, I thought I'd wash the bag. *(Beat)* Max? Everybody's gone. *(She turns to leave, then notices that the room is a bit of a mess. She picks up some drink glasses, to move them away; as she does this, she spills on her dress.)* Oh darn. That's going to stain. *(She goes off to the bathroom, and closes the door.)*

*(*FREDDY *begins to come out of the closet again, but as he does so, he catches the pocket of his pants on the door knob, ripping them. The rip is large. For a moment he doesn't know what to do.)*

FREDDY: I can't go out into the hall like this.

(He looks in the closet and takes out a pair of MAX's *pants. He sets the pants on a chair and takes off his own pants.)*

(Suddenly the door to the hall opens and MAX *hurries in.* FREDDY *freezes.)*

MAX: *(To himself as he enters)* No, I should think first about what I want to say to her.

(He sees FREDDY, *pantless.)*

JULIE: *(From the bathroom)* Is that you dear? I'm just taking off my dress!

*(*MAX *looks toward the bathroom.)*

(Blackout)

Scene Two

(The same, later that evening)

*(*GEORGE *and* JOE *are laughing.* JOE *is lighting their cigars; both are now dressed in tuxedos.)*

*(*TONY *is entering, wheeling in a cart of champagne. He is a bit hungover.)*

TONY: Here's your champagne, Mr Williams.

GEORGE: *(Puffing on his cigar)* If it isn't Eugene O'Neill himself.

TONY: No, Mr Reilly. It's Tony.

GEORGE: *(To* JOE*)* I would have bet you a sawbuck that the next time we'd come across our friend here, he wouldn't be standing. Maybe you do have the makings of a playwright, Tony, you've certainly the liver for it.

TONY: Oh I haven't stopped standing, Mr Reilly. *(Beat)* Since Ingrid found me on the closet floor.

JOE: *(Opening the champagne)* What were you doing on a closet floor?

TONY: Mr Williams, today I have learned the real meaning of the word inspiration.

JOE: He found a dictionary, George. *(Laughs to himself, and begins to pour the champagne)*

TONY: When you and Mr Reilly wouldn't let me into your room, I decided to work by myself for a while.

GEORGE: That was humanitarian of you.

TONY: So I borrowed Mr Whitcomb's typewriter again. *(Takes the typewriter off the cart)* When you see Mr Whitcomb, tell him the glue hasn't dried yet. *(Puts it on the desk)*

*(*GEORGE *and* JOE *look at the typewriter, then shrug.)*

JOE: So you were saying about being inspired.

TONY: See I wanted a place where I wouldn't be distracted, so I went into a broom closet.

GEORGE: The obvious choice.

TONY: And then it happened. I wrote and I wrote until I wrote: "The end". Then like a great weight had been lifted off me, I fell asleep. *(Beat)* The next thing I knew Ingrid was waking me up.

GEORGE: Was she in there writing a play too?

TONY: No. *(Beat)* I don't think so.

GEORGE: Too bad. *(Takes his glass of champagne)* This could have been the start of a new Broomsbury Group. *(Sips; to* JOE*)* Sorry. *(To* TONY*)* So you finished your play.

TONY: Yes. I gave it to Ingrid, but if I'd known you were here, Mr Reilly, I'd have brought it with me. But if you've got a minute, I'll go and get it— *(Starts to leave)*

GEORGE: That really isn't necessary!

TONY: After all you've done to encourage me, I think it only fair that you be one of the first to read it. *(He hurries out.)*

GEORGE: That boy really holds a grudge, doesn't he?

*(*GEORGE *sips the champagne.* JOE *is at the cart; he has picked up the bill for the champagne.)*

GEORGE: Joe, you never did tell me why you wanted to wait in Max's room.

JOE: *(With the bill)* Here, sign Max's name. It's his cabin. *(Looks up)* What did you say?

GEORGE: *(Taking the bill)* Nothing. Never mind, you just answered it. *(He signs* MAX*'s name. Phone rings.)*

JOE: Maybe that's the Colonel!

*(*GEORGE *picks up the phone.)*

GEORGE: *(Into the phone)* Hello? Yes. As a matter of fact he's right here now. *(To* JOE*)* It's for you. You've just received a cable.

JOE: Tell them to read it.

GEORGE: *(Into the phone)* You can read it to me. *(To* JOE*, repeating what he hears)* It's from William Morris. Dear Joe: On your recommendation are presently negotiating to secure exclusive representation of *Communist Manifesto* Stop Please advise if intention is to use *Manifesto* for dramatic play Stop Or for musical. *(Covers the phone)* Musical of course. Why do they even bother to ask?

JOE: What do you think of that agency now, George?

GEORGE: Wait, there's more. *(Repeating)* P S: Strongly urge you to consider our client Lillian Gish for role of ingenue in *Manifesto* Stop. *(Puts down the phone)* That's it. *(Beat)*

JOE: Well?

GEORGE: Well what?

JOE: Is she right for the part?

(Beat)

GEORGE: She's not really my idea of the role, Joe.

JOE: But could she do it? She's a name, George! *(Beat)* Okay, I'll cable back William Morris tonight and string her along. We don't want to lose her.

GEORGE: Good thinking.

*(*JOE *writes a note to himself.* GEORGE *looks out, thinking.)*

GEORGE: Joe, be honest now.

JOE: *(Writing)* When have I ever not been honest?

GEORGE: What do you think Max'll think about my changes in his play?

JOE: *(Putting his pad away)* If he has half a brain he'd get on his knees and kiss the ground you walk on, George. If the Colonel ever read what he wrote—

GEORGE: Then you don't think he'll be upset that I changed the location from the Chicago stockyards to the backstage of a Broadway show?

JOE: Why should he? They're almost the same thing.

GEORGE: Precisely what I thought. *(Beat)* Hell, what can he complain about? All I've done is clarify. Take that one line—"There is no tomorrow only today!" *(Beat)* It makes a whole lot more sense to me having a chorus girl in an audition say that rather than some what? Union organizer, wasn't it?

JOE: And take Max's title.

GEORGE: *(As if seeing it in very small lights)* "The Greedy and the Hungry."

JOE: Yours is a lot better, yet it still makes the same point.

GEORGE: *(As if seeing it in big, big lights)* "Some Have It, Some Don't"!!!

(MAX enters from the hallway. He is dressed as he was and carries a large envelope.)

JOE: Max!

GEORGE: What a surprise. I thought you'd be busy hobnobbing with the poor people.

MAX: I changed my mind. I'm not moving.

GEORGE: *(To JOE)* I guess Miss Rose just couldn't pull enough strings.

MAX: *(With fury)* To hell with Eva Rose!!

(Beat. JOE and GEORGE look at each other.)

MAX: She's just a critic. And we know what they're like.

(Short pause)

JOE: Anything the matter, Max?

MAX: Everything's just fine. Everything's just wonderful. As you will soon see.

JOE: What is that supposed to—?

MAX: *(At the champagne cart, having looked at the bill)* Since I see I am paying for it, I don't suppose you'll mind if I have some champagne.

GEORGE: Help yourself.

JOE: *(Whispers to GEORGE)* What did he mean by—?

GEORGE: There's nothing Max can do to us now, Joe, so stop worrying.

MAX: *(Pouring himself some champagne)* I hear you've been busy, George.

JOE: He knows!

GEORGE: Of course he knows. Max isn't stupid. He knew I'd get his play one way or the other. I'm just sorry it had to be the other. *(Beat)* No hard feelings?

MAX: No hard feelings.

GEORGE: We'd give you back your room but we've promised to meet the Colonel here. *(Looks at his watch. To* JOE*)* Any time now.

MAX: Actually that is one reason why I'm here.

JOE: What do you mean, one reason why—?

MAX: *(Noticing the typewriter)* What's happened to this?!!

JOE: I didn't have anything to do with it!

*(*MAX *picks up the insides of the typewriter—it is a gluey mess.* JOE *and* GEORGE *watch him. Pause.* MAX *tenses, almost cries as he touches parts of the ruined machine.)*

*(*GEORGE *shrugs.* JULIE *enters.)*

JULIE: *(Entering)* I just heard the Colonel was on his way here.

MAX: *(To* JOE *and* GEORGE*)* I assume you won't mind if Julie stays as well.

GEORGE: It's your room.

JULIE: Max, did you hear me—the Colonel is coming *here.* Shouldn't we go?

MAX: Why should we, Julie. As George says—this is my room.

JULIE: You've told me what you think of the Colonel, Max.

MAX: I haven't told him yet.

JULIE: All you'll do is cause another scene.

MAX: What do you mean—another scene? *(Beat) (Yells)* I have nothing to apologize for!! You were taking off your dress. Freddy had his pants off—

JULIE: I know—it is all my fault!

MAX: I'm not saying that. But if the shoe fits—!

GEORGE: Wait a minute! *(Beat)* Freddy without his...Julie without her... *(Beat. To* JOE*)* Why does that sound so familiar?

*(*JOE *shrugs.)*

MAX: Anyway, Julie, let's forget about that. What's done is done. It's *c'est la vie. (He sits in front of the typewriter and plays with the parts, with a certain longing.)* Mistakes will happen. *(He sighs.)*

JULIE: My God, what's happened to Max's typewriter?

MAX: *(To himself)* And life goes on. *(Puts pieces back. Smiles.)* Oh well. *(He laughs and shakes his head.)*

JOE: He's laughing, George. Why is he laughing?

*(*MAX *takes the script he has with him and goes to sit on the bed.)*

MAX: I hope no one minds if I do a little reading. There's this script I am quite anxious to take a look at.

GEORGE: Suit yourself.

*(*MAX *lies on the bed and opens the script.)*

JULIE: I don't know if I want to stay here or not.

CONKLIN: *(Off, knocking)* Mr Williams! Mr Reilly!

JOE: That's the Colonel now! *(Calling)* Coming!!!

*(*JOE *and* GEORGE *straighten up the cabin a little.)*

GEORGE: Stay, Julie. The Colonel's not at all what you think. With a man like that, you have to remember his bark is a lot worse than his bite.

JOE: I'll get the door. *(Goes to the door)*

MAX: *(Reading)* "Act One. Scene One. *Some Have It, Some Don't.* The backstage of a Broadway theater".

JOE: *(Opening the door)* Colonel, it's good of you to—*(He suddenly slams the door in the* COLONEL'*s face.)* That's your play, George!

MAX: *(Reading)* "We first meet our heroine as she waits to audition—"

GEORGE: *(Grabbing for the script)* Where did you get that?!

CONKLIN: *(Knocking; off)* Mr Williams! Mr Reilly!

MAX: You're awfully grabby. Joe, aren't you going to let the Colonel in?

JOE: *(Realizing)* I slammed the door in his face.

GEORGE: I asked you where you got my script?!!

MAX: From the Colonel's room, of course. While you all were at dinner, I had a maid exchange it for my original play. A copy of which I fortunately kept in the ship's safe.

CONKLIN: *(Off)* Open this door!

GEORGE: Joe, the Colonel's read the wrong play.

JULIE: Max, your play attacks everything the Colonel stands for!

MAX: True. *(Beat)* That's why I put George's name on the title page.

GEORGE: My name!!

JOE: Oh my God.

GEORGE: You won't get away with this.

CONKLIN: *(Off)* I said—open this door!!

JOE: We are going to swim home.

GEORGE: *(To* MAX*)* You ingrate. Without me you'd be nothing. I made you.

*(*MAX *gets up and moves toward the door.)*

JOE: Don't Max!

GEORGE: Max, please, we've been like brothers!

JOE: No!!!

*(*MAX *is at the door.)*

GEORGE: We're family!

*(*MAX *opens the door. The* COLONEL *enters with* CONKLIN*; he is a small, elderly businessman, and as will soon be apparent, always speaks through his secretary.)*

(Pause)

COLONEL: I would like to know, Conklin, why Mr Williams slammed the door in my face.

CONKLIN: *(To* JOE*)* Why did you slam the door in the Colonel's face?

JOE: I—*(He looks to* GEORGE *for help, but he nods as if to say "Tell him".)* I—I didn't, Colonel. *(Beat)* I mean, I didn't mean to. There was a sudden rock of the ship. That's what made the door slam. Didn't you feel it?

*(*COLONEL *looks at him. Short pause.)*

JOE There. Feel that? There's another one.

*(*JOE *tumbles around as if the ship was rocking— no one else moves. Pause)*

MAX: Champagne, Colonel Face?

GEORGE: *(Approaching the* COLONEL*, grabbing his arm, trying to move him away)* Colonel, could we have a little talk, man to man.

COLONEL: *(To* CONKLIN*)* He's touching me.

CONKLIN: *(To* GEORGE*)* You're touching the Colonel. *(Beat;* GEORGE *lets go.)*

COLONEL: *(Taking the champagne from* MAX*)* Have we met?

CONKLIN: Max Whitcomb, Sir.

COLONEL: The mysterious other member of Whitcomb and Reilly.

MAX: To be honest, Colonel, it's only George who is writing plays now.

GEORGE: That's a lie!

MAX: I have retired and invested my savings in a short-term loan business. I have three storefronts in Harlem.

JULIE: What are you saying? You'd never invest in—

MAX: Julie. Remember, it's George who is now the revolutionary.

COLONEL: Revolutionary? *(Beat)* Hear that, Conklin. You two should get together. *(Suddenly laughs and laughs. Others look at him. Finally winds down)*

CONKLIN: I'm glad my recent incarceration has amused you, Sir.

GEORGE: Colonel, that play you read—

COLONEL: Tell him to shut up.

CONKLIN: Shut up.

COLONEL: Conklin, tell Mr Whitcomb—

MAX: Max. Please—just Max.

COLONEL: *(Smiles)* Tell Max I find what he's done very— *(Beat)* Patriotic, I believe, is the word. In a depression I can think of no better way to serve one's fellow man than by loaning him money. What does he charge, Conklin, twenty percent?

MAX: The rate in Harlem's twenty-five. Of course the bigger lenders are even getting thirty, though I'm not in their league yet.

COLONEL: "Yet!" *(Smiles and nods)* I do like it when a man knows where he's going and what he's about.

GEORGE: He's about five feet from my fist.

COLONEL: Tell Max we all had to start small. I myself was an orphan. No American should ever feel ashamed at having had to start small.

JULIE: *(To* JOE*)* Why does he only talk through his secretary?

JOE: That's what businessmen always do. Have you ever tried to get one on the phone?

GEORGE: Colonel, getting back to the play—

CONKLIN: He said—shut up.

COLONEL: I don't think I have ever come across a playwright—

MAX: Ex-playwright. Remember George is the playwright. That's him over there.

GEORGE: You son of a bitch.

*(*JOE *holds him back.)*

COLONEL: With such an understanding of business.

MAX: I stayed a playwright this long only because—well, you know this, Colonel, in the theater it's so easy to hide your profits.

COLONEL: I like the way he thinks.

MAX: You know, I don't think I've paid income tax for— oh, at least ten years. And I'm sure it's the same for you.

GEORGE: Please, can't I say something?

CONKLIN: No.

MAX: To throw money away—on taxes! To flush it down the toilet of government with all its misguided namby-pamby social programs. Well, that would be a crime in my book. Especially—when one can invest it oneself.

GEORGE: *(To* JOE*)* I do not believe this.

JOE: Sh-sh. I'm interested in investments.

MAX: We both know that without unrestrained investment America would not be what it is today! The simple truth is—what's good for a man like you, Colonel, is good for all of us. *(Beat)* But I'm sure you would agree.

CONKLIN: Oh he agrees.

COLONEL: I do like the way he thinks.

MAX: But forgive me. I've allowed us to stray from the real reason for this visit, which I believe is that play you have in your hands.

GEORGE: Colonel, I had nothing to do with that play!!

MAX: *(Winks at the* COLONEL*)* You've come across modest playwrights before.

COLONEL: Uh. *(Beat)* No.

JOE: Colonel, an error has indeed been made.

MAX: The author's name is on the title page.

GEORGE: To hell with who it says is the author!

CONKLIN: That's just what you always say, Colonel.

COLONEL: *(Shaking the manuscript)* This play is—how shall I say it?

MAX: Loud.

*(*JOE *has begun to creep away.)*

GEORGE: *(To* JOE*)* Where are you going?

JOE: I'm your agent, I was going to stand behind you.

COLONEL: This play is—it is without doubt....

GEORGE: *(To JOE, who is behind him)* Quit breathing on my neck.

COLONEL: It is without doubt—the most....

MAX: Yes?

COLONEL: Moving work of art I have read in my life in the theater.

ALL: What?!!!

COLONEL: I cried when I read it. I laughed. Never have I been more touched by art.

JOE: *(To GEORGE)* It must have touched him all right. *(Points to his head)*

COLONEL: Words cannot describe the profound effect this work has had on me. I have cancelled my next six productions to devote all my energies to producing this masterpiece. But not on Broadway!

OTHERS: No?

COLONEL: I am going to rent Madison Square Garden for this! And do you know why?

OTHERS: Why?

COLONEL: Because this is a working man's play! A play for the common man to inspire him! What an idea! I'll give away an apple with every ticket. I'll dress the ushers as factory workers! *(Beat)* No, damnit, I'll hire real factory workers to be ushers. *(Turns to CONKLIN)* Non-union.

CONKLIN: Of course.

COLONEL: It will be the show of the century. Colonel Face presents—

(TONY runs in.)

TONY: Mr Reilly there's been a big mistake!

COLONEL:—*From Rags to Riches* by Richard Anthony the Third!!!!

ALL: Who???

TONY: Mr Reilly, Ingrid made a terrible mistake. Someone told her to exchange the scripts, but she got them mixed up. She gave away mine by mistake.

CONKLIN: That's Mr Anthony right there, Colonel.

COLONEL: So this is the author of this masterpiece. *(Holds up the script)*

TONY: Where did you get that? Give it back to me!

COLONEL: When you see what I will pay for the rights to produce this work I do not think you will want it back. *(Beat)* Give him the check, Conklin.

(CONKLIN does.)

TONY: *(Looking at the check)* I don't understand.

MAX: *(Sinking fast)* Me neither.

COLONEL: I have scheduled auditions to begin immediately upon my arrival in New York. I'll have the best actors in the city lining up to read.

GEORGE: I hear Lillian Gish is available.

COLONEL: Of course I shall insist on a few rewrites from Mr Anthony. He doesn't object, does he?

TONY: I want a drink. *(He goes and takes the bottle of champagne and starts drinking.)*

COLONEL: And tell Mr Reilly—

GEORGE: What, Colonel?

COLONEL: That as a token of my gratitude for having brought me this work of genius—

*(*TONY *belches.)*

COLONEL: —I am prepared to pay him a fee to assist Mr Anthony with his revisions.

GEORGE: That's very kind of you, Sir.

*(*TONY *is almost chugging the bottle now.)*

COLONEL: Now—I believe we should go, Conklin. *(Beat; to the others)* A young woman is in the lounge, and I have promised her an audition tonight.

*(*COLONEL *and* CONKLIN *leave. Stunned pause.)*

GEORGE: I don't understand. I heard the first act of that play. It was awful!

MAX: *(Head in his hands)* Julie, a workers' play! In Madison Square Garden! With factory workers! *(Beat)* It's everything I tried to write.

JULIE: I know.

GEORGE: *(Getting up and moving to* MAX*)* Oh well. *(Slaps* MAX *on the back)* It's not the end of the world. Things could be worse. *(Beat)* We still have each other, Max.

MAX: George—

GEORGE: We can still work together—

MAX: I can't.

GEORGE: *(Suddenly turns on him)* Haven't you got all this out of your system yet?!!

MAX: Is that what you think all this was about—getting it out of my system?

GEORGE: The thought did cross my mind, once or twice.

MAX: We live in different worlds.

GEORGE: I'm in the real one, where are you?

MAX: *(Turns to* JULIE*)* Julie, it doesn't seem fair. I have beliefs. I've struggled. I've been willing to renounce everything I have—everything I was. What more can I do?

JULIE: I think you've done all you could, Max.

(Knock at the door)

MAX: Come in!

*(*FREDDY *enters, now dressed as a civilian. He carries a small suitcase.)*

MAX: Freddy!

FREDDY: Mr Whitcomb.

MAX: Freddy, anyone would have—

FREDDY: Please. *(Beat)* That's not why I'm here. I only came to find one thing out before I leave.

JOE: Leave? We're in the middle of the ocean.

FREDDY: In about an hour we'll be passing a French liner, the captain has been kind enough to make the necessary arrangements for me to board it.

GEORGE: You're going to France?

FREDDY: Back there, yes.

TONY: I told you there was a big difference between France and America. *(Drunk, to the others)* A very big difference.

JOE: Well, we'll miss you. Freddy, it's people like you that the American theater is lacking.

FREDDY: I know. But the question I came to ask is: Mr Reilly, why did you put me in the closet this afternoon?

(Pause. GEORGE *is uncomfortable.)*

GEORGE: Because there was already someone in the bathroom? Ha ha ha.

(Others laugh nervously. FREDDY *turns, stops, then turns back.)*

FREDDY: I nearly forgot. I came across one of your published plays in the ship's library. I wonder if you two would mind autographing it.

GEORGE: Anything for a friend. You got a pen?

MAX: Freddy, the way I acted before, that wasn't the real me. You understand that, don't you?

FREDDY: I understand. *(Beat)* Here's the book. *(Opens the bag and pours out burnt pages. Sniffs at it.)* What do you know, it smells of lighter fluid.

*(*FREDDY *turns and goes. Phone rings;* JULIE *gets it.)*

JULIE: It's Eva Rose, Max!

MAX: Ask her what she wants. I don't want to talk to her. *(Goes to* TONY*)* Tony, did you get your idea for the play from experience or from something you read?

TONY: I don't read very well, Mr Whitcomb.

MAX: From experience! I knew it! *(He slams his hand down.)*

TONY: Actually I got my idea from Louie in the barber shop.

MAX: You wrote about his life, did you?

TONY: Oh no. See, this morning Louie was giving this man a haircut and this man told Louie his whole life story. He said to Louie that he wanted his life to be an example to people, about how good America can really be if you only try.

JOE: I've tried. I've tried.

TONY: And it was this man's life that my play's about.

MAX: I see. Maybe what I need to do is listen more to other people. Who was this man, do you know?

TONY: Louie told me his name, but I forgot. It was something to do with shaving, though.

GEORGE: Shaving??

TONY: Like whisker. Or beard...

GEORGE & MAX: *(Suddenly)* Or Face!!!!!

TONY: That's it! Face!

GEORGE: He's written a play based on the life of Colonel Face! No wonder he liked it.

JOE: *(To* GEORGE*)* Why didn't you think of that?!

JULIE: *(Hanging up the phone)* Max, you won't believe what's happened!

MAX: What now?

JULIE: Miss Rose talked to a couple of members of the W P A Theater who happened to be on this ship—

MAX: The W P A!

JOE: What's that?

GEORGE: The biggest commie theater in New York, Joe.

JOE: Bigger than the Theater Guild?

JULIE: And she told them about your interest in political theater.

MAX: And?!

JULIE: And Max, they want to commission you to write a play for them!

MAX: *(Stands triumphant)* Commission me?!! What do you think about that, George?! Julie, that's just what I've been waiting for!

JULIE: I know!

MAX: *(Going to his desk)* I already know just what I want to write!

JULIE: Wait, Max, that's not even the best part. *(Beat)* They said that because they were almost broke, they need something light so it will move to Broadway!

(GEORGE looks at MAX and smiles. MAX sits down.)

JULIE: What's wrong, Max? And they think you're the perfect writer for it! It's that wonderful? *(Beat)* What's the matter?

(Short pause. GEORGE watches MAX closely.)

JULIE: Max? *(Beat)* They also wanted to know if you could get George to help you.

(Pause)

(MAX is broken; he tries to fight back tears. Finally he looks to GEORGE, who has been smiling a very big smile.)

GEORGE: It's an unfair world Max. *(Beat)* If you need any more proof—look behind you.

(MAX looks back and sees TONY, who is holding the bottle and staggering. Suddenly TONY smiles and falls, passing out.)

GEORGE: *(Quietly, putting his arm on MAX's shoulder)* Max—call it fate.

JOE: Like Astaire and Rogers.

GEORGE: Like Sacco and Vanzetti.

MAX: So...? We just start all over? *(Beat)* Pretend like nothing has happened?

JOE: What's happened?

(Short pause)

MAX: Julie, I wasn't the only one who wanted to change things. What about your beliefs?

JULIE: You can't have everything.

(Short pause)

MAX: So George gets what he wants. *(Beat)* He gives up nothing.

GEORGE: I'm not the lamb who strayed, Max.

(Short pause)

MAX: So everyone thinks the right thing is for us to work together again?

GEORGE: *(Jumping up, rolling up his sleeves)* And the sooner the better, Max. We can start right away. Any ideas for a title?

MAX: *(To all of them)* So we just put our blinders back on?????!!!

(Beat)

GEORGE: Too long for the marquee, Max.

MAX: *(Yells)* George!!!

GEORGE: Sorry.

(Pause)

MAX: Okay. I guess you win. *(Beat)* I'll write a play with you. *(Beat)* But listen to me! Damnit, every chance I get I'm going to sneak my beliefs into it. Does everyone understand that?!!

JOE: Sneak. Sneak. Who's looking?

MAX: Then write this down.

*(*GEORGE *is poised to write.)*

MAX: Act One. Our curtain rises on three cabins on an ocean liner. One first class. One second class. One third—

JOE: Max, I thought we were talking Broadway.

MAX: Okay. Okay. *(Beat)* Forget second and third class.

JOE: They're forgotten.

GEORGE: I didn't even write them down.

(Short pause as MAX *thinks, then:)*

MAX: As the lights come up, we hear—the Communist *Internationale*. *(Suddenly turns to the others)* Anyone have a problem with that?!

OTHERS: *(As they shake their heads)* No, no problem.

MAX: Good. *(Continues)* The Communist *Internationale* sung—by the masses.

JOE: The masses, Max? You know how much that'll cost? *(To* GEORGE*)* Even non-union, you got all their costumes—

MAX: Then sung—by a lone revolutionary.

GEORGE: What's a revolutionary doing in a first class cabin, Max? He doesn't belong there. Why can't it— *(He looks around, then:)* —just play on a victrola?

JOE: That's cheap!

MAX: Okay. On a victrola. *(Beat)* And alone on stage sits— *(He hesitates, then:)* —a young man whose head is bursting with ideas about—justice, about what is right and wrong in the world, in our country.

GEORGE: *(Excited)* That's good!

JOE: Is it?

GEORGE: I can have real fun with that! The jokes are starting to come!

*(*GEORGE *suddenly begins to write furiously.* JOE *hurries to him and reads over his shoulder.* MAX *tries to continue.)*

MAX: And though he may be young—

(No one is paying any attention to him.)

MAX: —and spoiled, and naive, and though his beliefs may be as yet unformed, even crude—

*(*JOE *bursts out laughing, having read one of* GEORGE*'s jokes.)*

JOE: This is great stuff, George!

*(*JULIE *joins them.)*

MAX: *(Trying to continue) —even crude, there is no denying that in this young man's heart—he feels something cannot be ignored.*

*(*JOE*,* GEORGE*, and* JULIE *laugh as they read* GEORGE*'s jokes.* MAX *is alone and ignored.)*

END OF PLAY

JITTERBUGGING: SCENES OF SEX IN A NEW SOCIETY

A free adaptation of Arthur Schnitzler's LA RONDE as translated by Helga Ciulei

JITTERBUGGING: SCENES OF SEX IN A NEW SOCIETY was first produced at River Arts Repertory (Lawrence Sacharow, Artistic Director) on 8 August 1989 with the following cast and creative contributors:

G I/HUSBAND .... Chris Sarandon
WHORE/YOUNG MARRIED WOMAN .... Karen Young
MAID/SINGER .... Laura Innes
MANAGER/MAYOR .... Dan Butler

Director .... Lawrence Sacharow
Set designer .... Anne Servanton
Costume designer .... Marianne Powell-Parker
Lighting designer .... Mark London
Sound designer .... Aural Fixation

CHARACTERS & SETTING

G I
WHORE
MAID
MANAGER
YOUNG MARRIED WOMAN
HUSBAND
SINGER
MAYOR

The play takes place in 1947 in and around a small New England city on the Atlantic Ocean. The central location is an older hotel where on a Saturday night crowds come to hear the latest big band and singer from Boston.

At numerous points in the play band music is called for—this music should be of the forties and could include such tunes as A String of Pearls, American Patrol, Chattanooga Choo Choo, I've Got a Gal in Kalamazoo—*all of which are highly optimistic and romantic.*

The play is written to be performed by four actors.

ONE

THE WHORE & THE G I

(Bathroom on the main floor of the hotel. Saturday night. Loud band music can be heard from the hotel's ballroom. Each time the door is opened, the music becomes quite loud.)

(G I enters, goes to the mirror to comb his hair.)

(Stall door opens and WHORE *comes out. At first he doesn't notice her.)*

WHORE: Come here, boy.

(He looks toward the door.)

WHORE: I'm over here.

G I: Excuse me, I didn't know someone was.... *(He realizes what she is.)* Oh. I see. *(He looks back at the door.)*

WHORE: Look, I have a room just down the street.

G I: *(Continues to comb his hair)* Sorry, I'm with some friends.

WHORE: *(Comes up to him)* What's wrong—don't you like me?

G I: I wouldn't say that. *(He grabs her ass and squeezes it.)*

WHORE: *(Pulls away)* Watch it, the door's not locked.

(He shrugs and combs.)

WHORE: Come on, let's go.

G I: I told you I'm with some friends. Besides, I'm broke.

WHORE: For a soldier there's no charge.

G I: You must be the one Hubie told me about.

WHORE: Hubie? Sorry, I don't remember a Hubie.

G I: You're serious about no charge?

WHORE: Ask Hubie.

G I: *(Looks at his watch)* Okay. Come on.

WHORE: Why the big rush all of a sudden?

G I: I said I didn't have much time.

WHORE: How long have you been in the service?

G I: None of your business. How far's your place?

WHORE: About a ten minute walk.

G I: I can't take that long. Sorry.

WHORE: Wait. Come here—least let me give you a kiss. That's the best part anyway.

G I: Not for a man.

(They kiss)

G I: Don't you know a place closer?

WHORE: Why don't you come later tonight after you've left your friends.

G I: What's the address?

WHORE: You won't come, will you?

G I: If I say I'll come, then I'll come. What's the address?

WHORE: How about in there? *(Points toward the stall)*

G I: Sorry, I'm not that desperate.

WHORE: If you knew more about me, you might be. We only live once.

G I: *(After a pause)* Okay, but fast.

WHORE: Lock the door.

(He goes to the door and locks it, then turns off the light.)

WHORE: Why did you do that?

G I: I have my reasons.

WHORE: Be careful, the floor's wet.

(He almost slips in the dark.)

WHORE: There's a puddle just to your right.

G I: You seem to know your way around here.

(They go into the stall.)

WHORE: You know, I wouldn't mind having a lover like you.

G I: I'd wear you out in a week.

WHORE: We'd see who wears out first.

(Knock at the door)

WHORE: Someone's knocking.

G I: So what? Come here.

WHORE: Maybe the police.

G I: Come here.

WHORE: Hold me.

G I: You're safe with me.

(During this, the band music becomes very loud.)

(Lights come on. G I *is at the door.)*

WHORE: *(Coming out of the stall)* It would have been more comfortable in a bed.

G I: Maybe. Maybe not. *(He goes to unlock the door.)*

WHORE: What's the rush?

G I: I told you I have friends.

WHORE: Wait. What's your name?

G I: None of your goddamn business.

WHORE: Mine's Mary.

(He opens the door.)

WHORE: Hey!

G I: What is it now?

WHORE: How about a little change for the attendant?

G I: You got all you're going to get. *(He goes.)*

WHORE: Bastard!

(End of Scene One)

TWO

THE G I & THE HOTEL MAID

(The woods near the hotel. Later that Saturday night. The band continues to play, though now in the distance.)

MAID: Frank, why were you in such a hurry to leave?

G I: Oh, I don't know.

MAID: They're a fantastic band, aren't they. Maybe even one of the best the hotel's had.

G I: Sure.

MAID: I wouldn't be at all surprised if one day we heard them on the radio.

G I: Yeh, they're okay.

(He puts his arm around her waist—she lets him.)

MAID: You don't have to hold me anymore—we've stopped dancing.

G I: What was your name? Kathy?

MAID: You must have Kathy on the brain.

G I: Now I remember; it's Joan.

MAID: It's too dark out here. It's sort of scary.

(He grabs her arm.)

G I: Don't forget you're with a G I.

MAID: There's nobody else out here.

G I: *(Lights a cigarette)* It's getting lighter all the time.

(Puts the match up to her face)

G I: You *are* cute.

(Blows out the match, tries to feel her behind)

MAID: Hey, what are you doing? If I'd known you wanted to....

G I: I'd bet a weeks pay there's not another as soft and round back in that whole hotel.

MAID: I see—you've tried them all then.

G I: A guy can learn a lot watching girls dance. *(He laughs.)*

MAID: And the blond with the big nose I saw you dancing with?

G I: A friend of a friend.

MAID: Of that corporal's?

G I: Nah, the other one—with the loud voice.

MAID: Oh—*him.*

G I: What the hell's that supposed to mean? He didn't try anything with you, did he? If he so much as...

MAID: He didn't do anything. I just watched him with the others.

G I: Oh. Tell me about it.

MAID: Hey, you're going to burn me with that cigarette.

G I: Pardon moi. Did you know I served a year in France?

MAID: I better go, I have to be at work by six.

G I: *(Grabs her arm)* Hey, look over there—there's another couple just like us.

MAID: Where? I don't see anybody. And what do you mean— "just like us"?

G I: Well, I mean...that they like each other too.

(Pulls her toward him)

MAID: Watch it! It's not so easy to walk on this grass in these heels. You want me to fall down?... Let me take them off. *(She sits down.)*

G I: Let me help you.

MAID: Hey, I'll scream—is that what you want?

G I: Not so loud. Sh-sh.

MAID: What are you doing...what....

G I: We're alone.

MAID: I don't want to be alone.

G I: We don't need anyone else for...to do...

MAID: Please, mister. Look if I knew...if I...oh...oh...hurry...

(Loud band music plays)

G I: Come on—again!

MAID: I can't see your face.

G I: Forget the face!

(Loud band music plays again)

G I: *(He is standing over her.)* You better get up that grass is wet.

MAID: Give me your hand.

G I: Come on, come on.

MAID: I have to get my shoes back on.

G I: Listen to that.

MAID: To what?

G I: They're still playing Elmer's Tune. We didn't take as long as I thought.

(She gets up.)

MAID: Hug me, will you?

G I: Just a second, I'm lighting a cigarette. *(He does.)*

MAID: It's so dark.

G I: It'll be light in the morning.

MAID: You do like me, don't you?

G I: What do you think all that was about? Come on.

MAID: What do we do now?

G I: Go back. What else?

MAID: Can' t we stay here for a little while?

G I: It's too dark.

MAID: Frank, I'd hoped you'd walk me home.

G I: Why would you hope that?

MAID: I'd just like it, Frank.

G I: *(Looks at his watch)* Okay—where's home?

MAID: Not too far—on Water Street.

G I: That's in my direction too. But I'm not ready to go home just yet. I still have a little energy left.

MAID: So now it's the blond with the big nose.

G I: Her nose isn't so big.

MAID: Frank, please, no more tonight. Stay with me.

G I: Okay, okay—but maybe you'll give me your permission to have just one more dance?

MAID: I don't want to dance anymore.

G I: Fine. Here's a quarter—buy yourself a beer while you're waiting.

(He goes, she follows.)

(End of Scene Two)

THREE

THE HOTEL MAID & THE HOTEL MANAGER

(The MANAGER'S *office desk, phone, radio, etc.)*

*(*MANAGER *sits at his desk, smoking a cigarette—going over the books and bills. Monday morning)*

(Phone rings.)

MANAGER: *(Into phone:)* Hi Ted... No, that's no problem. You Chamber of Commerce boys are always first in line here, I've told you that.

(The MAID *enters with a dust cloth.)*

MAID: *(Seeing the* MANAGER*)* I'm sorry, I didn't realize anyone was in here. *(She goes.)*

MANAGER: *(Who has watched her go; into phone:)* I'm writing it down now—back room, Saturday night, Chamber of Commerce meeting. Don't mention it. *(He hangs up. He looks at the door. He gets up and goes to the radio, turns it on—big band music plays. He goes back to the phone.)*

MANAGER: *(Into the phone:)* Lil, get me the Mayor again.... Ted, it's me. I forget to tell you we're trying out a new singer this Saturday. I've only seen her picture. I don't know if she'll strip, but I'd guess it being her first night she'd...from the picture, I'd offer her twenty... Okay, I'll talk to her. See you Saturday. Sure. *(He hangs up. He sits back at his desk and starts to work, stops, calls:)* Joan!

*(*MAID *returns.)*

MAID: Did you call me?

MANAGER: Was there something you wanted, Joan?

MAID: I was just going to straighten up a little; but I didn't know you were working in here.

MANAGER: Oh. *(He looks at her.)*

MAID: I'll come back when you go to lunch. *(She starts to go.)*

MANAGER: Oh Joan!

MAID: Yes?

MANAGER: I wanted to ask you to do something...but I just forgot what it was....

(Pause)

MAID: It'll come to you. *(She starts to go.)*

MANAGER: Joan, I remember—would you close the blinds, it's so damn hot, maybe that'll help.

*(*MAID *closes the blinds.)*

*(*MANAGER *goes back to his books.)*

MAID: You certainly do work hard, Mr James.

MANAGER: *(Over the books)* There's a lot that needs to be done.

*(*MAID *starts to go to the door, stops.)*

MAID: You know you'd be cooler if you took off your jacket.

MANAGER: Oh. *(Notices)* Thank you, Joan.

(He watches as she leaves. Pause)

MANAGER: Joan!

(She returns.)

MAID: Yes sir?

MANAGER: Joan...what *was* I going to say...oh right—could you get me a bourbon and soda, please.

MAID: The liquor's locked up, Mr James.

MANAGER: You don't have the key?

MAID: The bartender has it, but doesn't come in until twelve.

MANAGER: Oh.

MAID: I could go around the corner to the Blue Moon.

MANAGER: Forget it, it's hot enough already without any bourbon. Just get me a glass of water—and let the tap run so it's good and cold.

(She goes.)

(He starts to work again, stops, takes off his jacket and goes to hang it up behind the door.)

*(*MAID *enters with the glass of water, at first doesn't see him.)*

MAID: Oh, I didn't see you!

MANAGER: I'm sorry if I scared you. I was just hanging up my jacket.

MAID: Here's your water. I'll set it on your desk. *(She does, but almost spills it on the papers)*

MANAGER: Be careful!

MAID: I'm sorry.

(She tries to wipe it up; he takes a hold of the end of her apron and also wipes—they are very close together. She moves away.)

MANAGER: What time is it?

MAID: Almost ten.

MANAGER: Oh, it's only ten.

(After a pause, she goes to the door; she turns back and sees him looking at her, she smiles and leaves. He tries to go back to work, goes to the radio and tries another station—more music.)

MANAGER: Joan!

(She immediately enters as though she were waiting for him to call.)

MANAGER: Joan...why do I keep forgetting what I want to say...right—is the boss in yet?

MAID: Not yet, Mr James.

MANAGER: That's odd, it's already ten.

MAID: There's a meeting of the church deacons this morning, Mr James.

MANAGER: Then that's where he is. Thank you.

(She starts to go.)

MANAGER: Joan?

(She turns back. Pause.)

MANAGER: Joan, I was wondering....

MAID: Wondering what?

MANAGER: Wondering...if...that blouse of yours—what is it made of?

MAID: My blouse? I really don't know. Don't you like it?

MANAGER: Come here, come here.

MAID: What do you want, Mr James?

MANAGER: A little closer, I won't bite.

(She comes closer.)

MANAGER: That's a nice shade of blue. *(He holds the blouse.)* That's a cute outfit, Joan. *(He begins to unbutton the blouse)*

MAID: Please...

MANAGER: What's wrong? *(He opens her blouse.)* You have very nice skin, Joan.

MAID: Thank you. *(He kisses her breast.)*

MANAGER: See, that didn't hurt did it.

MAID: No.

MANAGER: It didn't look like it did. You enjoyed that, didn't you, Joan?

MAID: What if someone comes to the door?

MANAGER: Who's going to come to the door?

MAID: It's too light in here.

MANAGER: You have nothing to be embarrassed about. In front of me or anyone else for that matter, Joan... Even your hair smells nice, did you know that?

MAID: Mr James...

MANAGER: What's the big deal? It's not like I've never seen you like this before. In fact, just the other afternoon, I was passing by the maid's closet and the door was opened and you were changing into your....

MAID: You have to keep the door open a little or you'd suffocate!

MANAGER: I saw everything...this...and this...this....

MAID: Please, stop...

MANAGER: Come closer...and here...here...

MAID: If someone knocks!

MANAGER: Stop it. We just won't answer that's all....

(Band music from the radio grows very loud.)

(Knocking at the door)

MANAGER: Sh-sh! Someone's at the door.... Maybe he's been out there the whole time and we just didn't hear him.

MAID: Oh no, I was listening.

MANAGER: Quick, go look through the key hole.

MAID: Alfred...I didn't know you cared about me....

MANAGER: I said go and see who it is.

MAID: *(Goes to the door)* Whoever it was is gone now. Maybe it was Mr Parker back from the deacons' meeting.

MANAGER: *(He has opened the blinds and now fixes his clothes.)* Joan, you can go now.

(She gets closer to him, he withdraws.)

MANAGER: I said—go. Please. I'm going to the Blue Moon.

MAID: This early? It's only ten.

MANAGER: I said I'm going to the Blue Moon. And if anyone asks, that's where I've been all morning. *(He slowly opens the door, checks outside, starts to go, stops and returns.)* I almost forgot my jacket—it could be a little chilly out there. *(Grabs the jacket and goes.)*

*(*MAID *looks around, sees a pack of cigarettes on the desk, takes one out, lights it, then takes the whole pack and leaves.)*

(End of Scene Three)

FOUR

THE HOTEL MANAGER AND THE YOUNG MARRIED WOMAN

(An automobile: we see both front and back seats. Wednesday afternoon. It is raining.)

(The MANAGER *sits behind the wheel, smoking and waiting. He looks in the rear view mirror—combs his hair. He sees someone on the street, starts instinctively to wave—then hides his face. He drums with his fingers on the steering wheel; takes out a silver flask and drinks, puts it back in his pocket; takes out his pocket watch and checks the time, puts it back. He notices something sticking out from between the seat, pulls it out—it is a woman's stocking; he panics, doesn't know where to put it, then jams it into his pocket. He opens the glove compartment and takes out a box of chocolates—eats one just as—)*

(The young MARRIED WOMAN *jumps into the passenger seat. She has an umbrella which she quickly folds. She wears a half-veil hat and a scarf, so one can hardly see her face.)*

(The MANAGER *is startled, but pleased, and tries to swallow the chocolate and clean his face as—)*

MARRIED WOMAN: *(Getting in)* Quick, let's go.

MANAGER: *(Trying to swallow)* You made it!

MARRIED WOMAN: Alfred, I said, let's go.

(He starts the car; the sense of them driving off.)

(He reaches over to try to touch her.)

MARRIED WOMAN: Leave me alone for just a little while, would you please?

(He nods and drives.)

MANAGER: Chocolate?

(She shakes her head.)

MARRIED WOMAN: I'm so confused—I don't even know where I am.

MANAGER: You're with me—in my car. I just bought it actually—what do you think?

MARRIED WOMAN: It's nice. Give me a cigarette.

(He does.)

MARRIED WOMAN: Where are we going?

MANAGER: Not very far.

MARRIED WOMAN: I passed two men on the street right back there.

MANAGER: Friends of yours?

MARRIED WOMAN: I don't know. I don't know.

MANAGER: You don't know who you know?

MARRIED WOMAN: I couldn't look.

MANAGER: So what's the problem—in that getup I doubt if even I would recognize you.

MARRIED WOMAN: Is there something wrong with the way I'm dressed?

MANAGER: Nothing. You look splendid.

MARRIED WOMAN: I'm not exactly used to this sort of thing, Alfred, so if I'm not dressed right...

MANAGER: Forget it. Just take your hat off and relax.

MARRIED WOMAN: Alfred, I told you five minutes...not a second more....

MANAGER: I know, I know. But at least let me see you.

(She takes off the hat.)

MARRIED WOMAN: You do like me, don't you, Alfred?

MANAGER: Emma, you have to ask?

MARRIED WOMAN: It's awfully hot in here.

MANAGER: You have a heavy coat on. *(Reaches over and rubs his hand against her face)*

MARRIED WOMAN: What are you doing?

MANAGER: You know, I've never seen you like this.

MARRIED WOMAN: Like what?

MANAGER: Alone.

MARRIED WOMAN: Alfred, stop the car. I should really go. Please.

MANAGER: We'll be there in a minute.

MARRIED WOMAN: You promised to behave yourself.

MANAGER: I know. *(He drives.)*

MARRIED WOMAN: It's suffocating in here.

MANAGER: I can't open the windows any more—if you'd just take off your.... *(Starts to unbutton her coat with his free hand)*

MARRIED WOMAN: I'll do it. *(Takes off her coat, throws it in the backseat)* Turn around, the five minutes must be up by now, Alfred.

MANAGER: It's hardly been one minute, Emma.

MARRIED WOMAN: What time is it—exactly.

MANAGER: *(Takes out his pocket watch)* Three fifteen.

MARRIED WOMAN: I should have been at my sister's by now.

MANAGER: You can see your sister anytime.

MARRIED WOMAN: Alfred, why did I let you talk me into this?

MANAGER: Because I...love you, Emma.

MARRIED WOMAN: And how many others have you said that to?

MANAGER: To no one—since I met you.

MARRIED WOMAN: I'm so stupid—if only I'd known this would happen. To think just a week ago, even yesterday—

MANAGER: It was the day before yesterday that you agreed to meet me.

MARRIED WOMAN: All you do is confuse me—I didn't want to come here. I swear it. Yesterday I was completely decided against it. I even wrote you a letter last night.

MANAGER: I didn't receive it.

MARRIED WOMAN: I ripped it up. But I should have sent it.

MANAGER: I'm happy you didn't.

MARRIED WOMAN: I don't understand myself anymore. Alfred, please—let me out.

MANAGER: We're here, Emma. *(He stops the car.)* It's quiet, isn't it? *(Pause)*

MARRIED WOMAN: Keep your promise, Alfred.

MANAGER: One kiss.

MARRIED WOMAN: And no more.

(He kisses her, she responds—it lasts quite a while.)

MANAGER: You make me very happy. *(He kisses her again.)*

MARRIED WOMAN: Alfred, what are you doing to me?

MANAGER: It's not too bad like this. It's certainly better than meeting the way we have.

MARRIED WOMAN: Don't remind me. Remember the club party?

MANAGER: How could I forget: with you sitting next to me, close to me, your husband pouring the champagne.... *(She looks at him.)* I only meant to bring up the champagne. Do you want some bourbon? *(Takes out his flask)*

MARRIED WOMAN: Do you have a glass?

MANAGER: Maybe in the back seat. *(Starts to climb back)* It's more comfortable back there anyway.

(She pulls him back.)

MARRIED WOMAN: I'm comfortable enough here. *(She takes the flask and drinks.)* Alfred, I want to ask you something, and I want you to promise to tell me the truth.

MANAGER: I promise.

MARRIED WOMAN: Has there ever been another woman in here...like I am, I mean?

MANAGER: But Emma, I bought this car used.

MARRIED WOMAN: You know what I mean, Alfred!

MANAGER: I don't understand why that's important.

MARRIED WOMAN: Because you...know should I...no, it's best that I don't say anything. I won't ask again. I have only myself to blame for what I've done.

MANAGER: Okay Emma—let me say this: if you really feel you shouldn't be here, if I mean so little to you, if you don't care how much I love you...then, you're right, I think we should drive back.

MARRIED WOMAN: Yes. Let's go back.

MANAGER: Look, Emma, I'm not like a lot of other men. I can't talk fancy talk. I wouldn't even know how to begin. Maybe I'm just naive, but....

MARRIED WOMAN: But what if you are like other men?

MANAGER: If I were, then you wouldn't have come today, because you're not like other women.

MARRIED WOMAN: How do you know that?

MANAGER: Because I do. *(He puts his arm around her, and pulls her to him.)* Because we're very similar people, Emma. We're both unhappy. But Emma, life's too short to always be unhappy.

MARRIED WOMAN: *(Opening the glove compartment)* Chocolate?

MANAGER: Just a half.

(She puts one into her mouth and passes it to him in her lips. He grabs her and begins to fondle her.)

MARRIED WOMAN: *(Pushing him away)* Alfred, you promised!

MANAGER: Life's so short, Emma. *(He swallows the chocolate and tries to feel her again.)*

MARRIED WOMAN: That's no reason to....

MANAGER: Yes it is!

MARRIED WOMAN: Alfred, I'm here because you promised to behave...besides there's not enough room.

MANAGER: There is in the back seat.

(He climbs into the backseat, tries to help her back)

MARRIED WOMAN: Wait a little, Alfred.

(He reaches and tries to undo her blouse.)

MARRIED WOMAN: You're going to rip it.

MANAGER: You don't wear underwear?

MARRIED WOMAN: I didn't feel like it today. *(She's in the backseat now.)* My friend Irene doesn't sometimes either. You can take off my stockings. Oh I'm cold. *(She covers herself with her coat.)*

MANAGER: You'll get warm soon.

MARRIED WOMAN: How do you know?

MANAGER: *(Piqued:)* What do you mean by that? *(He undresses.)*

MARRIED WOMAN: Hurry. Hurry. Alfred! *(She hugs him.)*

MANAGER: You smell sweet.

MARRIED WOMAN: It's the chocolate.

(Quiet band music plays.)

MANAGER: I don't know what's wrong.

MARRIED WOMAN: It's okay, Alfred.

MANAGER: I was afraid all day something like this would happen.

MARRIED WOMAN: Don't worry about it.

MANAGER: It happens to a lot of men, you know.

MARRIED WOMAN: I know....

(He looks at her.)

MARRIED WOMAN: I mean, I wouldn't be surprised, Alfred.

MANAGER: I think I'm just too excited.

MARRIED WOMAN: You're just nervous, try to calm down.

(Pause)

MANAGER: You wouldn't happen to know the works of Stendhal, would you?

MARRIED WOMAN: Stendhal, Alfred??

MANAGER: Specifically his *Psychology of Love.*

MARRIED WOMAN: You want to talk books now, Alfred?

MANAGER: There's one story in it that you should read, Emma.

MARRIED WOMAN: Why?

MANAGER: It's about a group of army officers and they're sitting around talking together....

MARRIED WOMAN: So what?

MANAGER: So—what they're talking about is their love affairs. And do you know, Emma, that every one of them confesses that when he was first with the woman he had loved the most, well...that she, that he—to make a long story short, Emma—the same thing happened to each of them that's just happened to...us.

MARRIED WOMAN: Oh. To us.

MANAGER: You see, it happens all the time.

MARRIED WOMAN: Uh-huh.

MANAGER: Well there was one officer who swore that it had never happened to him—but Stendhal goes out of his way to tell you that this man is a famous liar.

MARRIED WOMAN: I guess I'll have to read this Stendhal.

MANAGER: You should, Emma. He's a very important writer.

MARRIED WOMAN: You'll have to loan me the book—I'll read it in bed.

MANAGER: Sure. So you see it's really no big deal, just one of those stupid things that seem to happen.

MARRIED WOMAN: Look at it like this, Alfred—at least you kept your promise and behaved yourself.

MANAGER: That's not very funny, Emma. You're just going to make things worse.

MARRIED WOMAN: I didn't mean it to be funny, Alfred. That Stendhal does sound interesting. You know I always thought it only happened to old men.... *(He looks at her)* ...I mean...you know...to men with a lot of life experience.

MANAGER: Who the hell told you that? You women don' t know anything.... I almost forgot the best part of the story—there's this one officer who tells how he spent three...or maybe it was six nights—I can't remember exactly—with this woman who he really loved—who he *desiree*—that's the French word for it—and they did nothing all those nights except cry—cry because they were so happy to be together. That's all they wanted to do.

MARRIED WOMAN: The woman too?

MANAGER: Sure. Why not? I can understand that.

MARRIED WOMAN: Did the other officers all cry too?

MANAGER: No. They did other things as well.

MARRIED WOMAN: Oh, that's good. I thought Stendhal was saying all army officers cry at these times.

MANAGER: Now you're making fun of Stendhal.

MARRIED WOMAN: Don't be stupid, Alfred, I've never even read him.

MANAGER: Well, then you're making me nervous. I keep thinking you only have one thing on your mind.

MARRIED WOMAN: Really, I'm not thinking about it at all.

MANAGER: It would help if I thought you cared about me.

MARRIED WOMAN: I'm still here, aren't I?

MANAGER: See what I mean.

MARRIED WOMAN: Come here, hold me, Alfred. *(She holds him.)* In one way, Alfred, maybe it's all for the best. I mean, we always said we only wanted to be good friends.

MANAGER: You're doing it again, Emma.

MARRIED WOMAN: Don't be crazy, isn't that what you kept telling me you wanted—to be good friends and nothing more. I remember you saying that at the club party, at the town picnic, at my sister's...oh my God, I should have left ages ago...my sister's waiting for me, what am I going to tell her.... Let's go, Alfred.

MANAGER: Emma, we can't go now!

MARRIED WOMAN: Why not?

MANAGER: Five more minutes, please.

MARRIED WOMAN: Okay. Five more minutes—but only if you promise to behave yourself, Alfred. Now you lie there and don't move and I'll give you one more kiss...don't move or I'll leave right...my love...my love....

MANAGER: Emma...my...

(Loud band music plays)

MARRIED WOMAN: My Alfred...

MANAGER: My darling...

MARRIED WOMAN: Now we really have to go.

MANAGER: Your sister can wait.

MARRIED WOMAN: I'm too late for my sister now, I have to get home. What time is it?

MANAGER: How should I know?

MARRIED WOMAN: Look at your watch.

MANAGER: It's in the front seat in my vest.

MARRIED WOMAN: So get it!

(He reaches into the front seat and gets his watch. She starts to dress.)

MANAGER: Three forty five.

MARRIED WOMAN: Oh my God—hand me my stockings. What am I going to tell him?

MANAGER: *(Getting dressed slowly)* When can I see you again?

MARRIED WOMAN: Never.

MANAGER: But Emma, why?

MARRIED WOMAN: Because I love you too much. Give me my shoes.

MANAGER: Here they are.

MARRIED WOMAN: My compact's in my purse. Hurry, please.

MANAGER: I can't find it.

MARRIED WOMAN: Give it to me then. And start driving, please.

(He climbs into the front seat.)

MARRIED WOMAN: He'd kill us both, if he found out, you know that?

MANAGER: Really?

MARRIED WOMAN: What am I going to say if he asks where I've been?

MANAGER: At your sister's?

MARRIED WOMAN: You know I'm no good at lying.

(He starts the car.)

MARRIED WOMAN: Alfred, give me a kiss.

(He turns and kisses her.)

MANAGER: My love.

MARRIED WOMAN: I think it was better than just crying.

MANAGER: Emma, a woman shouldn't talk like that. *(He starts to drive.)*

MARRIED WOMAN: How are we going to act if we happen to run into each other?

MANAGER: Happen to? Won't you be at the library meeting tomorrow? I thought you were on the new building committee.

MARRIED WOMAN: You're coming to that?

MANAGER: I volunteered to be on the new building committee.

MARRIED WOMAN: Then I won't go. I won't go. I wouldn't know how to...everyone would...hand me a chocolate....

(He does.)

MANAGER: We'll see each other tomorrow at the meeting, Emma.

MARRIED WOMAN: No. I'm sorry, I can't.

MANAGER: Then the day after tomorrow...I'll pick you up.

MARRIED WOMAN: You can't be serious.

MANAGER: At...two.

MARRIED WOMAN: Drop me off at the next corner. I'll walk from there.

MANAGER: Emma, say yes. *(He stops the car.)*

MARRIED WOMAN: We'll talk about it at the meeting.

MANAGER: *(He embraces her.)* Emma...

MARRIED WOMAN: You'll mess my hair. *(She opens the door.)*

MANAGER: Tomorrow at the library, the day after, here.

MARRIED WOMAN: Goodbye.

MANAGER: And what are you going to tell your husband?

MARRIED WOMAN: Don't ask. I'll think of something. Why do I love you so much?!! What have I done?!! *(She goes.)*

(Alone he smiles to himself; looks into the mirror.)

MANAGER: Well—what do you know, Alfred, you're finally having an affair with a woman with class!

(End of Scene Four)

FIVE

THE YOUNG MARRIED WOMAN & THE HUSBAND

(Their bedroom. Later that night. WOMAN, *in bed, reading. The* HUSBAND *[a newspaper publisher] enters, rubbing his eyes.)*

WOMAN: You're not going to work anymore?

HUSBAND: No. I'm too tired.

WOMAN: Aren't you feeling well, you usually work a lot later?

HUSBAND: I feel fine. I just...

WOMAN: *(Reading)* You just what?

HUSBAND: Started to get sick of that damn newspaper.

WOMAN: Oh. I can understand that. *(She reads.)*

(He starts to undress.)

HUSBAND: Also I...

WOMAN: *(Reading)* Yes?

HUSBAND: I thought I should spend some time with you.

WOMAN: Oh really?

(He sits on the bed.)

HUSBAND: You'll strain your eyes reading so much.

(She closes the book.)

WOMAN: Is there anything wrong?

HUSBAND: Nothing. I just wanted to tell you how much I love you, but I'm sure you know that.

WOMAN: There've been times when I've wondered, Carl.

HUSBAND: Well you know how busy I've been.

(She nods.)

HUSBAND: And besides, I think it's good for us to wonder about how we feel. It adds a little mystery.

WOMAN: Oh.

HUSBAND: No, I'm serious. If we always felt the same for each other, it'd get pretty monotonous, wouldn't it?

WOMAN: Why?

HUSBAND: I see it like this, Emma; instead of a marriage, what we've really had is maybe ten or twelve affairs with each other.

WOMAN: I haven't counted.

HUSBAND: And that I find very exciting. If I had let myself throw all my energies into this when we first got married, we'd be like everybody else now: tired of each other.

WOMAN: Oh I see—that's what you mean.

HUSBAND: And believe me, Emma, when we first met it wasn't easy holding myself back.

WOMAN: For me either...when we first met.

HUSBAND: But it's a good thing we did—or we wouldn't be able to feel now how we do.

WOMAN: You mean how we feel every two months?

HUSBAND: Yes. And sometimes more often.

WOMAN: And now you feel like starting another affair with me?

HUSBAND: That's possible.

(He pulls her toward him.)

WOMAN: What about how I feel?

HUSBAND: I'm sure it's the same for you, Emma. You're very beautiful, did you know that? *(He gets into bed.)* I don't know—maybe mystery's more meaningful for a man. Women do seem to know right from the start what *they* want.

WOMAN: You think so?

HUSBAND: I do, yes. By the time a woman like yourself gets married, she may have talked a little, may have read a little—actually in your case maybe a bit too much—but what has she experienced? Nothing. So she's had nothing to confuse her. Whereas when a man gets married, he's already experienced *too* much and so is totally confused. No wonder love is still a mystery to him.

WOMAN: *What* kind of experience?

HUSBAND: You wouldn't want to know, Emma....

WOMAN: Then *with* whom?

HUSBAND: Sweetheart, there are women in this world who do things you've never dreamed anyone would do.

WOMAN: The kind of women you've been attacking in your paper?

HUSBAND: That's right. Though I haven't been *attacking* them, Emma.

WOMAN: No?

HUSBAND: It's my hope that a more severe penalty for this kind of...sin, will in fact deter other young women from taking their first step down a road from which there's never any turning back.

WOMAN: I could think of worse fates.

HUSBAND: *(Angry:)* Don't talk like that, Emma, you don't know how stupid you sound.

WOMAN: Sorry. I wasn't thinking.

(He reaches for a cigarette, moves a bit away from her)

WOMAN: Talk to me some more. I like it when you talk to me like this.

HUSBAND: What do you want me to talk about?

WOMAN: *(Snuggling to him)* Tell me about the affairs you had before we were married.

HUSBAND: Emma, please!

WOMAN: Why not? We're alone aren't we?

HUSBAND: Why would you want to know?

WOMAN: Can't I be curious?

HUSBAND: It wouldn't be right, Emma.

WOMAN: You say that, but how do I know how many other women you've held like you're holding me?

HUSBAND: Don't be crude. And I don't like it when you refer to yourself in the same breath as those kinds of women.

WOMAN: Either answer me one question or you can just go to sleep. *(She turns away.)*

HUSBAND: You talk to me like you talk to our daughter.

WOMAN: *(She snuggles to him.)* I'd also like to have a son to talk to.

HUSBAND: Emma.

WOMAN: Come on, forget I'm your wife, pretend I'm your mistress.

(Pause)

HUSBAND: What do you want me to do?

WOMAN: First, answer my question.

HUSBAND: What is it?

WOMAN: Were any of your women—married?

HUSBAND: What do you mean?

WOMAN: You know what I mean.

HUSBAND: What makes you want to know?

WOMAN: I just do. Aren't there wives who....

HUSBAND: Yes, Emma, there are. Do you know someone who...?

WOMAN: I really don't know.

HUSBAND: One of your girlfriends?

WOMAN: How should I know?

HUSBAND: You're with them all the time, has one of them said something....

WOMAN: No.

HUSBAND: Do you suspect one of them?

WOMAN: Suspect? I wouldn't even know how to suspect someone.

HUSBAND: Sweetheart, this is important—are you sure there isn't....

WOMAN: Carl, certainly not. It's ludicrous to even think about it.

HUSBAND: Not even one?

WOMAN: None of *my* friends.

HUSBAND: Promise me something, Emma.

WOMAN: What?

HUSBAND: That if you ever even suspect...that you'll stop seeing her immediately.

WOMAN: Do I really have to promise this?

HUSBAND: Emma, I know you too well—you're still naive about the world.

WOMAN: I must be. You keep telling me I am.

HUSBAND: And it would be just like you, Emma, to risk your own reputation, by trying to help a woman like this.

WOMAN: How could I help her, Carl?

HUSBAND: Just being seen with respectable women makes it much easier for such a woman to continue her lies.

WOMAN: Oh, I see....Then I promise to restrict myself to only respectable women, Carl.

HUSBAND: Good, Emma. You know it's just that I want you to be careful.

WOMAN: So do I, Carl. *(She snuggles up to him.)* So was there a married woman in your past or not?

HUSBAND: Yes, Emma, there was.

WOMAN: Really?! Who was she? Do I know her?

HUSBAND: Emma!

WOMAN: When was it? How long before we were married?

HUSBAND: Don't ask, please, Emma.

WOMAN: But Carl!

HUSBAND: She's dead.

(He pulls away. Pause)

WOMAN: Really?... Oh.

(Pause)

HUSBAND: This may sound ridiculous, but I have the impression that these women always die young.

WOMAN: Uh-huh...Did you like her a lot? *(She snuggles more.)*

HUSBAND: *(Looks her in the eyes)* It was a long time ago.

WOMAN: Did you hold her like you hold me?

(Pause, he rubs her hair.)

WOMAN: Was she beautiful?

HUSBAND: *(He kisses her on the forehead.)* Yes.

(Pause. She kisses him.)

(She reaches to turn off the light.)

WOMAN: Was she as beautiful as me? *(She turns off the light.)*

(Band music)

WOMAN: Do you know what I kept thinking about all day?

HUSBAND: Tell me.

WOMAN: About...our honeymoon.

HUSBAND: Really? I wish I had the time to think about such things.

WOMAN: And I was....

HUSBAND: You were what?

WOMAN: I was wondering if you still love me as much....

HUSBAND: As much today as...?

(She nods.)

HUSBAND: Yes, Emma. I do.

WOMAN: Do you think....

HUSBAND: What?

WOMAN: Do you think you always will?

HUSBAND: Yes...always... *(Short pause)* Though, my baby, that doesn't mean a man will always *show* his love—there is a world out there which *he's* forced to face. And that can take its toll sometimes.

WOMAN: *My* poor baby, you should get some sleep.

HUSBAND: Marriage, I think, must be more than just loving—it's two people growing old together.

WOMAN: Hold me.

HUSBAND: *(He does.)* Goodnight, sweetheart.

WOMAN: Goodnight.

(End of Scene Five)

SIX

THE HUSBAND & THE SWEET YOUNG SINGER

(A hotel room. Boston. Thursday night. Couch, radio, etc)

(From the radio, we hear an upbeat big band tune—something like American Patrol.*)*

(The HUSBAND *and the sweet young* SINGER *are dancing [maybe even jitterbugging]. It should at first appear to us that it is difficult to believe that this man who is dancing with such verve is really the same husband of the last scene. But that is what a business trip can do, isn't it?)*

(They dance for quite a while. The song ends. They laugh, out of breath. He goes and turns the radio down.)

HUSBAND: I think that's about all I can take.

(She sits and takes out a cigarette.)

HUSBAND: Could I have one?

SINGER: Oh sure.

(She gives him a cigarette.)

HUSBAND: *(Noticing:)* You need another drink. *(Takes her glass)*

SINGER: Please...I'll just end up leaving it.

(He goes to the bureau, where he keeps a couple of bottles and pours her another drink. He looks at her, then at his watch.)

SINGER: It was awfully nice of your Chamber of Commerce to send you up here.

HUSBAND: They didn't exactly send me....

SINGER: But I thought...

HUSBAND: They knew I had some business in Boston—and so...

SINGER: I see.

HUSBAND: *(Pulling a ticket out of his jacket)* By the way here's your train ticket for Saturday. Mr Franklin asked me to....You know how the mail is.

SINGER: That was very nice.

HUSBAND: *(After a pause)* Mr Franklin owns the hotel where you'll be singing.

SINGER: I know.

HUSBAND: His manager will pick you up at the station.

SINGER: I'd hoped someone would.

HUSBAND: *(He sets her drink down.)* You'll need an ashtray. *(He goes to get one.)*

(She takes a sip of the drink.)

SINGER: My head—it's already spinning.

(He brings the ashtray, puts out his cigarette; he stares at her.)

SINGER: *(After a pause:)* What are you doing?

HUSBAND: I want to kiss you.

(He takes her chin and kisses her. Pause)

SINGER: Mr Jones, I should be going, you know I still haven't packed....

HUSBAND: Carl.

SINGER: Yes.

HUSBAND: You know I've seen you sing.

SINGER: You have, really?

HUSBAND: Last month I was up here on business....

SINGER: Like today.

HUSBAND: Yes... Maybe you remember me?

SINGER: I'm sorry.

HUSBAND: I bought you a drink.

SINGER: I'm sorry—a lot of men buy me drinks when I'm singing.

HUSBAND: They do?... Do they also ask you up to their hotel rooms?

SINGER: Some try, yes.

HUSBAND: And what do you tell them?

SINGER: I ignore them. I pretend I haven't heard them.

HUSBAND: You didn't ignore me.

SINGER: Should I have?

(He kisses her. She responds.)

HUSBAND: You have beautiful lips.

(She takes another sip of her drink.)

SINGER: Do I?

HUSBAND: But I suppose you've been told that before.

SINGER: So often I've lost count.

HUSBAND: No, tell me the truth—how many men have kissed those lips?

SINGER: Why should you want to know that?

HUSBAND: I just do. Tell me.

SINGER: If I told you, you wouldn't believe me.

HUSBAND: Then let me guess—twenty.

SINGER: Oh sure, twenty. Yeh, that sounds about right. I think I better....

(She starts to get up, he pulls her down.)

HUSBAND: Ten then.

SINGER: Ten, twenty, five thousand, what's the difference—just because I come to your room....

HUSBAND: I'm sorry.

SINGER: You should be. *(She sits. Takes another sip of her drink)*

HUSBAND: There's nothing wrong with coming to a man's hotel room to pick up a train ticket.

SINGER: That's what I thought.

HUSBAND: Have you ever been to a man's hotel room before?

SINGER: Actually, I have.

HUSBAND: It's best to be honest with each other.

SINGER: Though it's not what you think—I was with some friends. There was a party.

HUSBAND: It wouldn't have been the end of the world if you had been...say with a boyfriend....

SINGER: Who said it would be the end of the world? I just don't have a boyfriend, that's all.

HUSBAND: Oh, come on.

SINGER: I don't.

HUSBAND: You don't think I'm going to believe....

SINGER: Not for a few months at least.

HUSBAND: Who was he then?

SINGER: What's it to you?

HUSBAND: I'm curious, that's all. *(He presses himself closer to her.)*

HUSBAND: Tell me who he was.

SINGER: He looked kind of like you.

HUSBAND: He did?

SINGER: Maybe that's why I....

HUSBAND: You what?

SINGER: You know. Do I have to say everything in plain English?

HUSBAND: Why you're here?

SINGER: Yes.

HUSBAND: I don't know whether that should make me happy or not.

SINGER: The way you talk—it's like him too. And the eyes...

HUSBAND: My eyes?

SINGER: Why are you looking at me like that?

(He goes to kiss her, she tries to get up.)

SINGER: I have to go home.

HUSBAND: Later.

SINGER: No. I really have to.

HUSBAND: You worried about what you're going to tell your father?

SINGER: I'll tell him I was rehearsing. I'm always rehearsing. Anyway, what I do is my business not his.... Hey, how do you know I live with my father?

HUSBAND: *(He shrugs.)* And don't you have a sister?

SINGER: Yeh. How do you know?

HUSBAND: A guess. Older or younger?

SINGER: She's thirteen now. And what a brat; when I was her age I never dreamed of doing half the things she does. You know I caught her sneaking out to meet a boyfriend.

HUSBAND: I don't know what the world's coming to.

SINGER: Yeh. That's what I told her. *(She takes another sip.)*

HUSBAND: Can I have another cigarette?

(She gives him one.)

HUSBAND: You need another drink. *(He takes her glass.)*

SINGER: I've had plenty, thank you.

HUSBAND: You still haven't told me anything about your boyfriend.

SINGER: What's to tell? He left me that's all.

HUSBAND: That was a mistake. Was he in the army?

SINGER: No. He was too old. Like you.

HUSBAND: I see.... *(Brings her the drink)* At first I thought you had blue eyes, but now they look green.

SINGER: Don't you like green eyes?

(He kisses her, she responds.)

SINGER: Let me up for a minute...

HUSBAND: No

SINGER: I feel dizzy.

HUSBAND: Then hold onto me.

(He holds her; she hardly resists.)

HUSBAND: Was he your first boyfriend?

SINGER: Oh sure.

HUSBAND: Tell me about the others...

SINGER: There weren't any others....

HUSBAND: You want to go home?

SINGER: Yes. *(She doesn't move.)*

HUSBAND: I thought so. *(He unbuttons her blouse)*

SINGER: Really...I shouldn't.... I drank too much....

(He takes off her blouse.)

HUSBAND: You are very beautiful, Ruth....

SINGER: My name's not....

(Band music)

SINGER: You're married, aren't you?

HUSBAND: Why do you ask?

SINGER: I knew you were married. I could tell.

HUSBAND: You better get yourself dressed, I'll walk you home.

SINGER: It's not so late.

HUSBAND: I'll get your hat. *(He gets up.)* Do you still live in the same house?

SINGER: How do you know where I live?

HUSBAND: I didn't think you'd move.

SINGER: I don't understand what you're talking about.

(He approaches her.)

HUSBAND: *(Tenderly:)* You do look so much like her.

SINGER: Like who?

HUSBAND: Here's your coat. *(Picks up her coat)* Don't you remember?
...The three of us went on a picnic together. Just before the war.
You couldn't have been more than eleven.

SINGER: The three of us?

HUSBAND: You. Me. And your Mother. I knew her for a few weeks.

SINGER: My Mother's dead.

HUSBAND: I know. Come on, let's go.

(End of Scene Six)

SEVEN

THE SWEET YOUNG SINGER & THE MAYOR

(Small back room—really almost a closet—in the hotel. Saturday night)

(The band plays dance music in the distance.)

(The room is quite dark.)

(The SINGER *sits, staring at the floor. She wears only a slip.)*

(The door opens. Light comes in.)

SINGER: *(Jumping up)* Who is it? Who's there?

(The MAYOR *enters.)*

MAYOR: I just came to see how you were doing?

SINGER: Close the door.

(He does.)

SINGER: I'll be ready in a minute.

MAYOR: You can hardly see anything in here.

SINGER: Your eyes adjust.

(Short pause)

MAYOR: Then I'll go and tell the others that you're almost ready.

SINGER: Please.

MAYOR: Would you like a drink?

SINGER: Not while I'm singing, thank you.

MAYOR: Is there anything we can get for you?

SINGER: I don't think so.

(He turns to go.)

SINGER: You have a cigarette?

(He takes one out, but can't quite see her.)

SINGER: Just hold it out, I can see *you.*

(She takes it, he lights a match—she lights her cigarette.)

MAYOR: You've been doing this long?... Singing, I mean.

SINGER: Oh sure. For years and years.

MAYOR: So you have must been out on the road before.

SINGER: A million times.

MAYOR: You seem quite young to....

SINGER: I'm old enough.

MAYOR: Oh, I wasn't saying....

SINGER: Now you're going to tell me you have a daughter my age....

MAYOR: Actually...

SINGER: I don't believe it.

MAYOR: No, I wasn't going to say.... Mind if I have a drink?

SINGER: Why should I care?

(He takes out a flask and drinks.)

SINGER: Do the other singers...?

MAYOR: Most of them, yes. That is, the ones we ask. The Chamber of Commerce only meets four times a year.

SINGER: So four times a year—whoever's singing?

MAYOR: It hasn't been a problem. Do you have a problem?

SINGER: Why would I? I told you, I've been on the road before. I was just asking because...I know other places but this is my first time here, that's all.

MAYOR: I understand.

SINGER: I know what goes on.

MAYOR: Sure...Alfred was wondering....

SINGER: Alfred?

MAYOR: The hotel manager. He's the one who talked to you.

SINGER: Oh him. What about him?

MAYOR: He wasn't so sure if you'd ever.... I mean, very often...

SINGER: Don't listen to Alfred.

MAYOR: We didn't.

SINGER: Do me a favor and hand me my dress there.

(He picks it up and starts to go to her. She takes off her slip—she is naked now. Pause)

SINGER: So the other singers...I mean, they would just take off...?

MAYOR: *(Handing her the dress, trying not to be too obvious that he is looking her over)* Yes. They...yes.

(She holds the dress in her lap. She is obviously nervous, if not scared.)

SINGER: So you're with the Chamber of Commerce too, huh?

MAYOR: I'm the mayor.

SINGER: Oh. The mayor. *(Pause)* I thought I'd sing while I did it.

MAYOR: I think that's expected.

SINGER: Oh yeh. Of course. *(She turns away, trying not to cry.)*

MAYOR: Look, dear, I can talk to the others—we don't want to make you do anything you don't....

SINGER: Hey, quit it, okay? I took this job, didn't I? I know what I'm doing, so just leave me alone, okay?

(Pause.)

MAYOR: Do you know what you'll sing?

(After a pause; she looks up and nods. She puts out the cigarette.)

SINGER: *(She sings quietly:)*
"Don't sit under the apple tree
With anyone else but me
With anyone else but me
With anyone else but me
No no no
Don't sit under the apple tree
With anyone else but me
'Til I come marching home."

(Pause. Then he starts to sing and they sing together:)

SINGER & MAYOR:
"Oh don't go walking down lovers lane
With anyone else but me
With anyone else but me
With anyone else but me
No no no..."

(They stop, look at each other.)

MAYOR: Come here. Please.

(She looks down; sings:)

SINGER: "I just got word
From a guy who heard
From the guy next door to me.
That the girl he met
Just loves to..."

(She stops.)

MAYOR: Please. I'll help you with your dress....

(She nods.)

(Band music—maybe: Don't Sit Under the Apple Tree.*)*

SINGER: Do you have another cigarette?

(He gives her one. She starts to put on her dress.)

SINGER: Come on. I have another set to do after this.

*(*MAYOR *doesn't move. He takes out his flask and drinks.)*

SINGER: What's wrong with you?

(He shakes his head.)

SINGER: Look—I like you, okay?

(He looks at her and nods)

MAYOR: You know....

SINGER: What?

MAYOR: Besides being mayor—I'm also a dentist here.

SINGER: That's nice. Good for you.

MAYOR: I mean—so if you ever...while you're here...if you happen to want me to look at your teeth....

SINGER: Sure. *(Pause)* I'll give you a call. *(She goes to the door.)*

MAYOR: I sometimes take evening appointments.

SINGER: Great. Thanks.

(She opens the door—music louder. She goes, and we hear the cheers and whistles of the Chamber of Commerce.)

(End of Scene Seven)

EIGHT

THE MAYOR & THE WHORE

(The bathroom—same as the first scene. Later that Saturday night)

(In the distance we hear the singer and the band playing for the crowds.)

(The MAYOR *is on the floor—unconscious. His pants are pulled around his feet.)*

(The WHORE*, obviously frightened, is at the sink, wetting paper towels.)*

(She goes to wipe his face with them, then goes back to make more, then he stirs.)

(She looks back at him and freezes.)

MAYOR: *(With pain:)* What...? Jesus Christ, what...? *(He groans in pain)*
My chest... *(Tries to breathe deeply, grimaces)* Ah... *(Deep breaths)*
What happened? Where...? *(Looks around)* Who are...?

*(*WHORE *just watches him.)*

MAYOR: Oh my God. Now I... Damn, that's all I would have needed—to die of a heart attack in...with.... My wife would kill me. *(Feels the pain)* Ow. Get me a glass of water, please. *(He tries to sit up.)* It couldn't be just gas, could it?

(She gives him the water.)

MAYOR: How long have I been...like this?

WHORE: Five minutes...maybe...

(He nods.)

MAYOR *(Feeling his own pulse)* God, my hands are freezing. *(Feels his chest again—again pain)* I better just sit here for a second. *(He props himself up against the stall.)* Am I very pale?

(She looks at him and nods.)

MAYOR: What about my eyes? The pupils. How big are they?

(She looks.)

WHORE: Big.

(He nods.)

MAYOR: I'm lucky.

(He feels on his neck and notices the wet towels. He looks at the WHORE.*)*

MAYOR: You did this?

(She nods.)

MAYOR: Thank you.

(He smiles to himself, then suddenly reaches for his wallet—thinking she had probably stolen it—he feels it and takes it out.)

WHORE: I didn't touch it.

MAYOR: I see.

(He puts it back. She takes out a cigarette and smokes, watching him.)

WHORE: I better go.

(He nods. But there is a knock at the door)

MAYOR: Wait.

(The door is tried from the outside. He calls:)

MAYOR: I'll be a few minutes! *(To her:)* You better stay here until he goes away.

WHORE: *(Offering)* Cigarette?

MAYOR: *(Starts to accept)* No. I better not. *(Breathes heavily, feels his arm)* My arm's still a bit numb. Tell me something—has this... what's your name, anyway?

WHORE: Why do you want to know?

MAYOR: I see. Forget I asked. But tell me—has this sort of thing...happened to you before?

WHORE: *(Shakes her head)* Never.

MAYOR: I wasn't sure if it was an occupational hazard. *(He struggles to pull up his pants.)*

WHORE: You want me to help you?

(He looks at her and nods. She pulls up his pants.)

MAYOR: How old are you by the way?

WHORE: What do you think?

MAYOR: Twenty...four?

WHORE: Oh yeh. Sure.

MAYOR: Twenty two?

WHORE: Why do you care?

MAYOR: *(Shrugs)* I don't know. I've got a daughter who's nineteen. *(He holds out a towel.)* Could you wet this again?

(She takes it and wets it. He feels his head, sees there's a little blood.)

MAYOR: Did I fall?

(She nods.)

WHORE: Your head just missed the edge of the sink.

MAYOR: Oh.

(Takes the towel. He tries to stand up—she just watches him.)

WHORE: Be careful—the floor's slippery.

MAYOR: Thank you. *(He starts to move toward the door; stops.)* Have you ever thought about doing something else?

WHORE: Why? Like what?

MAYOR: You're pretty enough to have boyfriends.

WHORE: Who says I don't.

MAYOR: I mean just one...two.

WHORE: I'm choosy now who I go with.

MAYOR: I see. *(He goes to the door, stops, reaches for his wallet, takes out a bill, goes back and puts it on the sink counter.)* Lock the door behind me, and wait in here for a few minutes.

(She follows him to the door.)

WHORE: What time is it?

MAYOR: *(Checks his watch)* What do you know—it's nearly one.

(With one hand on the door, he stops and looks at her.)

MAYOR: Come here.

(She hesitates.)

MAYOR: Come here.

(She goes to him.)

MAYOR: Is that a broken tooth?

WHORE: So?

(He takes out his wallet again.)

MAYOR: Take this card.

(She takes it and looks at it.)

MAYOR: Call the number. I'll fit you in—some morning.

(She nods. He holds out his hand. She shakes it. He opens the door. For a brief moment the music and singing can be heard very loud. He leaves. She locks the door. The music is distant again. She goes to the sink, fixes her hair. Sees the money and takes it. Pause)

WHORE: *(To herself, sighing:)* One o'clock. Another hour and I can go to bed.

(She goes to the door, unlocks it, opens it. As she leaves, we hear the singer and the band very loud again—)

(End of Scene Eight)

END OF PLAY

RIP VAN WINKLE, OR "THE WORKS"

ORIGINAL PRODUCTION

RIP VAN WINKLE premiered at the Yale Repertory Theater (Lloyd Richards, Artistic Director) on 4 December 1981. The cast and creative contributors were:

RIP VAN WINKLE .... Seth Allen
GRETCHEN .... Laura Esterman
MEENIE *(girl)* .... Patricia McGuire
MEENIE *(woman)* .... Kaiulani Lee
HANS DERRICK .... Gerry Bamman
COCKLES .... Alan Rosenberg
HEINRICH VEDDER *(boy)* .... Jon Walker
HEINRICH VEDDER *(man)* .... Stephen Lang

PART ONE

FOREMAN .... John E Harnagel
FIRST WORKER .... Kevin McClarnon
SECOND WORKER .... Dan Desmond
AUNTIE .... Mary Van Dyke
SURVEYOR .... Vic Polizos
SOLDIER .... Steven Ryan
REV JOHNSON .... Richard Jamieson
MRS JOHNSON .... Jane Kaczmarek
NICK VEDDER .... Baxter Harris
HUDSON GHOST .... Michael Grodenchik

PART TWO

HENRY .... Richard Jamieson
FRANCIS .... Steven Ryan
JACK .... Vic Polizos
BOY .... Jon Walker
SECRETARY .... Dan Desmond
HOUSEKEEPER .... Zakiah Barksdale
SERVANT GIRL .... Becky London
MAN ON PUMP .... Michael Grodenchik
MAN WITH BUCKETS .... Baxter Harris
BURNING MAN .... Kevin McClarnon
CONSTABLE .... John Lloyd
GUARD .... Charles S Dutton

SGT JONES .... Baxter Harris
LOOKOUT .... Kevin McClarnon
CORPORAL .... Michael Grodenchik
SCHOOLTEACHER .... Warren David Keith

PART THREE

CLYDE .... Charles S Dutton
EDWARD .... Warren David Keith
RICHARD .... John Lloyd
JONATHAN .... Steven Ryan
JUDITH .... Mary Van Dyke
DUTCH .... Kevin McClarnon
GEORGE .... Michael Grodenchik
SHEPHERD .... Frank Maraden
SHEPHERD'S BROTHER .... Vic Polizos
LAWYER .... Baxter Harris
POSTMASTER .... Richard Jamieson
PAUL .... Dan Desmond
SAM .... John E Harnagel

Director .... David Jones
Set design .... Douglas O Stein
Costume design .... Gene K Lakin
Lighting Design .... Jennifer Tipton

for David Jones

PART ONE
"DRUNK"

Scene One

(Near a muddy road. Morning. FOREMAN *and* FIRST WORKER *look off. Noise of wagons, shouts, horses)*

FOREMAN: Help him!

VOICE: Stuck!

FIRST WORKER: Stuck.

FOREMAN: Help him!

FIRST WORKER: Get his face. Pull!

FOREMAN: Pull! Pull! Goddamn mud.

FIRST WORKER: *(To himself)* Pull. Please. Pull. Pull.

FOREMAN: Get to him! That's a man! A man!

FIRST WORKER: *(Under his breath)* Flesh and blood. They can't get close.

FOREMAN: The head! Get his head!

FIRST WORKER: They can't stand up. He's choking.

FOREMAN: By the hair then!

FIRST WORKER: The mud. Gonna drown.

FOREMAN: Stupid. It's just stupid!

FIRST WORKER: Mud.

(Horse screams off.)

FOREMAN: Now what?

VOICE: Stuck!

FOREMAN: What the hell is that horse stopped for?!! Move it!

FIRST WORKER: Stuck. He's gonna drown. Pull. Pull.

FOREMAN: Move that horse!

FIRST WORKER: Reach him. Please.

FOREMAN: You don't move it we're going to have two hundred stuck horses!

VOICE: Stuck!

FOREMAN: Unstuck it! Oh, Christ, it's down.

VOICE: Help! I need help!

FOREMAN: It's down. No. No.

FIRST WORKER: They reached him.

FOREMAN: No get it back up! Come on. Please. Please. Please.

VOICE: Stuck!

FOREMAN: Then shoot it! Either get that horse up or shoot it!

FIRST WORKER: Out. He's out. The mud.

(Gun shot off)

FIRST WORKER: They shot it.

(Horse screams.)

FOREMAN: Wounded. Don't believe this. Wounded. Stupid. In the head! Not in the back!

*(*SECOND WORKER *struggles in, coughing, covered with mud, exhausted.)*

FOREMAN: Stupid!!

(Horse screams.)

FIRST WORKER: Dying.

FOREMAN: I don't want it dying, I want it dead! Shoot it! *(Runs out)*

SECOND WORKER: Water.

FIRST WORKER: *(Points)* There's a stream.

*(*SECOND WORKER *nods.)*

FIRST WORKER: Here. *(Offers his hand; helps him up.)*

SECOND WORKER: Slippery. Fell down. Wouldn't let go.

FIRST WORKER: What wouldn't?

SECOND WORKER: The mud. *(Starts to leave; stops)* Didn't know a man could drown in mud, did you? *(No response)* Well, now you know.

(Horse screams in pain.)

FOREMAN: *(Off)* Shoot!!!!!!

Scene Two

(Edge of a stream. Large rock. GRETCHEN *and* AUNTIE *scrub clothes.* MEENIE, *a young girl, sits, she stares off right. Far upstage a* SURVEYOR *with tripod. He surveys off left.)*

MEENIE: So many wagons! Mother, what comes after twelve?

(Short pause; GRETCHEN *ignores her.)*

MEENIE: Thirteen comes after twelve, doesn't it? Twelve. Thirteen. Fourteen. Fifteen. Seventeen. Mother, I never saw so many wagons before in my whole life! Have you, Mother?

*(*GRETCHEN *ignores her.)*

MEENIE: Seventeen wagons going to the works. I wonder what's in all those wagons, Mother? Do you know? Do you have any idea? Oh there's my favorite! That one there with the six mules! That's the prettiest of them all, don't you think so! *(Short pause)* Mother, which one is Father driving? I'll bet it's that one with the mules. I'll bet that's the one, don't you?

*(*GRETCHEN *just continues working.)*

AUNTIE: Meenie, why don't you go and get a little closer. Maybe then you can see your father. But don't get too close. And stay out of everyone's way. And don't go getting that dress dirty. And...

MEENIE: *(Almost off)* Can I, Mother? Can I?!

AUNTIE: Go.

*(*MEENIE *runs out. Pause. They scrub.)*

AUNTIE: So you don't talk to your own daughter anymore?

GRETCHEN: And say what?

AUNTIE: She's your daughter.

GRETCHEN: *(Shouts)* And say what?!!!

AUNTIE: Relax. Relax.

GRETCHEN: That her father is a drunkard?

AUNTIE: You don't have to say a word about him, if you don't...

GRETCHEN: That if it weren't for my working myself half to death we'd all of us be starving? That every time he has so much as a penny in his pocket it ends up being poured down his throat? Or his so-called pals' throats?

AUNTIE: Gretchen...

GRETCHEN: That all we got left in this world after all his father left him is one shed that my mother left me, and that he'd have drunk that too if I hadn't kept it in my name? That her father didn't come home last night, and that I'd bet my soul he isn't on one of those wagons but passed out under some tree—even though it's the first bit of real work he's got in years? That my daughter's got a father who's got a wife who is not only worn down, but pretty nearly worn out from trying to reform him and trying to convince herself that he still can be reformed? Is that what I tell her? Is it?

AUNTIE: No.

GRETCHEN: Then right now I have nothing else to say to anyone. *(Looks at some clothes)* Beer stains. How I'd give anything to clean dirt for a change.

AUNTIE: You take things too much to heart.

GRETCHEN: I have to go to work.

(They start to pick up the clothes; MEENIE *runs in;* SURVEYOR *exits with tripod.)*

MEENIE: I couldn't see him, Mother. I could see all the drivers, but I couldn't see him. Maybe he's coming later with a bigger wagon. Maybe he's coming with eight mules!

GRETCHEN: Maybe. *(They start to leave; gunshot in the distance; horse screaming.)*

AUNTIE: What's...?

MEENIE: Look, it's a horse! They're shooting a horse!

AUNTIE: Let's go, Meenie. Come along.

MEENIE: But why would they shoot a horse?! Look, he's...!

AUNTIE: Don't look. Come here. Don't look.

MEENIE: But...!

GRETCHEN: Why shouldn't she, she sees more suffering every day of the week in her own home. *(She exits.)*

MEENIE: *(Crying)* Mother! Stop them!

AUNTIE: *(Holding* MEENIE*)* Did I ever tell you the story about the horse who died and then turned into a Prince?

MEENIE: I'm too old for fairy tales.

AUNTIE: Then I'll just tell it to myself. Once upon a time there was a handsome prince....

MEENIE: But the horse!

AUNTIE: You hold your horses and I'll get to him. First—the prince.

(They have exited. A SOLDIER *enters. He is wet, carries some of his clothes.)*

SOLDIER: Where'd he go now? Peter! Peter! I saw him just a minute ago. Peter!!

VOICE: *(From behind the rock)* Ahhhhhhhh!

*(*SOLDIER *is startled, grabs his rifle.* RIP *appears from behind the rock, holding his head.)*

RIP: Put that thing down. What did you think I was, an Indian? Well, then you'd be a damned fool 'cause there ain't no Indians around here no more. Though I wish there was, 'cause Indians know how to whisper. They know how to respect a man's sleep. They wear moccasins. You got anything to drink?

SOLDIER: The stream. *(Calls)* Peter!!

RIP: Ah! What's that? Thunder?

SOLDIER: Huh?

RIP: Nah, must be in the head. Yeh, there it is again. Sure sounds like thunder though. *(Sitting down)* Oh where are the birds? Where are the crickets chirping? This town's getting too crowded for me.

SOLDIER: You seen a surveyor around here?

RIP: If he was up in the clouds I might have seen him, 'cause that's where my head was pointed. But my eyes, they were closed. How about a drink?

SOLDIER: Got nothing.

RIP: Me too. I swore off.

SOLDIER: Must have thought I got lost. Told him I'd be a minute, that was half an hour ago. Went to take a bath, left my clothes on the bank, then two women and a kid come by. Have to hide in the trees 'til they go. Even though I'm travelling I still keep my pride.

RIP: Pride. That's a good thing to keep. I got mine somewhere here. *(Checks his pockets)*

SOLDIER: *(Looking)* Is that him? Peter! ... No.

RIP: You want to know what I think?

SOLDIER: No.

RIP: I think your friend, he strolls down to the inn, he props his feet up on the table, and he has himself a morning beer. A nice cool morning beer. That's the best beer of the day.

SOLDIER: The morning beer.

RIP: Or the best beer of the early part of the day.

SOLDIER: Of the morning.

RIP: Exactly.

SOLDIER: The morning beer's the best beer of the morning.

RIP: No doubt about it. That's what I think, and you can have that thought for free. See, that's how we are around here—generous. We help each other out; watch each others' kids; look after each other when we're sick; buy each other drinks.

SOLDIER: Here he comes. Peter! *(Takes out a bottle and drinks)* Peter!

(RIP clears his throat.)

RIP: Thought you had nothing?

SOLDIER: *(Puts bottle away)* Don't. I swore off.

SURVEYOR: *(Entering)* Where the hell you been?

RIP: Naked and in the bushes.

SOLDIER: It's a long story. See, these women...

RIP: Ah! Women! It's always women, isn't it?

SOLDIER: I...

SURVEYOR: Who's he?

RIP: A thirsty man.

SOLDIER: Peter, wait, it's not what you....

SURVEYOR: Forget it, I don't have time. You find anything out?

SOLDIER: Not yet, but...

SURVEYOR: Right. Too busy running around in the bushes...

RIP: Naked.

SOLDIER: I...

RIP: With women!

SOLDIER: *(Yells)* Who asked you????

RIP: Just trying to be helpful. See, that's how we are around here—helpful. Watch each others' kids; look after each other when we're sick; buy each other drinks.

SURVEYOR: *(Has taken out a bottle and a map)* Here!

(Throws RIP the bottle.)

RIP: Ahhh! Dawn is breaking.

SURVEYOR: *(To SOLDIER)* We ought to make friends with the natives. *(Looks over the map)*

RIP: *(Takes a drink)* A new day has begun! Ahhh!

SURVEYOR: This *(The map)* is a piece of crap. Seen better maps of Heaven than this of this county. I got about eighteen acres sketched in so far. Put on your clothes, we still have a lot of work left to do.

RIP: *(Drinking)* Let there be light *(To* SOLDIER*)* Nice man. Drink?

*(*SOLDIER *stares at him.)*

RIP: Oh that's right, you swore off.

SOLDIER: You want help or should I go into town?

SURVEYOR: First, the land. I want to walk the hills to the north, they could be strategic.

SOLDIER: Fine by me.

SURVEYOR: Later we can both go and look up this Mr Rip Van Winkle.

SOLDIER: Whatever you say.

RIP: *(He chokes; quietly.)* Who?

SURVEYOR: What he say?

SOLDIER: "Who?"

SURVEYOR: Him.

SOLDIER: No, that's what he said—"Who?"

SURVEYOR: Who what?

RIP: Who did you say you were going to look up?

SURVEYOR: Mr Rip Van Winkle. Why?

RIP: No no no reason. Just... You know. I heard you say and... Are you from the works?

SOLDIER: What's he talking about?

SURVEYOR: The works. They're building some works down the way. Saw the wagons.

SOLDIER: No, we are not from the works. We're from Boston. We are part of an army.

RIP: Ah.

SOLDIER: Come on, we got work to do.

SURVEYOR: Wait. Maybe he knows him.

RIP: Me? Do I...Rip Van Winkle? Uh, well, I guess you could say, he's sort of a friend of mine. Close friend. Very very close. You've never met him?

SURVEYOR: No.

SOLDIER: Never.

RIP: I see. What exactly do you want with good ol' Rip? If I may ask.

SURVEYOR: Show him the map.

(SOLDIER does.)

RIP: Of course it's none of my business.

SOLDIER: This is the most recent we could come up with. Twenty years old.

RIP: *(Looking)* Ah.

SOLDIER: *(Pointing)* Look at that.

RIP: Ah.

SOLDIER: And there.

RIP: Ah.

SOLDIER: And there.

RIP: Ah.

SOLDIER: And this area here.

RIP: Ah.

SOLDIER: You see what we mean now?

RIP: Ah. I don't read.

SURVEYOR: *(Pushes SOLDIER away)* What we're trying to show you is that each of these large plots are labeled as being owned by a certain Rip Van Winkle. And, as it's part of our task at this point to gain the support of the more wealthy gentlemen of the community, we are, as you can understand, rather anxious to meet up with this Mr Van Winkle.

RIP: I see. Hmmmmmm. *(Takes a drink)* And you really don't...? Not even the color of his hair?

SURVEYOR: He's a name on a map.

RIP: Interesting. Excuse me. *(Drinks)* He's a busy man.

SURVEYOR: Our business won't take long.

RIP: I guess in that case...after all, who am I to deny you such a pleasure.

SOLDIER: Mr Van Winkle?

RIP: He... is there any more?

(SURVEYOR nudges SOLDIER to give RIP his bottle.)

RIP: Thank you. *(Drinks)* Mmmmmmmm.

SOLDIER: You were saying?

RIP: Saying? What was I saying? Oh right. I believe with my whole heart that no more true or decent, no kinder man has ever breathed God's air, than Mr Van Winkle. *(Drinks)* Ahhhh. Of course, I can only really speak for myself, but for myself this I can swear—I would not be alive today, if it weren't for Rip Van Winkle. I would not be here, or there, or anywhere for that matter. In fact, I would have no breath at all, if it were not for....

(HEINRICH, a boy, runs in.)

HEINRICH: There you are. Mr Derrick sent me looking for you.

(RIP shushes him and winks.)

HEINRICH: What? He said you never showed for work, and that if I was to find you, and you weren't dead or almost dead then you'll never get to drive no wagon for him.

RIP: *(To men)* Rip Van Winkle will give me work. I have nothing to worry about.

HEINRICH: Huh? What are you talking about, Rip...?

RIP: Van Winkle. That's just who we're talking about. Sh-sh!

SOLDIER: *(To SURVEYOR)* Derrick.

SURVEYOR: Who?

SOLDIER: Derrick. The letter. That rider at the inn in Pittsfield gave us a letter for a Mr Derrick. *(To Rip)* Gave us two shillings to deliver it.

RIP: Come along gentlemen, I know a comfortable little inn which, besides its obvious charm, is often visited by Mr Van Winkle. Come. Come.

(They start to go. SECOND WORKER enters, still covered in mud, on his way to the stream.)

SOLDIER: God, what happened to him?

SECOND WORKER: Fell in the mud.

RIP: Come on, come on. Let's not dawdle.

SECOND WORKER: What's the hurry? Got a couple of suckers to buy you a drink, Rip?

(Pause)

SURVEYOR: Rip?

SOLDIER: Rip?

RIP: Rip? Rip? What's ripped? Did something rip? *(Pause; he looks up at the sky.)* Going to rain. *(Pause; then he puts on a big toothy innocent smile.)* Do you want your bottle back?

Scene Three

(Beer garden. Tables. Late morning. REV JOHNSON, MRS JOHNSON, *and* COCKLES *[*DERRICK*'s nephew] stand, looking out a telescope toward the works.* DERRICK *sits and watches them.)*

REV JOHNSON: *(Looking)* Mmmmmm. How wonderfully inspirational to witness a beginning. The effort alone fills one with hope.

DERRICK: Yes.

REV JOHNSON: God bless you, sir, and He thanks you. You are making our work all the easier.

COCKLES: How so?

REV JOHNSON: My flock, it appears, shall be quite exhausted by Sunday. And tired muscles cannot the Lord resist.

DERRICK: And what do you think, Mrs Johnson?

(She slowly goes to the telescope and looks through.)

MRS JOHNSON: *(Finally; quietly, without conviction)* It's lovely.

REV JOHNSON: *(Laughs)* Lovely!

DERRICK: Very sweet. *(Laughs)*

REV JOHNSON: That's a woman for you.

DERRICK: I'm not sure "lovely" is the right word, Mrs Johnson. I think "serviceable" might be more appropriate for a works.

*(*MRS JOHNSON *tries to hold back tears.)*

MRS JOHNSON: Excuse me. *(She runs off sobbing.)*

DERRICK: I hope it was not what I said.

REV JOHNSON: I can assure you it was not, Mr Derrick. My wife is rather high strung. She has not yet learned the art of adapting.

DERRICK: I see.

REV JOHNSON: It will take time. Six months of marriage after all is nothing. One will have to work at it. And that, of course, takes time.

DERRICK: Of course.

REV JOHNSON: She is still quite young. And girls as I am sure you are aware still have their heads full of dreams. I think she was rather distraught at my not getting a more—shall we say—urban parish.

DERRICK: In time, Rev Johnson, this shall be an urban parish, if I have my way.

REV JOHNSON: You and I can see that. You and I see the house when only the foundation is built, but my wife unfortunately when she looks at your works all she sees is dirt. It is theaters and boulevards she wishes to see through your telescope.

DERRICK: Yes.

REV JOHNSON: *(Moves away from the telescope.)* If there is anything I can do, Mr Derrick, please do not refrain from calling. As you are now servicing this town, I shall strive to service you. It is my belief that God's will must be seen to on more days than just one. I am unlike most ministers, I don't mind getting dirty.... I should go and see to my wife. Trust me, she has it in her to be both charming and delightful. *(Starts to go.)* Tell me something, Mr Derrick. How can a girl who has spent her entire life on a farm be so repulsed by dirt?

DERRICK: She'll change.

REV JOHNSON: *(Nods)* Theaters. She wouldn't even know how to behave in one. *(Leaves)*

DERRICK: *(Stands)* Cockles, let me see. *(Looks through the telescope)* It's lovely.

(HEINRICH appears around the corner. He watches for a moment, then pretends to run in out of breath.)

HEINRICH: I found him. *(Pants)* Just let me catch my... *(Pants)* You wouldn't believe all the places I'm looking. *(Pants)*

DERRICK: And...?

HEINRICH: And! He was just lying there, poor Rip. Seems he's on his way to the works real early this morning. Real real early and... *(Pants)* he gets kicked by this horse. It's hard to believe, but there's this horse and it kicks him right in the head. Poor Rip. And he looks up at me and he says to me, "Heinrich, help me get to work". And I says, "Rip you can't go to work today, you've been kicked in the head". And he says, "Help me up". And I says, "No, don't move, Mr Derrick he's going to understand". And he says, "But". And I says, "But". And then he's trying to stand by himself, but his legs they won't hold him up, so he looks up at me and he says, "Yes, Mr Derrick is a nice man" and then he groans. Poor Rip.

DERRICK: "Poor Rip." *(Turns away)*

(Short pause)

HEINRICH: *(Pants)* And then I start running *(Heavier panting)* and I don't stop for nothing because I know that Mr Derrick he wants to know what I know so I'm running *(Even heavier panting)* and I keep running 'til I get here. *(Very heavy panting)*

(Finally DERRICK *reaches into his pocket, gives him a coin, and* HEINRICH *stops his heavy breathing, smiles and starts to walk off.* NICK*—the owner of the Gardens and* HEINRICH*'s father—has entered and grabs him.)*

NICK: *(Slaps* HEINRICH *across the face; he stutters.)* Where-wherewhere you been? He runs off for all morning. Now get inin there and get to work!

DERRICK: Your boy was doing me an errand, Nick.

NICK: *(To* HEINRICH*)* Open your hand! Open open it! *(Slaps him)* A shillilling. Now what were you going to do with a shilling?

DERRICK: I gave it to your boy, Nick. Not to you.

NICK: A boy don't need a shilling! This boy needs, he needs somethin' else. *(Grabs* HEINRICH*)*

DERRICK: Let him go.

NICK: I'm his father!

DERRICK: Don't blame the boy for that!

*(*GRETCHEN *has entered; she wears an apron; she counts change.)*

NICK: You shouldn't talk like that in front of my boy. It ain't right.

HEINRICH: Knock him down! Just knock him down!

NICK: IIIIII...

GRETCHEN: He can't. Or won't

DERRICK: *(Quietly)* Gretchen.

NICK: You got myyyy boy upset.

HEINRICH: *(Yells)* Knock him down!!!!!

NICK: Boy...

GRETCHEN: He can't! Because that man's got a county and a works and he's got an Inn that don't make him a pound a year. So he can't. Or won't. *(Pause)*

NICK: Boy? (He goes to HEINRICH *and tries to rub his hair.)*

HEINRICH: Get away from me!

NICK: Whaaaaat kind of talk's that?

HEINRICH: Why didn't you knock him down?

NICK: You can't go knocking people down, boy, not when they're payin'. You're oooold enough to know that.

(Pause)

GRETCHEN: Go inside, Heinrich. I want to speak with your father.

*(*HEINRICH *slowly leaves.* NICK *starts to clean up.)*

NICK: You shouldn't have sssssaid what you said, Mr Derrick. But just toooooo show I got no bad feelings, Gretchen, geeeeeet Mr Derrick another drink.

GRETCHEN: I'm not getting nothing until you explain why you paid me one and three when you know damn well I've earned one and six.

NICK: *(Screams)* Get him a drink!!!!!!

(Pause, she doesn't move.)

NICK: I paid what I owed.

GRETCHEN: But I...

NICK: It may be less than what you earned, but it's what I owed.

GRETCHEN: Come again.

NICK: Now don't you start something, Gretchen Van Winkle. I have never cheated nobody in my life.

GRETCHEN: There's a first for everything.

NICK: I told you—I paid what I owed!

GRETCHEN: But I earned...!

NICK: But there was a bill!

GRETCHEN: A what?

NICK: A bill. That was owed me. That's all.

GRETCHEN: A bill? What kind of...? *(Stops, realizes, suddenly very upset)* When was he here?!! When?!!!!!

NICK: I couldn't refuse him, could I? Rip without something to drink— that's paththethtic. I got a big heart.

GRETCHEN: With my money!! *(She sits, holds her head, fights back tears.)* Why do I even... Why bother. God I feel so foolish. I can't remember the last time I cried. As if tears were... What a waste.

*(*DERRICK *tries to give her a handkerchief)*

GRETCHEN: *(Screams)* Nooooo!!

(Pause)

DERRICK: *(Motioning for* NICK *to leave)* Nick...

*(*NICK *starts to leave but stops.)*

GRETCHEN: *(To* DERRICK*)* You. You've sucked out his acres and now he's bone dry. Go away.

DERRICK: I paid a fair price, Gretchen.

GRETCHEN: I wouldn't know. Went down his throat and into his *(*NICK*'s)* pocket. I wouldn't know. *(Slowly stands; yells)* Give me that handkerchief!!!!

(He does; she blows her nose.)

GRETCHEN: I don't know what's the matter with me. *(Rubs her eyes)*

*(*HEINRICH *has entered and watches.)*

DERRICK: *(To* NICK*)* The boy.

GRETCHEN: Let him see. Let him. Maybe then he'll think twice before he becomes a drunk like the rest of them.

(Pause)

NICK: Look, I don't want to stop a man from having a good ttiiiime.

GRETCHEN: A good time. Sure. Why not.

*(*NICK *exits with* HEINRICH*. Pause.)*

DERRICK: You hate him?

GRETCHEN: You'd like it if I did.

DERRICK: I wouldn't.

GRETCHEN: Funny, aren't I? Go ahead and laugh. Fifteen years ago I could have had you. But then I wanted a good time. I was a girl.... God, I try. It's that damn good humor that I just can't stand. What's to be so happy about? Sometimes I find myself just screaming at him—what's to be so happy about!

DERRICK: The boy said he got kicked by a horse. That's why he didn't show up at the works.

GRETCHEN: I wish. *(Pause. She starts to pick up things.)*

DERRICK: Gretchen...

GRETCHEN: Don't ask.

DERRICK: There's room, Gretchen. You could have a whole floor to yourself. You could be my cook. I'd pay. It's a job. Nothing more.

(Pause)

GRETCHEN: No. I can't change. *(She leaves.)*

COCKLES: She'll change.

*(*MRS JOHNSON *enters, she's very nervous, awkward.)*

MRS JOHNSON: I came back to apologize for my behavior.

DERRICK: There's no need to...

MRS JOHNSON: It must have been the heat. I am quite susceptible to heat.

DERRICK: I understand.

(She turns; REV JOHNSON *has entered. She turns back.)*

MRS JOHNSON: *(Holding out a book)* Have you read this?

DERRICK: I'm afraid I....

MRS JOHNSON: The characters are most exceptionally drawn. One almost gets the sense that one knows them. As if you could recognize them if they walked by... And they might recognize you and say "hello"... If you'd like to borrow it... *(She holds it out)*

DERRICK: *(Taking the book)* Thank you.

MRS JOHNSON: *(Nods)* Goodbye. *(She exits.)*

REV JOHNSON: See—charming and delightful. Good day. *(He exits; Pause.)*

DERRICK: *(To* COCKLES*)* Come on, boy, let's go to work.

(They leave. HEINRICH *enters, clearing off the tables.)*

VOICE: Psst. Pssst!

*(*RIP *enters.)*

HEINRICH: Sh-sh! *(Points to where his father is, off)*

RIP: How much did Derrick give you?

HEINRICH: Shilling.

RIP: Good work.

HEINRICH: My father took it.

RIP: That's life.

HEINRICH: You want a bottle? *(Takes out a bottle from under his shin)*

RIP: You stole it?

HEINRICH: He beat me.

RIP: Fair is fair. *(Takes the bottle, winks. He drinks. He saunters over to the telescope, looks through.)* What a lot of dirt.

Scene Four

*(*DERRICK*'s office. Table and chair. A telescope is set up at one window.)*

*(*DERRICK, COCKLES, SOLDIER *and* SURVEYOR. *As the scene opens,* COCKLES *stands at a distance, the other three are pushing their chairs back and standing.)*

DERRICK: *(Holding out his hand)* Gentlemen.

SOLDIER: Mr Derrick, the armies of the Continental Congress wish to thank you.

*(*DERRICK *suddenly turns his head.)*

SOLDIER: What is it?

DERRICK: A fly. *(Short, awkward pause)*

SURVEYOR: And I, sir, would like to add my own thanks. You must know how difficult it is to find a man with a works who's willing to sell to a rebel militia.

DERRICK: *(A bit distracted by the fly)* A man with a works can't help but be aware of the ways of His Majesty's government. The plans for these works, you know, had to be smuggled here.

SOLDIER: *(To* COCKLES*)* England doesn't want us to grow.

SURVEYOR: I have heard that of other works as well. That's why I admire your courage.

DERRICK: If I'm to keep what I own it doesn't take courage to know who has to be fought. And it's not just the English; they also have their supporters in this colony. Just west of here's a whole valley full of Canucks.

SOLDIER: Canucks, sir?

SURVEYOR: Canadians.

DERRICK: That is they still think of themselves as Canadians, though they've been south for years.

SOLDIER: Do they own a works, sir?

DERRICK: *(Shakes his head.)* Farmers.

SOLDIER: Then what do they know?

SURVEYOR: They may know how to fight.

DERRICK: I wouldn't be surprised if they had eyes on this valley as well.

SOLDIER: What do they want with two valleys?

DERRICK: Why wouldn't they?

SOLDIER: I see.

SURVEYOR: Again our thanks. You are a patriot, sir.

COCKLES: He happens to own a works.

DERRICK: Same thing. *(Swats the fly)*

COCKLES: Missed?

(DERRICK nods.)

SOLDIER: *(Pointing toward the telescope)* Would you mind?

DERRICK: *(Smiles)* No.

(SOLDIER looks through.)

COCKLES: It's delicate.

DERRICK: Tell me—what do you see?

SOLDIER: A country. *(They move to leave.)* Peter, the letter.

(SURVEYOR looks at him.)

SOLDIER: The letter. From Pittsfield.

SURVEYOR: *(Begins to look through his knapsack)* Excuse us, sir. But it seems we got so caught up in recounting our adventure with Van Winkle that we have left one errand uncompleted. I believe this is for you. *(Hands him the letter)* Good day.

SOLDIER: Good day. *(They leave.)*

DERRICK: *(Smiles)* Cigar, boy?

COCKLES: *(Taking one)* Stupid hicks.

DERRICK: Well, I liked them. They're young. They have their vision. They have hopes. They see the broad canvas. We need each other. I, their canvas; they, someone like me to draw on it.

COCKLES: *(Turns away)* What about me?!

DERRICK: What about you???? What are you talking about? You heard what he said—a country. Well a country must have its works, and a works must have its country. I feel fifteen years younger.

COCKLES: You know they weren't any older than me, Uncle.

DERRICK: No, I guess they weren't. So what?

COCKLES: I can have a vision too!!!!

DERRICK: Who said you couldn't, boy?

COCKLES: Maybe I'm not a boy!

DERRICK: Don't be childish. Of course you're not a boy. Who said you were a boy? Look, this is just silly. *(Opens the letter that he has been fiddling with. He reads. Pause. He slams his hand on the desk.)*

COCKLES: Get it?

DERRICK: Get what?

COCKLES: *(Confused, takes the letter)* From our lawyer?

*(*DERRICK *nods.)*

COCKLES: *(Reads)* "You must obtain from Rip Van Winkle a proper conveyance for the lands you have purchased from him. The papers he has signed are in fact only loans in the form of mortgages. Hence, the lands remain his legal property; and due to the improvements on the lands, which include the works, its value is now far greater then the amount which he owes. Hence, it is within Van Winkle's legal right to sell and/or lease part or all of the lands, pay what is owed to you, and accrue a very sizable profit for himself due to the improvements you have made on his lands." *(Pause)*

DERRICK: *(Quietly)* He's enclosed this deed for Van Winkle to sign.

(Long pause)

COCKLES: He'll sign. *(Short pause)* He will. *(Short pause)* Look, Uncle, I'll make him sign.

DERRICK: *(Erupts)* Use your head, boy!!!!

*(*FOREMAN *enters.)*

FOREMAN: Excuse me, Mr Derrick, but I've been unable to locate Van Winkle, so as you requested his wife's been told that his services will no longer be required by the Derrick Works.

DERRICK: And what was Mrs Van Winkle's reaction to this news?

FOREMAN: None. No reaction.

*(*DERRICK *nods, rubs his eyes.* FOREMAN *leaves.)*

DERRICK: Bugger.

COCKLES: Rip?

DERRICK: This fly... Cigar boy?

COCKLES: I have one, Uncle.

DERRICK: *(Noticing)* Ah. So do I.

(Pause. Door opens. MEENIE *appears.)*

COCKLES: I'm sorry miss—Mr Derrick is not accepting visitors.

MEENIE: *(Looks around the room.)* I. I. I. *(She starts to cry.)*

DERRICK: It's Meenie. Rip's daughter.

COCKLES: I'll get someone.

DERRICK: Yes. No. What's the matter, Meenie?

MEENIE: My fa...just because he got kicked by a... How could you?!!!! ! *(Cries)*

COCKLES: She's heard about her father.

DERRICK: Yes. To her he's still a father. Too bad she can't fire him too. So I'm a monster am I, Meenie?

MEENIE: Yes!!! *(Cries)*

DERRICK: I'm the villain, and I suppose you're the princess. And you've been terribly wronged. I understand. Everything. *(Plays with the letter; without looking at her)* How unfair it must seem. To a child's eyes. Your father. Your hope. How cruel. Everything you'd longed for, you believed was, everything you'd spent every inch of your strength to gain, it just melted. What you'd thought was stone, was ice, and you don't know what to think anymore, and the ground is moving beneath your feet, and you find yourself reaching for a cigar but you already have one....

MEENIE: What?

COCKLES: Uncle?

DERRICK: *(Screams)* I too am a princess!!!!!!!!!

COCKLES: Uncle would you like a glass of water?

DERRICK: What? *(Calm)* No. No... Meenie. I'm sorry. There's nothing I can do for your father.

(She cries.)

COCKLES: *(Quickly)* Except Uncle, hire him back.

DERRICK: Boy, I'm not a charity.

COCKLES: *(With much urgency)* Hire him back, Uncle! But this time not as a driver of mules.

DERRICK: Boy, she's not stupid.

COCKLES: This time, it'll be a better job. One that will take advantage of your father's talents.

DERRICK: What talents? I don't understand you, boy.

COCKLES: Your father's too intelligent a man to be a mule driver, Meenie. He was bored. That was the problem. He needed more of a challenge.

DERRICK: He's not going back to work!!

COCKLES: And we'll raise his salary. We'll double it!

DERRICK: I'm going to stop this. Foreman!

COCKLES: No, we'll triple it!

DERRICK: Triple it?!! Foreman!! Foreman!!

COCKLES: *(To* DERRICK*)* Use your head!!

DERRICK: You're out of yours. Foreman!!!!! Where is he?!!

COCKLES: But there's just one stipulation...

DERRICK: Foreman!!!!!

*(*FOREMAN *enters.)*

DERRICK: There you are. Would you kindly take my nephew....

COCKLES: ...that your father sign a paper...

DERRICK: *(Stops)* Sign a...? *(To* FOREMAN*)* Go. Go.

COCKLES: ...sign a paper...

DERRICK: Yes?

COCKLES: ...stating...

DERRICK: Yes?

COCKLES: That under no circumstances will he...ever touch a drop of alcohol again. And here's the paper right here. Have him sign it. And he's hired.

*(*MEENIE *grabs the paper, looks first at* COCKLES *and then at* DERRICK, *who nods, then suddenly squeals with delight and runs out. Pause.* DERRICK *sits and nods.* COCKLES *goes to the telescope.)*

COCKLES: *(Looking through)* We'll let him drive the big horses. If he's drunk with them, they'll crack his skull open. *(Short pause)*

DERRICK: What do you see, Cockles?

COCKLES: *(Turns back from the telescope.)* Whatever I want to see. *(Short pause)* You didn't call me boy. *(Suddenly slaps his arm.)* Got him.

Scene Five

(Hillside. Afternoon)

(Far upstage, REV JOHNSON *and* MRS JOHNSON *are having a picnic.)*

*(*SURVEYOR *with tripod stands far left.* RIP, MEENIE *and* HEINRICH *are down stage right.* HEINRICH *holds a plumb-bob for the* SURVEYOR. RIP *drinks.)*

RIP: This place it's getting crowded. Remember when you could sit up here for a week and nobody'd bother you. Except the jackrabbits. *(Drinks)*

REV JOHNSON: Blue sky. Green hills. Cool breeze.

MRS JOHNSON: Going to rain.

SURVEYOR: God damn it, stand still!!!!

(HEINRICH *does.)*

RIP: Ahhhhh, the sun. *(Pause)* What was I talking about?

MEENIE: You were getting the rope.

RIP: The rope. What rope? Oh, the rope. I was getting the rope for my Grandmother. She was a funny lady, Meenie. I mean, she weren't funny, but I thought she was. She had a face so sharp you could chop wood with it. Never saw her face make a smile except once but that only looked like a smile, 'cause in fact she was squinting into the sun. So that's Grandmother. Anyway, the rope. So I had this piece of thin rope, and I'm tying it to two little stakes I've pounded into the ground, oh they're about eight feet apart, and the rope I tie it tight, so it's about a foot maybe off the earth. And then I'm yelling, "Grandma, Grandma!", and I'm crying, I was always crying, I was a great crier, had soft little cries, and big scratchy cries, I could play my cries like I was an instrument or something, Jesus, I was good; anyway, I'm yelling to Grandmother, and she comes out, and already I know she's not going to believe whatever it is I'm crying about, but she knows I know, but anyway she comes out and I say, "It's a chicken, it's got out of the pen", and she says, "Well get it back in the pen", and I say, 'cause I'm trying not to let her see the rope, I say, "But it flew up into the tree", and she shakes her head and spits, she loved to spit, Grandmother she spits, course nobody ever saw her spit except me, 'cause she knew nobody believed what I said so she could spit around me, and she spits and says, "Chickens don't fly into trees", and I say, "That's what I thought", and I'm pointing out what tree and she's getting closer to the rope, and that's when I realize I'm holding my breath and not crying anymore, so I start up again and I can see she can't wait to find there's no chicken up there so she can beat me and so she says something like "humpf", whatever that means, so she walks quickly toward the tree but she never gets there because she trips over the rope and falls and also I put some water there, so it's mud she falls in and that was something I wouldn't have missed for the world. She was such a funny lady, 'cause she was always doing things like that, tripping over ropes and falling into the mud. *(Laughs, drinks)* Of course, she broke her leg. And of course, I'm the one everybody wants to talk to. 'Course "talk" isn't what they mean, but that's the word they use. So Father's standing there and Mother's looking over his shoulder, and both are asking where that rope had come from to say nothing about the mud, and I'm there giving a concert of crying but sooner or later I know I got to say something, so I say, "It was a trap for the jackrabbits", and Father says, "But it was too low to catch jackrabbits, they'd jump over it" and I say; "That's what the mud was for to make 'em slip", and they don't know whether I'm just a moron or the biggest bald-faced liar they've ever seen; so Father he calls me a moron and he beats me, and Mother she calls me a liar and she beats me, and I'm thinking, "Hey, I'm either one or the other so how about making up your minds". *(Pause, drinks)* And that just goes to show you, Meenie, the hardest thing in the world, the loneliest of professions, the job you got to work the hardest at is—having a good time. *(Pause; drinks)*

*(*REV JOHNSON *and* MRS JOHNSON *wander off)*

RIP: Nice to see her husband taking some time with her. Get her to relax.

SURVEYOR: Still, I said, damn it!!!!

RIP: *(To himself)* Shouldn't yell at a boy. Boys are boys. And they don't stand still. *(Drinks)* Ahhhh. So where's this paper I got to sign?

MEENIE: I gave it to Mother and she sent me out looking for you.

RIP: Seems everybody's always looking for Rip. "Where's Rip?" "Will somebody please go find Rip!" That's why I have so much time, I'm the only one who doesn't waste his days looking for Rip. Don't they know a man's gotta have time to himself?!

(Drinks; MEENIE *turns away.)*

RIP: I don't mean you child. I'm always glad to see you. Let me look at my girl. Stand up.

(She does.)

RIP: No, I don't think I deserve to have a thing like you.

MEENIE: I thought you hurt your head.

RIP: Oh, it's hurting all right, Meenie.

MEENIE: I thought a horse kicked you.

RIP: A horse? I get kicked by a lot of horses. There's one in there now, kicking the bejesus out of me.... No, you're too good for a drunk. Heinrich—boy, don't you ever drink.

HEINRICH: *(Trying to stand perfectly still)* Yes, Rip.

RIP: *(To* MEENIE*)* Give me that cup. Shouldn't drink from a bottle in front of children. *(Pours and drinks)* Did I ever tell you about how my Grandfather got all this land?

MEENIE: No.

RIP: *(Laughs)* I'm sure I have. You're a smart girl, Meenie. Only a girl and already she knows about men. You'll make a good wife.

HEINRICH: *(Still)* I know.

RIP: You do, do you?

MEENIE: I'll make a good wife for Heinrich.

RIP: For Heinrich? So it's settled, is it?

HEINRICH: *(Still)* We've worked it all out, Rip. *(Yells)* I'm standing still!!!!!

MEENIE: He's going to go with his Uncle in a ship to the North Pole, to catch whales.

RIP: The North Pole? That's a long way from here.

HEINRICH: My Uncle will pay me ten shillings a month and I'll send it all to Meenie.

RIP: He's going to send it all to you, Meenie.

MEENIE: And I'll give it all to you to keep for us.

RIP: I wouldn't do that, darling. No. Don't do that. *(Drinks)*

SURVEYOR: Come on, what's going on over there?!!

MEENIE: Shut up!!!!!

RIP: *(Holds his head.)* I thought I heard Gretchen there for a second. *(Drinks)* Heinrich?

HEINRICH: Yes, sir.

RIP: If you marry my daughter, you must promise me something.
You must promise me, never to drink.

HEINRICH: I already told you I won't, Rip.

RIP: That's a good boy. Then let's swear on that. The two of us. Not another drop—once I've finished this. *(Drinks)* I was going to tell you how Grandfather got his land. *(Drinks)* He got it by falling off a coach. And that's the God's honest truth. He was going north in the coach and he was drinking and he falls off and it's a hot day, so he takes off his clothes while he's trying to find his way. A coat there. His shoes over here. Well, after he'd made a few miles, he only has his drawers left, so he sits down and as he always slept in his drawers anyway, he's comfortable and he falls asleep. And that's how he got his land.

HEINRICH: Because he fell asleep?

RIP: Because, don't you see, all his clothes that he'd scattered around, they are like claims and as this land hadn't been claimed by nobody yet but some Indians, when he wakes up he finds he'd claimed half a county. He did. *(Drinks)* And that's what my Grandpa told me, little Rip, while I was on his knee. He says: my boy, some men they work all their lives and get nothin', and some men they get drunk and wake up owning half a county. You never know, he says. That's just life, he says. *(Drinks)* Now there's no more land to wake up to. *(Pause)* The time of the lazy fellas like me is over. *(Pause)*

(Stands up, finishes bottle.) Let's go see if your future father-in-law will give me a drink, Meenie.

HEINRICH: Rip, I thought you were quitting.

RIP: Don't be a smart ass. Give me that. *(Takes the plumbbob)*

SURVEYOR: Hey!!!!!!

*(*RIP*'s hands shake.)*

HEINRICH: Why are your hands shaking?

RIP: I said, don't be a smart ass.

(He throws down the plumb-bob; RIP, MEENIE, *and* HEINRICH *leave.)*

SURVEYOR: *(Throws down his map)* Discipline. No discipline.

SOLDIER: *(Entering with satchels)* What's the matter with you?

SURVEYOR: Those the supplies?

SOLDIER: Yes.

SURVEYOR: Let's go to the next village.

SOLDIER: Why the sudden rush?

SURVEYOR: *(Picking up map)* Problem with maps is they keep changing. *(He leaves.)*

SOLDIER: *(Picking up the equipment)* The problem with maps???? *(Leaving)* The problem with you is that you can't stand still!!

(They're gone. Pause. REV JOHNSON *and* MRS JOHNSON *enter. He holds her hand.)*

REV JOHNSON: They're gone. Come on, I know a shed just over the hill.

MRS JOHNSON: Not now. Please.

REV JOHNSON: Pick up the bed spread.

MRS JOHNSON: *(She does.)* No. I don't want to. Please.

REV JOHNSON: I'll carry something if you wish.

(She cries.)

REV JOHNSON: Come. *(He starts to undo her blouse.)* We won't be seen. *(He unbuttons his shirt.)* Do you want me to keep my collar on?

(She cries.)

REV JOHNSON: All you have to do is lie still. Just stay still... And relax.

(They leave; she cries. Wind)

Scene Six

(Beer Garden. On one pillar there is now a recruitment poster.)

*(*RIP *at a table. Bottles in front of him. He holds the paper and stares at it, tries to focus on it.* NICK *leans over him;* DERRICK *sits at a distance concentrating on* RIP; COCKLES *stands, anxiously watching* RIP.*)*

(Long pause)

(Suddenly RIP *passes out.)*

(Everyone sighs, shakes their heads, and looks at each other.)

*(*NICK *picks up a bucket of water and pours it over* RIP*'s head.)*

RIP: Ahhhhhh! *(Holds his head)* I don't feel so good. What's this? More liquor? When it rains is pours. I haven't seen so much liquor since a wake.

DERRICK: That's what this is, we're paying our last respects to the old Rip.

RIP: The old Rip? Oh right. I forgot. This is Rip's last meal. Once I sign this paper, I become a new man.... *(Holds his head.)* Sit down with me, Nick. I don't like it with everybody watchin' me. Here, let's the both of us drink, like we always do.... Except this'll be the last time, Nick. No more after this.

NICK: If you keeeeep your oath.

RIP: I will. This time I will. I never signed an oath before. Always just said it. Big difference. This here. I'll keep it alright. It's the signing that makes the big... *(Starts to nod off)*

NICK: Then for old times, Rip. *(Sits.)*

RIP: Huh? Good. That a boy, Nick. For old...for the old...Rip. Poor old Rip. He weren't so terrible, you know. We were friends, Rip and me. Brothers!... And I don't want to hear nobody say a word against... If I hear so much as a...they'll be sorry. Here's to Rip! My very best friend! *(Drinks. Pause; suddenly)* Who's got a pen!

*(*COCKLES *hurries to give him one;* RIP *feels the pen to see if it's right.)*

RIP: This the pen? Yes. *(Pause)* Somebody read me this again. I want to hear it again.

DERRICK: Cockles.

COCKLES: *("Reading")* "Know all men by these presents, that I, Rip Van Winkle, in consideration for...the monthly salary of sixteen shillings to be paid by Derrick Works, do promise from this time forward to suspend all consumption of liquor, wines, and spirits and thereby to announce to the world that I am a new man." *(Sets the paper back down)*

RIP: There it is again—"new man". I like that—"new man".

(He passes out. NICK *leaves.* GRETCHEN *enters.)*

GRETCHEN: *(To* DERRICK*)* He sign yet? *(He shakes his head.)* You think it's a good idea to get him drunk? If I know Rip, he'll say he wasn't in his right mind, so the oath won't count.

DERRICK: By tomorrow, with my foreman keeping him busy, you keeping an eye on him, Nick locking him out, and with every cent he earns going directly to you, I think there's a chance.

GRETCHEN: I pray you're right. *(Long pause)* Why doesn't he just sign it?!

DERRICK: He will.

GRETCHEN: Why are you doing this?

DERRICK: *(After a pause)* I...

*(*NICK *has entered with bucket. He pours it over* RIP's *head, who wakes up. He doesn't see* GRETCHEN.*)*

RIP: This fine schnapps.

NICK: High Dutch Schchchnapps. Fifteen years in the botttttle.

RIP: No.

NICK: Last time I touched that schnapps was your wedding. RRRRRRRip. Remember, we broached the keg under that tree.

RIP: This the same?

NICK: Yes.

RIP: I thought I knew my liquor. You had it fifteen years? I wouldn't have had it so long...that was more than fifteen years ago.

NICK: No.

RIP: Same day as I got married.

NICK: Yes.

RIP: Right. Right. The same day. Now don't argue with me, because I'll remember that day as long as I live.

DERRICK: *(Feet up, looks at* GRETCHEN*)* And I remember Gretchen then. I envied you, Rip.

(She looks at him.)

RIP: No! Yes? I guess I envied me too. *(Drinks)* You didn't know what was happening, did you Derrick?

DERRICK: *(Watching* GRETCHEN*)* She was lovely.

RIP: Who?

DERRICK: Your wife.

RIP: Gretchen lovely??? I guess she was. Yeh, she was my little girl then. We were handsome together.

DERRICK: To me, Rip, she was like some wonderful thing that was just out of my reach.

RIP: *(Sighs)* Too bad I've not been out of her reach. *(Rubs his face)* Nick, have another.

(NICK begins to pour water in his drink.)

RIP: Hey, stop that! I thought you were a drinking man. Don't you know good liquor and water is like a man and his wife?

NICK: How soooo?

RIP: They never agree! *(Laughs)* I always take my liquor single. Here's to your good health! May you live long and happy!

DERRICK: And prosper.

RIP: Yeh.

(They drink. GRETCHEN, still unseen by RIP, watches. Pause)

DERRICK: That's right, Rip; drink away and drown your sorrows.

RIP: Yes, but she won't drown.

(Everyone turns to GRETCHEN, except RIP, who drinks.)

RIP: My wife is my sorrow and you can't drown her. She came close once, but couldn't do it.

NICK: When? *(Turns to GRETCHEN)*

RIP: Didn't you know that Gretchen almost drowned?

NICK: No.

RIP: That was the funniest thing. It was the same day we got married; she was coming across the river in the ferryboat and...

DERRICK: And what, Rip?

RIP: And the boat, it turned over.

DERRICK: Turned over?

RIP: Yes. But too bad she wasn't on it.

(Pause. GRETCHEN, obviously hurt, just watches.)

DERRICK: *(More to GRETCHEN than RIP)* Why too bad, Rip?

RIP: You got to ask? Because she...

(Drinks)

DERRICK: Because?

RIP: See that's what I was sayin', Nick, if she had been in that boat like she was supposed to be, she'd have drowned. I don't know how she got left behind. Women are always late—always. *(Drinks)* Course if she were drowning I would have jumped in to save her....

(GRETCHEN sort of smiles.)

RIP: At least I think I'd have done that. Yes, I would have done that, because then it would have been more my duty than it would be today. If she was drowning today I don't know what I'd do.... *(Laughs)*

(GRETCHEN starts to go to RIP; DERRICK motions for her to stop.)

DERRICK: You wouldn't save Gretchen?

RIP: *(Drinks)* It's only when I'm drunk that I tell her what I think, and then she don't listen 'cause she says I'm drunk. *(Drinks)* I pity her.

DERRICK: You pity Gretchen?

RIP: Yeh. Why else would I keep her around unless I pitied her? I got a big heart, that's why I don't kick her out. Stupid woman.

(Pause)

DERRICK: *(To GRETCHEN)* Gretchen? *(She shakes her head.)*

RIP: Who else I been talking about? Of course, Gretchen. Stupid and ugly and dumb as a brick. *(Laughs)* Maybe I should just throw her out. Yah, maybe that's what I'll do. *(Laughs)*

(NICK, getting nervous, stands and starts to back away.)

RIP: Hey, where you going? There's still your drink.

NICK: I I I I I I...

RIP: I'm talking! I need to have my friends.

NICK: *(Looking at GRETCHEN.)* Riiiiiip...

RIP: You think I'm boasting, don't you? Well you just wait and see what I do to that bitch of mine, you'll see that I'm not... *(Sees GRETCHEN. Pause)* Gretchen. *(Pause; looks at everyone's face. Breaks down and sobs)* Gretchen!

GRETCHEN: Sign, Rip.

RIP: I hate drinking. I don't want to drink. *(Sobs)* I didn't mean....

GRETCHEN: The liquor was talking.

RIP: I *(Screams)* Yes!!!!!!!!!! *(Pause, calms himself)* That liquor's got a big mouth. *(Looks at GRETCHEN, then back to the paper)* Does it take all that pen and ink to say just what Cockles said?

DERRICK: Yes, Rip.

GRETCHEN: Please, Rip.

RIP: And where does my X go, Derrick?

DERRICK: *(Stands, goes to* RIP.*)* There, you see that white space?

RIP: I see it. *(He practices Xs in the air.)*

COCKLES: Sign.

DERRICK: *(To* COCKLES*)* Easy... It's a new life, Rip.

*(*RIP *looks to* GRETCHEN.*)*

GRETCHEN: *(Nods)* Rip. *(Looks to* NICK*)*

NICK: Think of Meenie.

(Pause)

RIP: Why do you bother? *(Pause)* I'll sign. *(Pause)* But not like this. I'm not going to let the new Rip be born drunk...and looking like.... No. I want some clean clothes. And water so I can wash. And something like coffee to get me sober. And then we're all going to see a new Rip who doesn't look a thing like me. *(Looks up)* It's the least we can do for the new Rip, isn't it?

(Pause)

GRETCHEN: *(Finally)* I'll fetch his clothes. *(To* DERRICK*)* Keep an eye on him. *(She leaves. Pause)*

DERRICK: *(Throws down the butt of his cigar; to* COCKLES*)* I'm getting some more cigars. Watch him. *(He leaves. Pause.* RIP *takes a glass and pours it over his head to sober up.)*

COCKLES: Look after him, will you? I've got to get rid of this beer.

(Pause. HEINRICH *enters.)*

NICK: Don't let him leave. *(He leaves.)*

RIP: Tell me, do you ever cry, boy?

HEINRICH: Never.

RIP: *(Nods)* That's because you don't drink.

*(*HEINRICH *turns away.)*

RIP: Don't go away. So you're going to marry my daughter.

HEINRICH: Yes, sir. *(Turns again)*

RIP: I said talk to me. Stay here. *(Not really looking at* HEINRICH*)* Tell me about yourself. Do you go to school?

HEINRICH: Sometimes, when my father can spare me.

RIP: *(Not really listening.)* Ah. So you go to school?

HEINRICH: Yes.

RIP: And. And what do you learn in school? Important things?

HEINRICH: Yes; reading, writing, and arithmetic.

RIP: All that? I don't see how the little mind can stand it all. Can you read?

HEINRICH: I just told you I could.

RIP: I forgot. You aren't lying to me are you, 'cause if you can't read, I won't let you marry my daughter. I won't have anybody in my family who can't read. Except me. And Gretchen.

HEINRICH: I can prove to you I can read—I'll read you that poster.

RIP: You do that, boy. Read it to me.

HEINRICH: "All able bodied men bear arms. And fight for freedom against the tyranny of the King."

RIP: It says that?

HEINRICH: Yes.

RIP: The King, huh? I've never seen any King around here.... How do I know you're not making all that up? Here. You read this, because I already know what it says. *(Hands him the paper)*

HEINRICH: "Know all men by these presents..."

RIP: Yeh. That's right. What a wonderful thing reading is—why you read it pretty near as well as Cockles. Go on.

HEINRICH: "That I, Rip Van Winkle..."

RIP: That's my name. You'll be a good son-in-law. Go on.

HEINRICH: "...in consideration for sums received do hereby sell and convey to Mr Hans Derrick all my estate, houses, lands whatsoever—"

RIP: What are you reading?! That's not down there!

HEINRICH: See—"houses", "lands", "whatsoever". *(Pause)*

RIP: Are you lying to me, son? *(Stares at him.)* Go on with the rest.

HEINRICH: "Whereof he now holds possession by mortgaged deeds, from time to time executed by me." That's all there is.

(Pause; RIP *shakes his head.)*

RIP: You read it better than Cockles, my boy. Much better. *(Puts paper in his pocket; without looking up)* Now run along and leave me by myself.

*(*HEINRICH *leaves;* RIP *slaps his head.)*

RIP: Like a brick. *(He stands. Silence)* Whore.

(He starts to leave, stops, goes back and takes a bottle and leaves. Short pause. GRETCHEN *enters with clothes;* DERRICK *enters with cigars;* COCKLES *enters buttoning up his pants, and* NICK *enters to clear off more bottles—all at the same time, all from different directions. They stop.)*

DERRICK: Where'd he go?

NICK: He's gone.

GRETCHEN: He's gone.

COCKLES: He's gone.

(Short pause)

GRETCHEN: I'll kill him. *(Short pause)*

COCKLES: *(To* DERRICK*; hopeful)* Maybe she will.

(Crash of thunder)

Scene Seven

*(*RIP*'s cottage. Night Storm rages.* MEENIE *at the window. Pause.* GRETCHEN *enters, wet.)*

GRETCHEN: Where's your father?

MEENIE: He's not come home.

GRETCHEN: Coward. He's got the courage of a mouse. Let him just try to walk in like nothing's happened. I'd like to see that. If he's got a brain, he won't.

MEENIE: He's got a brain.

GRETCHEN: Meenie, don't talk to me now.

MEENIE: Mother, don't be so hard.

GRETCHEN: Me?!! Is that how you see this? I'm being too hard? Meenie, don't make me hit you... I'm not the one who's thrown away two good jobs in one day!... Now what are you crying for?

MEENIE: Because my father's out in the rain.

*(Thunder—*MEENIE *screams.)*

GRETCHEN: He gets what he deserves. Do him good to get soaked from the outside for a change. *(Pause)* Is supper ready?

MEENIE: It's there by the fireside. Shall I lay the table?

GRETCHEN: Yes. *(Thunder)* What an awful night. I'm exhausted. *(She sits.)* Who's there? *(To herself)* The wind.

MEENIE: Shall I lay the table for two or for three?

GRETCHEN: Two! He won't get supper here tonight. Let him eat the mud. *(Thunder)* Just like him to go running around in this weather. I'll have him sick and on my hands for a week. And that will be his excuse to do nothing. *(Short pause; listens—nothing)* Where is he?!... This time I am putting my foot down—going to put it down hard on his head. *(Fighting back tears)* If he only knew how he hurts me. *(Thunder)* I don't know why I bother to even worry; I could be on my death bed, and he'd still expect me to wait on him. *(Lightning)* That was quite a flash. He's out there drunk and when he's drunk he doesn't know the first thing about taking care of himself... Oh Meenie, the gall he had to say he pitied me. And that little boy face—how he looked when he saw me, I...I fell for it. Again. Again I fell for it. *(Stands)* Go ahead and kill yourself!!!! *(Knock at the door; pause)*

MEENIE: There he is now!

*(*MEENIE *opens the door;* HEINRICH *enters.)*

GRETCHEN: Where's Rip? He's not with you?

HEINRICH: I thought he'd be here.

GRETCHEN: He's passed out in the hills, that's where that drunk is. Dogs come in from the rain. Not your father.

HEINRICH: Should I run out and look for him? I know the paths; we've often climbed together.

GRETCHEN: No. I'll bring him back myself. *(Puts on her coat)*

MEENIE: But Mother—if he hears your voice, he'll only run away that much faster.

GRETCHEN: *(Hurt)* Don't Meenie.

MEENIE: But it's true!

GRETCHEN: Then I can't help that. Let him run. Least then the neighbors will know I tried and won't go blaming me. *(She leaves. Pause)*

HEINRICH: I hope your father hasn't gone to the mountains tonight, Meenie.

MEENIE: He'll die from the cold, I know it!

HEINRICH: *(Seriously)* It's not that. I've just heard old Clausen over at father's saying that on this night every fifteen years, the ghosts—

MEENIE: *(Catching his wrist)* The what?

HEINRICH: The ghosts of Hendrick Hudson and his pirate crew visit the Catskills.

MEENIE: Ghosts?! Father!!!!

HEINRICH: Sh-sh! And the spirits have been seen there smoking, drinking, and playing tenpins.

MEENIE: Tenpins? *(Short pause; as she thinks.)* Don't be silly. I don't believe it.

HEINRICH: And every time that Hendrick Hudson lights his pipe, there is a flash of lightning.

(Lightning; MEENIE *gasps. Pause)*

HEINRICH: And when he rolls the balls along...

(Rolling thunder)

HEINRICH: ...there is a peal of thunder.

(They both listen, then crash of thunder; MEENIE *screams. Door bangs open.* RIP *enters helping in* MRS JOHNSON, *whose face is bruised.)*

MEENIE: Father!

HEINRICH: Rip!

RIP: I found Mrs Johnson out in the hills. She's hurt. Get her dry.

MRS JOHNSON: I'm not hurt bad. Don't go to any trouble. I can take care of myself.

HEINRICH: What was she doing out there in this storm?

RIP: Get something hot, Meenie. There, sit by the fire. Where's your Mother—over at Derrick's would be my guess.

MEENIE: She went out looking for you.

RIP: Ah, I'm sure she did. Looking to finish off what she wounded. *(Takes out the paper, pats it, puts it back)* Well, let her try.

HEINRICH: Heinrich, look at her face! What did you do—fall down?

MRS JOHNSON: Yes. Yes. I fell.

MEENIE: Father, where have you been?

RIP: *(Looks at her)* Washing my wound.

*(*GRETCHEN *enters, stops, stares at* RIP *then suddenly sees* MRS JOHNSON.*)*

GRETCHEN: Mrs Johnson!

MEENIE: Her face, Mother.

GRETCHEN: *(Quickly)* She's soaked. Meenie, hurry and get my Sunday dress. *(To* RIP*)* You, I'll talk to later—when we don't have company.

RIP: I'll talk to you now, you whore.

GRETCHEN: What? What?

RIP: *(Slaps her)* Whore! Whore!

(She screams.)

MEENIE: Father!

GRETCHEN: You drunk!!!!! *(She pulls away from him, turns to* MEENIE*)* Take Mrs Johnson into the other room. And please close the door.

*(*MEENIE *and* MRS JOHNSON *leave.)*

RIP: *(Looking at his hand)* Like a rabid dog, that's what you scratch like.

GRETCHEN: Why Rip? *(Suddenly erupts, grabs a chair and throws it at him)* Why?!!!!!!!

RIP: *(Very frustrated)* That's my question!!! Why? Why does my wife want to keep me begging and crawling? Who else knew? Nick? Meenie? I hurt so much.

GRETCHEN: Suffer.

RIP: You hate me?

GRETCHEN: *(After a short pause)* Yes.

RIP: You hate me?

GRETCHEN: Yes.

RIP: *(Nods)* She admits it. You and Derrick were pretty smart. Jesus Christ, she admits it to my face!!!! Give me a cane, 'cause I'm a blind man. Keep me drunk so I don't see what's in front of my own nose.

(He reaches for a bottle, GRETCHEN *grabs it away.)*

GRETCHEN: Mine. Because it's in my house.

RIP: The bottle.

GRETCHEN: Empty.

RIP: No.

GRETCHEN: Will be. *(She opens it)*

RIP: The bottle or I break apart the house.

GRETCHEN: No, Rip.

RIP: Will.

GRETCHEN: Here. *(She starts to pour some on the floor.)*

RIP: Stop, or I don't stop me. *(Picks up a plate)*

GRETCHEN: You wouldn't.

RIP: Done it two or three times before, haven't I?

(She hesitates then pours some more on the floor. He smashes a plate.)

GRETCHEN: Stop him!!!!!

MEENIE: *(Who has returned)* Father!

RIP: Maybe I'm your father and maybe I'm not.

*(*MEENIE *cries.)*

GRETCHEN: Rip how can you?!!!!

RIP: *(With more plates)* Sign—you said. Sign. Well here's my X! *(Smashes more plates)*

HEINRICH: I'll get my father. *(Runs out)*

GRETCHEN: All for a bottle. Of course. That's appropriate. That always has come first.

RIP: What else do I have?

(Long pause)

GRETCHEN: Nothing.

MEENIE: Father, what are you doing?

RIP: Packing.

GRETCHEN: You're not walking out on me, because I'm throwing you out.

RIP: I was thrown out years ago. But this is the first time I'm walking out... Why don't you cry—maybe clean your soul.

GRETCHEN: Out! Out! You disgrace this house!!

RIP: Yes. If not being a sinner in a house of sin is a disgrace, then that's just what I am. *(Starts to leave with his gun. Stops)* If I weren't drunk, I'd do the Lord a favor and butcher you myself.

GRETCHEN: Try it! Try it!

(He leaves; slams the door)

MEENIE: Father!!! Father!!!

*(*GRETCHEN *sits. Pause. Knock on the door. They look up. Door opens.* REV JOHNSON *appears. Long pause)*

GRETCHEN: *(Quietly)* She's in there. *(Points to the other room)*

*(*REV JOHNSON *goes into the other room. We hear him beating his wife. She screams and sobs.)*

Scene Eight

(A path in the mountains. The storm. Night. RIP *enters with his head down, coat-collar up. He protects his gun with the skin of his jacket.)*

RIP: *(To himself)* Cold. Cold and wet... Except inside. In there it's hot like an oven. Strange... I better look for someplace, maybe a cave, that's dry. Looks like this'll go on all night... *(Looks around)* Funny how everything sort of reminds me of her. The way the wind howls—that's how she talks to me. The way the ground feels—those are her kisses. But better. The ground's better. *(Starts to go)* Hey, what happened to my dog? He was with me just a moment ago. Something must have scared him. The thunder. *(Nods)* Too bad—I could have used the company. Wet. *(Lightning)* What a flash that was. Old Hendrick Hudson's lighting his pipe tonight. *(Laughs)* Now we'll hear him roll his big bowling balls along. *(Listens—thunder)* There it is. *(Looks to his left)* Is that my dog? No. Whatever it is it's got two legs, not four. Looks like a boy. Does. Didn't think I'd see anyone up this high, least not on a night like tonight. Hey! Over here! You! *(Moves to his left)* He's gone. Where'd he go? That's funny. I would have sworn I saw somebody over there. Must have been a shadow. *(Looks to his right)* There's another one. Hey, you! Mister! Don't run away! I don't want to hurt you!

*(*RIP *runs off right. A strange dwarfish* FIGURE *enters left. He has a long beard, carries a keg on his shoulders.* RIP *returns, backing in, doesn't notice the* FIGURE.*)*

RIP: Strange. He was there a second ago. Boy, my eyes must be playin' tricks. I better find me a place soon or God knows what I'm going to start seeing. *(Bumps into the* FIGURE. *Screams)* Ahhhhhh! You scared me. Jesus. Where'd you come from? I didn't see you. *(Pause. No response)* Were those your pals I was seeing? What are you doing up here? You got a cabin somewhere?... Talkative aren't you... But a good listener, I'll bet.

*(*FIGURE *sets down the keg.)*

RIP: What's that in the keg? Not liquor, is it? I ain't had any liquor myself for...well, not since I finished my bottle, and that was a good half hour ago.

*(*FIGURE *tries to light his pipe—lightning.)*

RIP: Feels like it's getting closer. Where you going with that? Far?

(No response. Thunder)

RIP: That's old Hendrick Hudson and his bowling balls.

(Laughs, FIGURE *stares at him;* RIP*'s laugh peters out.)*

RIP: Tell me something, are your women folk as quiet as you? If they are I'd really like to meet 'em. I'd never believe that a woman could keep her mouth shut unless I saw it with my own eyes. *(Laughs, no response)* You know you're an awfully small fellow to carry such a big keg. You need some help? You see, that's how we are around here—helpful. We help each other out; watch each other's kids; look after each other when we're sick; buy each other drinks.

(FIGURE *tries to light his pipe again—lightning.)*

RIP: Whoa. See what I mean? Feel how close it's getting?

(FIGURE *tries again—lightning.)*

RIP: Having trouble lighting that thing? Here, let me help you. I know how hard it is when it's windy.*(He tries to light the* FIGURE*'s pipe—each try—lightning. Finally succeeds)* There you go.

(FIGURE *picks up the keg and starts to go.)*

RIP: How far's the cabin?

(FIGURE *turns back and looks at him.)*

RIP: Don't worry, I'm right behind you.... You know, it's a good thing you came along, I was beginning to wonder whether I was going to get any sleep tonight.

(They exit. Roll of thunder)

END OF PART ONE

PART TWO
"HUNGOVER"

Scene One

(The mountains. Fifteen years later. Dawn. RIP *lies on the ground, his hair and beard are long and white, his clothes are rags, his hands old and weather beaten, and when he speaks, his voice is hoarse and feeble. Long pause.* RIP *starts to wake up. He groans, in obvious pain.)*

RIP: Hurt. Hurt. The neck. Feels like someone's got their hands around my neck. Ow!... What's the problem with my elbow? *(Tries to rub it, screams in pain)* Ahhhhhhh!!!!!... The other one hurts even more.... Bright sun. All I see are spots. *(Pause)* Where the hell am I? Did I sleep out here all night? No wonder it hurts to move. You get rheumatism sleeping in the wet grass. And that's just what I got. *(Coughs, then chokes)* Throat's like a bone. *(Tries to get up, grimaces)* Never had rheumatism like this. *(Suddenly cries out)* Pain!!!... My body's pretty angry with me. *(Suddenly remembers)* Wait a minute.... Nah, I must have dreamed it. Though those queer fellas seemed real enough. And strange things do happen.... *(Laughs to himself)* especially when you're drunk. *(He rises—reaches for his gun, which falls apart.)* My gun's got rheumatism too.... Someone must have took my good gun and left me this thing.... Maybe them?... Nah, that was a dream, Rip. *(Looks out over the valley)* What's that? That's not my village. That's more than twice the size of my village. But it sort of looks like my village, but bigger.... Maybe I'm still dreaming. Maybe. *(Shakes his head)* I don't know. *(Starts to go slowly)* My backbone is broke. *(Moves a few more steps)* My head's full of rocks. *(Few more steps)* This is the worst hangover I ever had. *(Falls; slowly gets up)* I don't know. *(He leaves.)*

(Pause)

*(*HENRY *enters. He is a Canuck.)*

HENRY: Ho! Ho!

*(*FRANCIS *and* JACK*, two Canucks, run in.)*

FRANCIS: Sh-sh. Light.

HENRY: *(Nods, whispers)* I've seen him.

FRANCIS: Who?

HENRY: Him!

FRANCIS: Yes? Yes?

HENRY: He's going to bring more money.

FRANCIS: He's with us then.

HENRY: Yes.

JACK: Wooed and won.

HENRY: Yes.

FRANCIS: And his uncle?

HENRY: He's lost everything.

FRANCIS: His uncle?

HENRY: No, Cockles. He's been cut out. There was a party. He's with us.

FRANCIS: Good. Good. So he brings more money.

HENRY: And he says, we fight. He says the offices are first. We should burn 'em.

FRANCIS: The offices?!

HENRY: That's where the deeds are.

FRANCIS: I know. I know. But who cares about deeds? They'll just make more deeds. They made the deeds they got now, didn't they? We want the land back. Not deeds.

HENRY: He says, first the offices, because that'll confuse 'em.

FRANCIS: Fuck the offices.

HENRY: Because that'll confuse them! Then the works.

JACK: The works?

FRANCIS: Oh.

HENRY: Yes.

FRANCIS: Burn 'em?

HENRY: Yes.

FRANCIS: That sounds more like it. Burn the works. Good.

JACK: They'll give us back our valley then.

FRANCIS: Give us nothing. We take it.

JACK: And take theirs.

HENRY: Maybe.

JACK: They take ours. We take theirs.

HENRY: What we want with two valleys?

JACK: What they want with two valleys?

FRANCIS: Where's he now?

HENRY: Getting the money.

FRANCIS: Oh.

JACK: You weren't seen?

HEINRICH: There was a party. Everybody drunk. This morning everybody going to hurt.

JACK: Good. Good.

Scene Two

(The garden of DERRICK'S *house. Morning. Chairs. Picket fence. Gate. Path, upstage of the fence. Bottles, dishes, etc. about—the aftermath of a party)*

(Servant GIRL *and* HOUSEKEEPER *are cleaning up.* DERRICK'S SECRETARY *sits; he drinks coffee.)*

GIRL: And then?

SECRETARY: *(To* HOUSEKEEPER*)* Big nose on that girl.

*(*HOUSEKEEPER *nods.)*

GIRL: Can I help it if I was made to stay in the kitchen? So what happened then?!!!

SECRETARY: Mr Derrick—well, you could tell something was on his mind, because he had a little smile that sort of ran across his lips, and relaxed, I hadn't seen him so relaxed in months—so you could tell something was up, but you didn't know what. And he's filling everyone's glass, and then when he's through, he bangs the table....

GIRL: This table?

SECRETARY: I think so.

GIRL: So he was here and Miss Meenie?

SECRETARY: She was—standing there I think.

GIRL: With the schoolteacher.

SECRETARY: No. No. The schoolteacher he leans against the fence. He doesn't talk to anyone. He just smokes a pipe and leans.

HOUSEKEEPER: He doesn't lean.

SECRETARY: He does. He's leaning.

HOUSEKEEPER: He's sitting.

SECRETARY: Leaning. On the gate. It was the gate he was leaning against.

HOUSEKEEPER: And he doesn't smoke a pipe.

GIRL: So Mr Derrick pounds.

SECRETARY: Yes. And everybody stops talking, and so they're looking at him and he says—"allow me to make a personal announcement." And everybody is looking at everybody because nobody has said to anybody anything about any personal announcement.

HOUSEKEEPER: I knew.

SECRETARY: No you didn't. How could you? Nobody knew. I didn't know. Did you?

(HOUSEKEEPER *shrugs and smiles.)*

SECRETARY: *(To* GIRL*)*She didn't know. And so he says—and he has his glass raised—he says: "to my dear step-daughter Meenie, and to her betrothed!"

GIRL: Oh!

SECRETARY: And everyone's craning their necks to look at everyone who's craning their necks.

GIRL: So no one did know.

SECRETARY: No one knew. Not even me.

HOUSEKEEPER: I knew.

SECRETARY: *(Trying to ignore her)* And then the schoolteacher he takes his pipe out of his mouth—he was smoking—and he moves away from the fence—on which he had been leaning—and slowly he approaches Meenie—and the faces on everybody, one small breeze would have knocked us all over—and the schoolteacher, he is taking Meenie's hand, now he's kissing it and Meenie is blushing and Mr Derrick, he shouts: "to the bride and groom!" And everybody applauded! But while they applauded they're looking around to see who knew while at the same time trying to look like they knew.

GIRL: No.

SECRETARY: Yes.

HOUSEKEEPER: No.

SECRETARY: Yes! ... Like bees in a hive, there's buzzing. And the men, they slap the schoolteacher on the back and he looks embarrassed—but happy too; and the women they're saying: "how wonderful" to Meenie and they grab their husbands and say "did you know?" and Seth, the fiddler, plays and Mr Derrick, I didn't know he could play the mouth organ, but he can and does and that's about when everybody starts to dance—first Meenie and the schoolteacher, of course, but then everybody—but only Meenie and the schoolteacher are really dancing, the rest are just sort of moving their feet because they're busy talking, and then Mr Derrick dances with Meenie, and Gretchen with the schoolteacher and she looks like a mother all right—she has tears in her eyes but she can't stop laughing and she steps on the schoolteacher's foot and almost falls down but he holds her up and then everybody dances with Meenie or with the schoolteacher and that's pretty much what happened.

HOUSEKEEPER: No, it isn't. He didn't say "to the bride and groom," Mr Derrick said "prosit" and pointed.

SECRETARY: He said "to the bride and groom."

HOUSEKEEPER: "Prosit" and pointed. I know, because I wasn't drunk. *(Pause)*

GIRL: And what about Cockles? I thought Mr Derrick had been so set on Meenie marrying him.

SECRETARY: Must have changed his mind.

HOUSEKEEPER: He wasn't there.

SECRETARY: He was there. He left early.

HOUSEKEEPER: He was invited, but he didn't come.

SECRETARY: They didn't invite him, but he came anyway, but only stayed for a minute or two.

GIRL: It's incredible, isn't it?

HOUSEKEEPER: What is?

SECRETARY: Everything. In a young girl's eyes, everything's incredible.

GIRL: No, that it could have been Cockles, instead of the schoolteacher. Everybody thought it'd be Cockles, nobody thought about the schoolteacher.

HOUSEKEEPER: I had my eye on the schoolteacher.

GIRL: And if she hadn't waited so long for the Vedder boy to come back from the war—

SECRETARY: *(To himself nodding)* Heinrich.

HOUSEKEEPER: I know who the Vedder boy is!

GIRL: If she hadn't waited it would have been Cockles, because nobody thought about the schoolteacher, not even Meenie, because he wasn't even here then.

SECRETARY: No. She's right. Poor Cockles.

HOUSEKEEPER: Nice man. *(Pause)*

SECRETARY: Yes. *(Pause)* I wonder if he knew.

GIRL: Sh-sh! Here he comes!

HOUSEKEEPER: Cockles?!!

GIRL: *(Loud whisper)* Yes!!

*(*COCKLES *comes around the corner—the servants become busy.* COCKLES *carries a small case. He comes through the gate. He is strangely distant.)*

COCKLES: I hear I missed quite the spectacular party.

HOUSEKEEPER: Told you he wasn't here.

SECRETARY: I'm sorry you had to miss it.

COCKLES: Whole town's buzzing with the news. Quite a surprise for everyone. Schoolteacher's a fortunate man. I couldn't be happier. *(To* GIRL*)* Do you believe me?

GIRL: Yes.

COCKLES: *(Shakes his head, laughs; to* SECRETARY*)* Is my Uncle in his study?

SECRETARY: He isn't up yet.

COCKLES: No. Of course not. It was a long evening.... For everyone... I haven't been to sleep myself.

SECRETARY: No?

COCKLES: I could hear the music. I love to dance. *(Awkward pause)* I'll wait in the study. *(Leaves)*

HOUSEKEEPER: Did you see his face?

SECRETARY: Chalk.

GIRL: He said he didn't sleep.

HOUSEKEEPER: Who could? I couldn't.

SECRETARY: *(To* GIRL*)* I forgot to tell you the other news.

GIRL: There's more?!

SECRETARY: Listen. Mr Derrick, well he's been drinking for quite a while now, and he pounds the table again and he begins to wave a piece of paper in the air like it was a banner and he says: "who knows what this is?" And of course nobody knows, though of course nobody says that they don't know, and he says: "it is my will."

GIRL: His will!

SECRETARY: His will. And then he says: "my wedding present" and he hands it first to the schoolteacher who reads it and his mouth it won't close, and then Meenie takes it and then Gretchen and then someone gets it and then finally I get it and I read it and it says...that when Mr Derrick dies, the works, they will belong to Meenie and the schoolteacher. That is what it says.

GIRL: To Meenie and the schoolteacher?

SECRETARY: Yes.

GIRL: But everybody has always said Cockles was going to inherit the works. What with him being Mr Derrick's nephew.

SECRETARY: I know. That's what everybody thought. That's what Cockles thought. *(Pause)*

GIRL: Poor man.

HOUSEKEEPER: He didn't know. You could tell.

*(*DERRICK *enters—hungover.)*

DERRICK: Who didn't know what? Is that coffee?

*(*HOUSEKEEPER *pours him some.)*

SECRETARY: We were talking about the party, sir.

DERRICK: I'm sure you're not the only ones. *(Smiles, flinches in pain, rubs his head)* The head. *(Sits)* The art of surprise is indeed an art. I proved it last night. Our neighbors think they know everything there is to know about the Derricks. But who knew? *(Smiles)*

SECRETARY: *(Points to* HOUSEKEEPER*)* She knew.

DERRICK: *(Surprised)* She did?

HOUSEKEEPER: Not really, sir.

SECRETARY: But she did. She knew everything, Mr Derrick. She told me so.

DERRICK: Then she must have had one eye on the housekeeping and one eye in the key hole.

HOUSEKEEPER: I didn't know. What do I know? Nothing. Nothing.

(She hurries out; DERRICK *and* SECRETARY *smile.)*

GIRL: *(As she's leaving, stops before* DERRICK*)* I hear it was a very lovely party, Mr Derrick.

DERRICK: It got the job done.

(She leaves.)

DERRICK: (Referring to the GIRL*)* Good worker?

SECRETARY: Talkative. *(Points to his nose)* Big nose.

DERRICK: Unlike us. Who mind our own business. *(Sips his coffee.)* I wonder if I shouldn't have been an actor. Obviously, I have the flair for the dramatic. I could have let our news slip out to one of those gossips, but I couldn't resist seeing those faces last night. I don't know why that gave me such a thrill, but it does. *(Pause)*

SECRETARY: Cockles is in the study.

DERRICK: That, unfortunately, is no surprise. I'll finish my coffee.

*(*GRETCHEN *enters—hungover.)*

GRETCHEN: Does it have to be so bright?!

DERRICK: I'll have someone close the curtains.

GRETCHEN: Don't make me laugh. My head jiggles enough just walking. Is that coffee?... *(Takes a cup)* Well, you saw the farmer's daughter in me last night. Two drinks and the literate elegant wife of the town's leading businessman went to bed. And the farmer's daughter rose from her grave. *(Sits, suddenly has a pain)* With a vengeance.

DERRICK: My memory's a bit blurred.

GRETCHEN: *(To* SECRETARY*)* Would you tell Maria, I'll skip breakfast this morning.

*(*SECRETARY *leaves.)*

DERRICK: Were you sick?

GRETCHEN: Did you hear?

DERRICK: No.

GRETCHEN: Let's say I gave up what I took.... Since when did you play the mouth organ?

DERRICK: Since when did you sing at parties?

GRETCHEN: Did I sing?

DERRICK: Did I play the mouth organ?

GRETCHEN: *(She laughs, then groans.)* Do you feel as awful as I do?

DERRICK: Worse...Cockles is here. In the study. I haven't seen him yet. *(Pause)*

GRETCHEN: Will he give it all back?

DERRICK: It's not the money that I care about. I just want him out of my sight. *(Pause;* DERRICK *stands.)* I'll get this over with.

GRETCHEN: Hans? Do you know where he'll go?

DERRICK: Where do crooks go? Your guess is as good as mine. *(Stands to leave. Stops)* He's my nephew. I raised him. It makes you sick.

(Leaves. GRETCHEN *sighs, pats her head;* MEENIE *appears; she is upset, she has been crying.)*

MEENIE: I'm ashamed.

GRETCHEN: Meenie! Have you been crying? What happened?

MEENIE: You happened! *(She goes to* GRETCHEN *and slaps her across the face.)*

*(*GRETCHEN *screams and collapses.)*

GRETCHEN: What did I do? What did I do?!

MEENIE: I haven't slept thinking about it. What are you?! You don't know anything!

GRETCHEN: *(Desperate)* Meenie, I don't understand!

MEENIE: Of course he didn't say anything. But I knew what he was thinking. And I wouldn't blame him a bit if he broke off the engagement. I wouldn't want to marry me either.

GRETCHEN: Why, Meenie?????

MEENIE: With a mother like you... How could you get so drunk?!!!!!

GRETCHEN: I got...???? Did I say something awful, Meenie? Did I!!!!!!

MEENIE: He's probably never seen a woman drunk before. He probably didn't know there were women who got drunk. How ashamed I am of you!

GRETCHEN: But it was because I was happy, Meenie.

MEENIE: You were sick. I heard you. I'm thinking—there's my mother and she's on her knees and drunk and retching. Every time you retch I want to scream. Why did you get sick???!!

GRETCHEN: That was after everyone was gone, Meenie.

MEENIE: I wasn't gone!

GRETCHEN: You're being unfair to me, Meenie.

MEENIE: You're a hick! You're a small town hick and you don't even know how to behave!!... He knew. He didn't say anything, but he knew. *(She runs out.)*

*(*SECRETARY, *who has entered and heard most of this approaches* GRETCHEN, *who is crying. Long pause)*

SECRETARY: If she were mine, I'd whip her 'til she screamed.

GRETCHEN: No.

*(*COCKLES *enters from the house.)*

COCKLES: *(As he passes them)* Happy? He didn't fire me....I quit. *(Starts to walk away, turns)* My life's in those works. *(Opens the gate; yells)* I'll bet everybody's happy now!!!!!! *(Slams gate, hurries off. Pause)*

*(*DERRICK *and* MEENIE *enter.)*

DERRICK: *(Entering)* Meenie, I can't understand a word. Can't this wait.

MEENIE: Talk to him. I think he likes you.

DERRICK: Talk to who? Can't it wait?

GRETCHEN: Hans, I don't her.

DERRICK: Blame her for what?

MEENIE: For what?!!!!

SECRETARY: Cockles quit?

MEENIE: Cockles???????

DERRICK: *(To* MEENIE*)* You want me to talk to Cockles???? But I just talked to him.

MEENIE: No, to James!

DERRICK: James????

MEENIE: Explain to him. Apologize to him.

DERRICK: James?????

SECRETARY: The schoolteacher.

DERRICK: I know who James is!

SECRETARY: Why did he quit?

GRETCHEN: Hans, I told you. I warned you.

DERRICK: About Cockles???

GRETCHEN: About me!! I'm just a farmer's wife!

DERRICK: What?! What?! Quiet!!!

GIRL: *(As she enters with breakfast)* Your breakfast. Mrs Derrick.

GRETCHEN: I said I didn't want breakfast!

MEENIE: Because she'd get sick!!

SECRETARY: It's for Mr Derrick.

DERRICK: I'm not hungry. I'm not hungry! Set it down. *(Screams)* Set it down!!!!!! *(Pause. Everyone is quiet.)* We'll get to this. Whatever it is. We will get to it. But first, Otto, get me the books from the safe...

*(*SECRETARY *leaves.)*

DERRICK: I'm going to rub his nose in this. How he has the gall to deny, to my face...

GRETCHEN: Who?

DERRICK: Cockles!!!!... It's not stealing, he says. It's a loan. A loan to Canucks!

MEENIE: Canucks????

DERRICK: I ask him, politely, very, very politely: a loan for what? So they can buy guns and shoot me in the back??! So they can farm, he says. So they can pay rent, he says. It's a good business, then why'd he have to fiddle with the books!!!! Otto!!! I didn't fight a war for Canucks! If they wanted to keep their land they should have thought about that when they picked sides. They supported the British, so let the British support them now! Otto!!

*(*HOUSEKEEPER *runs on.)*

HOUSEKEEPER: Mr Derrick!

DERRICK: Where's Otto?

HOUSEKEEPER: I don't know, but Mr Derrick!

DERRICK: Go get Otto!

HOUSEKEEPER: But...

DERRICK: I said.... What is it?

HOUSEKEEPER: Mr Derrick. Your offices. I saw from the window. They're on fire.

DERRICK: Fire?

HOUSEKEEPER: Yes, sir. *(He looks at everyone. Goes to the gate, opens it; looks down the path. Suddenly sees the fire)*

DERRICK: Oh my God. The bell! Ring the bell! Fire!!!

VOICE: *(Off)* Fire!!! Fire!!! Fire!!!

(Everyone runs out. MAN *runs on.)*

MAN: Water!! Water!! Water!!

(He runs off. Short pause. RIP *enters on the path. His face is bruised and cut.)*

RIP: Water, I'd like some water.... *(Stumbles; looks into the garden)* Ho! Hello! *(Sees the coffee)* Ah! *(Fumbles to open the gate, enters the garden, approaches the coffee, then sees the breakfast)* Oh! Hello. *(Shuffles to the breakfast and begins to stuff food in his mouth. With his mouth full, not really calling.)* Hello? *(To himself)* Teeth hurt. *(Eats)* Water. *(Goes to coffee)* Huh. *(Pours coffee in his hand)* Hot! *(Drinks; goes back to the food, eats some more)*

*(*HEINRICH *enters on the path, coming from the direction of the fire. He carries a satchel. He limps. Sees* RIP. *Stops)*

HEINRICH: Morning.

RIP: *(Startled, scared)* What?!

HEINRICH: Morning.

RIP: *(Nods)* Yes, it's morning. *(Eats, though keeps glancing at* HEINRICH. *Pause)*

HEINRICH: Big fire. *(Points)*

RIP: Yes? Oh.

(Pause. HEINRICH *starts to open the gate.)*

RIP: Don't!

HEINRICH: *(Stops)* I'm looking for someone.... Is there anyone in the house I can talk to?

RIP: No. *(Pause)*

HEINRICH: I guess everyone must be at the fire.

RIP: Yes.

HEINRICH: I'll come back then. *(Starts to leave)*

RIP: Wait!

*(*HEINRICH *turns back.)*

RIP: You don't want to knock me down?

HEINRICH: Why would I want to knock you down?

RIP: *(After a pause)* Come here come here come here come here.

*(*HEINRICH *enters the gate;* RIP *looks suspiciously around.)*

RIP: Tell me—is everyone mad here? Are you mad?

*(*HEINRICH *shakes his head.)*

RIP: Me neither. *(Whispers to* HEINRICH*)* They hit me.

HEINRICH: Who did?

RIP: They did. Look. *(Shows him his cuts)* I walk down from the mountains and I say—"hello,", and a boy, he says "old man, who's your barber?" "Who's my what" I say and that's when I find this. *(Touches his beard)* Strange, isn't it? Where'd this come from?... And then I fall down—I don't know why—I haven't been drinking. And one boy—I like him—he says "give him a stick so he can stand up." "Thank you" I say. "Give him a kick so he can sit down" says the other boy and he kicks me. And I say "do you know where I live?" and another boy, I didn't see him 'til then, he says: "looks like he's been dead and dug up again." And he says: "has the circus come to town?" I say: "why do you say this to me?" And somebody kicks me. And I hurt. Why?

*(*HEINRICH *just looks at him. Pause)*

RIP: Sit down.

*(*HEINRICH *does.)*

RIP: What do you want?

HEINRICH: I'm looking for Meenie Derrick. Is this where she lives?

RIP: Who?

HEINRICH: Meenie Derrick.

RIP: Which one? That's two people. I know them both. There's Derrick and I don't know where he lives except where he always lives. And there's my Meenie and I don't know where she lives either except at home and I can't find that. Two people. Two heads.

HEINRICH: I was pointed in this direction. They said the white fence on Park Street.

RIP: *(To himself)* They got names for streets here?

HEINRICH: Though I could have got turned around. Everything seems very different than when I was last here.

RIP: For you too? We can be friends. One head. Water?

*(*HEINRICH *nods.)*

RIP: It's wash water. That's why it's brown. Usually I don't drink wash water but today I do. It's hot.

HEINRICH: It's coffee.

RIP: I smell. You live here?

HEINRICH: Did.

RIP: Me too. I think—me too. You been away?

HEINRICH: For almost ten years.

RIP: Only ten years? I been away for one night.

HEINRICH: I was in the war.

RIP: Ah, the war... What war?

HEINRICH: With the British. My regiment surrendered, and I was impressed as a seaman in His Majesty's Navy five years. I jumped ship in the Canary Islands. Caught a schooner. Came home. Who else lives here?

RIP: Who else?

HEINRICH: Besides yourself. Who takes care of you?

RIP: Nobody takes care of me. I don't live here.

HEINRICH: But you're in the garden. Who makes your food?

RIP: Don't know, I don't live here.

HEINRICH: But you're here.

RIP: So are you. Do you live here?

HEINRICH: Of course not. I just walked through the gate.

RIP: Me too. I walked in like you. One head. Hungry?

HEINRICH: Then you're not somebody's old grandfather they keep in the garden?

RIP: *(Smiles)* Come in, just like you... You going to knock me down now?

HEINRICH: No, but I think maybe I should knock. It looks sort of suspicious the two of us just walking into somebody's garden.... *(He gets up, starts to approach the house.)*

*(*SECRETARY *runs out with an empty case.)*

SECRETARY: *(Running out)* Mr Derrick! The safe! It's empty! It's been robbed!... *(Sees* HEINRICH *and* RIP.*)* Who are you? What do you want? *(Suddenly screams)* Thief! Thief!!

Scene Three

(Street in front of DERRICK*'s burning offices. Pump. Buckets. The fire off left.* FIRST MAN *at the pump.)*

FOREMAN'S VOICE: (Off) Water!!!

FIRST MAN: *(Pumping)* Coming!!

SECOND MAN: *(Running in with buckets)* Keep pumping! Keep pumping!

FIRST MAN: I'm trying. Damn pump.

FOREMAN'S VOICE: (Off) Water!!!

FIRST MAN: *(To pump)* Get up! Get up!!!

SECOND MAN: *(Picks up one full bucket, waiting for another to be filled)* Harder! Pump harder!

FIRST MAN: It's not coming.

FOREMAN'S VOICE: (Off) Water!! Water!!

SECOND MAN: Use your muscles!!

FIRST MAN: I'm pumping. I'm telling you it's not coming up!!!

GRETCHEN: *(Running in with blankets)* Blankets! Blankets!

SECOND MAN: Pump! Pump!

FIRST MAN: You do it then!

FOREMAN'S VOICE: (Off) Water!!!

SECOND MAN: Damn it. *(Grabs the one bucket of water)* Coming! *(Runs out with bucket)*

GRETCHEN: Blankets! What do I do with the blankets??!!!

*(*THIRD MAN *runs in coughing, collapses choking.)*

FIRST MAN: *(To pump)* More! More! More!

THIRD MAN: *(Coughing)* I'm burning.

GRETCHEN: I've got the blankets now what do I do with them?!!!!!

FOREMAN'S VOICE: (Off) Water!

FIRST MAN: Coming!

GRETCHEN: Blankets! *(Suddenly looks up, screams.)* Ahhhhhhhhh!

*(*FIRST MAN *looks up.)*

FIRST MAN: The roof.

FOREMAN'S VOICE: (Off) The roof!!!

GRETCHEN: The roof! Back!!!!

FIRST MAN: Back.

FOREMAN'S VOICE: (Off) Back!!! The roof!!!!!

GRETCHEN: Ahhhhhhhhhhhh!!!!!!!!!!!

(The roof has collapsed; silence.)

THIRD MAN: I'm burning up.

*(*FIRST MAN *just touches the pump and water comes out.)*

FIRST MAN: Now it comes. *(Pause; he takes a bucket to* THIRD MAN.*)* Here.

THIRD MAN: *(Throwing water on himself)* Thanks. *(Pause)*

FIRST MAN: Now it comes.

(He walks off. DERRICK *enters, smeared with ash.)*

GRETCHEN: Senseless. *(Short pause)* Why? *(Short pause)* What do they want?

*(*DERRICK *just looks at the offices.)*

GRETCHEN: It makes you sick.

*(*DERRICK *nods.* CONSTABLE *and* SECRETARY *enter talking.)*

SECRETARY: One has a long white beard and the other—a limp. It's not likely that you'd lose them in a crowd.

CONSTABLE: Who said anything about a crowd? They're back in the hills with the rest of them. We've got dogs.

SECRETARY: They could be hiding in the cellar.

CONSTABLE: They *could* be on the moon. They are in the hills.

SECRETARY: Canucks?

CONSTABLE: You're not as stupid as you look.

GRETCHEN: But what do they want? I can understand robbing a safe, but torching a building?

CONSTABLE: They set the fire. You leave your house. So they can rob the safe. And escape.

SECRETARY: Simple.

CONSTABLE: And dumb. They picked the wrong town. Or the wrong constable. I'll find them. We'll track 'em and they'll lead us to the rest. We've got dogs. *(Starts to leave, stops.)* It's always this way, isn't it?

GRETCHEN: Which way?

CONSTABLE: From the outside. That's how you can catch it.

GRETCHEN: Catch what?

CONSTABLE: Disease. *(He leaves. Pause)*

SECRETARY: *(To* GRETCHEN*)* He's got dogs.

(FOREMAN *enters.)*

FOREMAN: *(To* DERRICK*)* He hasn't been seen since he left your house.

GRETCHEN: Who? *(Looks into* DERRICK*'s face)* No. Not Cockles?! That's not possible, Hans. You can't think, just because he took some... You don't really think...? Hans, he said they were Canucks!

DERRICK: *(To* SECRETARY*)* The safe, was it broken into or just open?

SECRETARY: Now that you mention it, Mr Derrick, it was open. But you can't think...? Maybe I should tell the constable. *(Starts to go)*

DERRICK: Otto. Leave the constable to worry about his dogs.

GRETCHEN: Hans you raised him!

DERRICK: I once raised pigs too. *(To* FOREMAN*)* The works. The northeast gate. Pull ten men and arm them. Keep them hidden. They'll try to sneak through there. Give the rest of the workers revolvers. But keep them working. Nothing should look out of the ordinary.

FOREMAN: Yes, sir. *(Leaves)*

DERRICK: *(To* SECRETARY*)* There's a Thomas Jones. A Sergeant Thomas Jones, he works at the Inn. You know who he is?

SECRETARY: Yes, sir.

DERRICK: Tell him I want to see him.

*(*SECRETARY *leaves.)*

DERRICK: He was the best Sergeant Major I had in the war. He can put together a little army within hours.

GRETCHEN: But Hans, the works? You don't think....

DERRICK: Even as a child, Cockles liked to play with fire. People don't change.

GRETCHEN: But how do you know it's Cockles?!!

DERRICK: I know. I know. *(Looks back at the fire)* Stupid bastard.

(They leave.)

Scene Four

(The hills. A clearing in the woods. JACK *up a tree, as a lookout,* FRANCIS *sits. A* BOY *fixes a shovel.)*

FRANCIS: Now what do you see?

JACK: More flame and more smoke.

FRANCIS: Good. They'll be watering ashes all night.... What's that you're doing, boy?

BOY: My father says, you fix your own tools, then you take good care of them.

FRANCIS: He's right, boy. He's.... How high the flames now?

JACK: Tall as three houses.

FRANCIS: Not high enough. Want 'em licking the clouds.

BOY: Why is that?

FRANCIS: 'Cause then our wives and fathers could see from over the hills, and they'd know we weren't flat drunk on our butts but doing what we said we'd do—gettin' our valley back. Tell me when they kiss the clouds, okay? *(To* BOY*)* Need some extra fingers?

BOY: No.

FRANCIS: Good boy. *(Pause)* What you see now, Jack?

JACK: Same as I saw the last time you asked.

FRANCIS: Oh. Must have built those offices with oak. 'Cause if it was pine you'd be seeing sparks too. See any sparks?

JACK: No.

FRANCIS: *(Nods)* Oak. *(Short pause)* Too bad. 'Cause no oak flame is going to reach the clouds. Looks like we'll have to wait for the works. Got to use powder with them as they're not wood but stone, so they won't burn but blast. My wife won't see it, but she'll hear it, I'll bet, 'cause the earth is going to shake when the works go up.... How you coming, boy?

BOY: Fine.

FRANCIS: Good boy.

*(*HENRY *enters.)*

HENRY: He's coming. He just crossed the stream.

FRANCIS: With a satchel?

HENRY: Two.

FRANCIS: Good. Good. Must have found a bank. Two satchels.

HENRY: How's it going down there, Jack?

FRANCIS: *(Laughs)* That's funny.

HENRY: What's funny?

FRANCIS: You say "down there", but you look up. That's funny.

JACK: It just keeps smoking, Henry. They must be pissin' in the coals.

HENRY: Let 'em piss, I say.

FRANCIS: Your boy, Henry, he's been fixing a shovel. Hasn't said boo, except when you ask him a question.

HENRY: Let me see, boy. *(Takes the shovel and smashes against the ground. Nothing happens. Smashes it again—the handle comes off.)* Good only for one bang, boy. That's not a shovel, that's a piece of straw. Try again, boy. Good for three bangs, that's a shovel, that's where I'll stop, so you'll know the next time. *(Hands him back the pieces)*

*(*BOY *starts to fix the shovel again.)*

FRANCIS: He's a good boy.

HENRY: That he is.

JACK: Oh! Oh!

FRANCIS: What, Jack?

JACK: It's the roof. The roof's fallen in.

FRANCIS: *(Laughs)* Good. Good. There won't be splinters left to pick their teeth with. Good.

*(*COCKLES *enters with satchels.)*

COCKLES: Where's the powder?

FRANCIS: Cockles, did you see? The roof's now the ground.

JACK: Climb up and see the picture, Cockles. It's such a lovely picture.

HENRY: A nice fire always warms the heart. Go watch.

COCKLES: If every building but one were on fire, I wouldn't stop to watch, I'd be too busy looking for a match to burn that one too.

HENRY: *(To* BOY*)* Yes. Yes. Frivolous to watch.

FRANCIS: Yes. Yes. Too busy to watch. I told Jack to come down, Cockles.

JACK: When did you tell me that? Cockles, he never told me that.

COCKLES: Where do you keep the powder?

FRANCIS: The powder? It's buried, of course. We're not stupid. Where'd we bury it, Henry?

COCKLES: Dig it up them. We're going to need it today.

FRANCIS: Today? We do the works today? We do two in one day?

COCKLES: They're like ticks, you got to keep squeezing them.

FRANCIS: Yes, like ticks. That's good. Also like fleas 'cause once they get on you they're hard to get off. Or like moths, 'cause they chew up and spit out everything you got. But ticks, that's good too.

HENRY: I don't know, Francis. The works, that's a lot for one day. I wouldn't want to be greedy.

FRANCIS: Who's being greedy, Henry. Think of it like this—we're locusts and we come to this valley. The offices, they were just breakfast, and a locust wouldn't leave a valley without having lunch, would he? And that's what the works is, lunch. Aren't you hungry for lunch, Henry?

HENRY: I'm hungry.

FRANCIS: Then let's say we're locusts and eat, Henry. And if we're locusts then we're not being greedy, but natural.

HENRY: I guess if you put it like that. Okay, Cockles, I'll eat the works.

COCKLES: Settled. We'll blast the works this afternoon.

HENRY: In the daylight?

FRANCIS: Of course. You don't eat lunch when it's dark, do you?

HENRY: No.

FRANCIS: Then what are you asking such a stupid question for?

COCKLES: *(Throwing down the satchels)* Here's all the money.

FRANCIS: I told 'em you found a bank.

COCKLES: The next best thing. It's from my uncle's safe. But there won't be any more. I'm coming with you.

FRANCIS: You? You want to be a farmer?

COCKLES: No. I mean, I want to be a part of your fight. This struggle. You can have my life. I won't disappoint you. That is, of course, if you want me.

HENRY: Yes. Yes.

COCKLES: Don't answer quite so quickly. You should know some things about me first. For four years I fought along side my Uncle, against the King and those like you Canucks who supported him. These hands may have killed one of your sons or a cousin or father. I sought to create a country, and to do that, I knew a great beast had to be killed. My hand was one of many which held the sword which severed his head. And when we won, I truly believed that a man would never again have to plow a straight furrow while glancing over his shoulder. He was to be left alone, his conscience better than a thousand laws. But the beast did not die, now not as one body but as many he lives— though each one smaller, like my Uncle.

HENRY: He's short? I've never seen him.

FRANCIS: I saw him once, but he was on a horse.

COCKLES: I mean less important.

HENRY: Not to me. He took our valley.

COCKLES: And we'll take his.

FRANCIS: Jack said we'd get two valleys.

COCKLES: A man becomes a believer but once in his life. You take away that belief and the rest is waiting to die. I still have my belief. I can help. Think it over.

(HENRY and FRANCIS move away and whisper. Pause. Finally they return to COCKLES.)

FRANCIS: With two satchels, we want you.

(JACK makes a bird noise.)

HENRY: What's he doing?

FRANCIS: I don't know. What are you doing, Jack?

JACK: That's the signal.

FRANCIS: What signal?

JACK: For someone coming.

FRANCIS: Hide. Hide.

(They run out. Pause)

*(*HEINRICH *enters pulling* RIP *along. Both out of breath)*

RIP: Stop pulling at me! Who are you? Who was that man that chased us? What did he want from us?

HEINRICH: Full of questions, aren't you?

RIP: I woke up. Walking so fast made me wake up. Where are we?

HEINRICH: Safe, I think.

RIP: Oh. Why did you drag me through that stream? There were stones. We could have walked on the stones.

HEINRICH: And who'd fish you out then?

RIP: Oh. Who are you?

HEINRICH: *(Looks around)* Sit.

(After a pause, RIP *sits.)*

HEINRICH: We'll stay here a while. Quiet.

RIP: Here. But not in here. *(Points to his head)* Loud in here. *(Pause)*

HEINRICH: Not exactly how I imagined my homecoming.

RIP: Agree. Agree. Except I don't know where my home is, so I can't be coming home.... Tell me...

HEINRICH: More questions?

RIP: One. One... Am I mad?

HEINRICH: You've had a bad hit. Here, let me look at that bruise. *(Goes to* RIP*)*

RIP: I have symptoms. What I see I don't know. And what I know I don't see. There is a great gap.

(As HEINRICH *touches the bruise)*

RIP: Ahhh!

HEINRICH: That boy really gave you a good kick. Lie back and stretch out.

RIP: And then?

HEINRICH: And then rest. It's been a long walk. And I had to pull you along at quite a fast clip.

RIP: And then sleep?

HEINRICH: If you can. Yes. We should be safe here for a while.

RIP: *(Lies back)* I can, but I won't. *(Short pause)* I'm afraid to wake up. *(Short pause)* Either I am mad or the world is. But those two things are the same.... But for you too, everything is changed?

HEINRICH: Pretty much, old man.

RIP: Good. It's nice to have company.

HEINRICH: From the moment I got off the ship, I've been seeing it. It's like the war never happened, or maybe it happened all fight, but they've buried it real good.

RIP: Ah, the war. An Indian war?

HEINRICH: The war with the British, old man; I already told you that.

RIP: Ah, that war. I don't know that war. One more thing I don't know. But who's counting.

HENRY: Everybody seems to be so busy. And everything's so clean.

RIP: Ah, clean. That is a sure sign of a madman. A madman is always clean. He washes at least ten times a day. So my Grandfather always said. That's why he never washed. Because he was sane. I smell. Will we stay the night?

HEINRICH: I don't know. Can you walk anymore?

RIP: I can walk. It's just that one night is a very long time. Anything can happen. *(Tries to get comfortable)* Wet. I have rheumatism. *(Short pause)* If I close my eyes will you become somebody else?

HEINRICH: Scared that I'll leave you? You're as safe here as anyplace else.

RIP: Oh. Then I'll rest. *(Pause. RIP laughs.)*

HEINRICH: What's funny?

RIP: I don't know. But I remember always laughing. I remember people always saying I was a happy man. I thought if I start to laugh I will remember what there is to laugh about. *(Laughs; stops)* Nothing. *(Closes his eyes)* Did you ever hear of a man whose name is Rip Van Winkle?

HEINRICH: Rip? Sure.

RIP: *(Sits up)* Yes?!

HEINRICH: When I was a boy, I knew Rip.

RIP: When you were a boy. Oh, must be another one... *(Lies down)* What was this Rip Van Winkle like?

HEINRICH: Rip, he was sort of the town drunk. Funny man, nice man, but a drunk.

RIP: Sounds like the same one. *(Short pause. Sits up)* What's become of Rip?

HEINRICH: What's become of him??? He's been dead for years.

RIP: Dead? *(Lies back down.)* Oh. *(Pause. Closes his eyes)* You won't leave me?

HEINRICH: Did I say I would?

RIP: Can I believe what you don't say?

*(*HEINRICH *open his satchel. Takes out first a handsome box, then reaches in and pulls out a canteen. Drinks)*

RIP: *(Opening his eyes)* What's that?

HEINRICH: Thirsty?

RIP: No. That. *(Points to the box)*

HEINRICH: Open it.

(Hands box to RIP*, who sits up and opens it)*

RIP: Razors? Is that what you do—cut throats? I have a throat. Is that why that man chased us?

HEINRICH: I'm a barber. Or was. That's how I earned my passage back here.... I was a barber in the army too. That's why I limp.

RIP: *(Lying back down.)* Makes sense.

HEINRICH: Does it?

RIP: Who cares anymore? *(Short pause)*

HEINRICH: I was shaving a major. He falls asleep.

RIP: He what?

HEINRICH: Falls asleep.

RIP: Poor man.

HEINRICH: Bee stings him. He jumps up and his gun goes off. Shoots my foot.

RIP: Oh... I wake up. I'm walking down from the hills. I'm knocked down. I'm kicked in the head. I'm eating in a garden. I meet a man with a limp.... What's your name?

HEINRICH: Heinrich.

RIP: I know a Heinrich. *(Falling asleep)* Nice boy... I'm eating in a garden. I meet a Heinrich who has a limp. We're running away. I don't understand.... I don't understand...anything.... *(Pause)*

*(*HEINRICH *goes to* RIP*, waves his hand over his face—he is asleep. He packs his satchel.)*

HEINRICH: Sorry, old man, but I didn't travel three thousand miles to sit up here with you. And besides you've caused me enough trouble for one day.

(He hurries out. COCKLES, JACK, HENRY, FRANCIS, *and* BOY *enter.)*

COCKLES: *(Looking over* RIP*)* Beast.

FRANCIS: He's a beast? He don't look like a beast.

COCKLES: Not him. The other one. There's a lesson for all of you. That's the kind of human beings they are. Drag the old up to the hills and leave 'em to die. Makes you sick. That's what we're fighting against.

FRANCIS: *(To the others)* Beasts. *(They nod.)*

HENRY: *(To* BOY*; pointing in the direction of* HEINRICH*)* Beast.

JACK: What do we do with him? Might wake up and hear us, if we just leave him here.

FRANCIS: Jack is right.

BOY: I'll watch him.

JACK: You'll do that, boy?

BOY: Yes.

HENRY: Good boy. You watch him.

COCKLES: Now let's get the powder.

FRANCIS: Yes. The powder. Where did we bury it, Henry?

(They start to go.)

COCKLES: *(Leaving)* Now at the works. There's a gate. The northeast gate. We'll get in through there....

(They are gone. BOY *still with shovel, goes to* RIP*. He pushes* RIP *with his foot.)*

RIP: *(Waking up)* What? You've gotten smaller. I knew I shouldn't have gone to sleep.

BOY: Get up.

RIP: Are you the same one or somebody else?

BOY: Get up.

RIP: In a minute, son, you can't rush these bones.

*(*BOY *hits him on the back with the shovel.)*

RIP: Don't hit, son. Don't hit.

BOY: Get up.

*(*RIP *slowly gets up.)*

RIP: Are you taking me home? Did someone send you to take me home?

*(*BOY *threatens him.)*

RIP: Don't hit!

BOY: Can you use a shovel?

RIP: Who you want hit?

BOY: My father wants a hole dug. A shit hole.

RIP: A shit hole? Go dig it, son. I won't stop you.

(BOY *threatens him.)*

BOY: And you're going to dig it.

RIP: Me? Oh, I'm no good at digging shit holes, son. You ask anyone and they'll tell you, I'm a bad shit hole digger, son.

(Threatens him again)

RIP: Where do you want it?

BOY: Follow me.

RIP: I'm following. I'm following. *(They leave.)*

Scene Five (a)

DERRICK: I am a cloud.

GUARD: A what, sir?

DERRICK: A cloud. To this ant, I'm a cloud. I'm also the wind. *(Blows on his hand)* It carries its food which is much bigger than it is, yet it doesn't appear to stumble. Strong.

GUARD: Yes, sir.

DERRICK: Through my palm, across my fingers—then onto the other palm and across my fingers—then back to the first palm and across those fingers. Sooner or later my hands will become the only world this ant remembers, and it will stop running and sit down and eat its food. Because here is the only home it's got.

(SGT JONES *and* LOOKOUT *enter.)*

SGT JONES: *(To* LOOKOUT*)* Tell the Colonel what you saw.

(DERRICK *lightly brushes off the ant.)*

LOOKOUT: Two men, sir. At least two men. Maybe three. They carry a barrel.

DERRICK: A barrel?

SGT JONES: Powder.

DERRICK: Yes.

LOOKOUT: I see 'em run down the steep side of this hill. Sort of slide down really on their backsides 'cause it's so steep, but they keep the barrel over their heads as they go down. They don't say nothing to each other. I thought I saw a third one at the top. They got rifles. They don't see me and I run back here.

SGT JONES: On their way to the works.

DERRICK: Yes. My foreman knows what to do. We'll squeeze them between the hills and the works. I'll cut them off at the north slope. You know the signal.

SGT JONES: I do, Colonel.

DERRICK: Then prepare yourself. *(Starts to leave)*

SGT JONES: Colonel. It'll be a turkey shoot.

*(*DERRICK *looks at him, nods slowly, then hurries off.* GUARD *who had left, now returns pushing* HEINRICH *before him.)*

GUARD: Sergeant, he was watching from those bushes.

HEINRICH: I didn't want to interrupt, are you from the town?

SGT JONES: Spy.

HEINRICH: Who's a spy? You don't think...? But a spy for what? The war is over! Look, my name is Heinrich Vedder. I grew up in this town. My regiment surrendered. For three years I was impressed in the British navy. I jumped ship....

SGT JONES: He's confessing. British sailor.

HEINRICH: I was impressed!

GUARD: *(Looking through satchel)* Razors.

HEINRICH: I'm a barber.

SGT JONES: Throat cutter. Tie him up.

HEINRICH: You're joking. Someone around here must know me. My name is Heinrich Vedder. I've come home.

*(*GUARD *grabs his wrists.)*

HEINRICH: What are you doing?

*(*GUARD *twists his wrists.)*

HEINRICH: Ahhhhhhh!!!!!!! What did I do? What did I do? *(Twists again)* Enough. Enough. Ahhhhhhhh!!!!!!! Stop!!!!!! Who are you...? What do you want? Someone must know who I am???!!!!

SGT JONES: He makes you weep, don't he? Get him out of my sight.

(Distant gun shot)

SGT JONES: Listen. That's the signal. Okay, boys! Attack!!!!!!!!

*(*SGT JONES *and* LOOKOUT *run out.)*

HEINRICH: *(Being pushed out by the* GUARD*)* My name is Heinrich Vedder.

GUARD: You think I care.

HEINRICH: I've come home.

GUARD: Lucky you. Move. Move. You've given me a headache.

(They leave.)

Scene Five (b)

(Another part of the woods. RIP *and* BOY *enter.* BOY *carries shovel,* RIP, *dirty from digging.)*

RIP: *(Entering)* I see what they mean when they say "dig your own grave". I got to rest now, son.

BOY: No.

RIP: What do you mean "no"? I said, I got to rest. Who's your father that lets you talk like to that me? *(Starts to sit)*

BOY: *(Threatens)* Don't.

RIP: How much more can I hurt. *(Starts to sit)*

BOY: *(Hits him)* Don't.

RIP: Why don't you go use that shit hole, now that it's dug.

*(*BOY *threatens him.)*

RIP: I think I have died and gone to hell and you are the devil. *(He looks around. He cries.)* Look at me, I'm crying, son. 'Cause I'm so lost. Don't you pity me?

BOY: *(Handing him the shovel)* Fix this.

RIP: The shovel? But the shovel's not broken.

*(*BOY *bangs the shovel on the ground. Bangs it again. On the third bang the handle comes off.)*

BOY: Fix it.

RIP: *(Taking the shovel)* You're a strange boy.

HENRY: *(Off. Yelling)* Boy! Boy! *(Runs on)* There you are, boy. Come with me. *(Grabs* BOY*'s arm)* Come. Come. Hurry. Don't look back boy. We got to run. They're coming. Run. Run.

(They run out. COCKLES *runs in.)*

COCKLES: Henry! Henry! What happened?!!!! Stop! *(Shoots in the air. Short pause)* Stop. What happened?

RIP: The hole's finished.

COCKLES: What?

RIP: I said, the hole's finished. Can I sit down now?

*(*FRANCIS *runs in, starts to run off.)*

COCKLES: Francis!

*(*FRANCIS *stops.)*

FRANCIS: Quick! Quick! Come!

COCKLES: *(Grabs* FRANCIS*)* Francis, what happened?

FRANCIS: Awful. Jack's killed. They were waiting for us. They had guards. Hurry! No time!

COCKLES: *(Holding him.)* And the powder—what happened to it, Francis?

FRANCIS: They didn't get it. We tuck it against the wall. That's when they shoot Jack. Poor Jack. He was the lookout. And we run like hell. Come, come, they got men in the hills. We saw them. Come.

COCKLES: Why didn't you light it?!!

FRANCIS: Poor Jack. In the head. I hear them!!!! *(Tries to push* COCKLES *off)*

COCKLES: Give me that rifle.

FRANCIS: Take. Take. *(Pushes away from* COCKLES *and starts to run off)*

COCKLES: Francis. *(Points rifle at* FRANCIS*)*

FRANCIS: What are you doing?

COCKLES: Come with me. We can ignite that powder with one shot.

FRANCIS: No. No.

COCKLES: Which wall, Francis? By the gate? By the northeast gate?

FRANCIS: Yes. Yes. Where's Henry?

COCKLES: Gone. Like a jackrabbit.

FRANCIS: Me too. Me too. Like a rabbit. Let me go.

COCKLES: No, Francis. Please.

FRANCIS: *(Screams)* I hear them!!!!!!

(He turns to run, COCKLES *shoots him.* RIP *moans.* COCKLES *looks at* RIP*, then turns away toward the works.)*

COCKLES: *(Walking off)* Burn. Burn. *(Pause)*

RIP: *(Standing over* FRANCIS*)* Take my advice and don't wake up. *(He leaves.)*

Scene Five (c)

(Another part of the woods. DERRICK, CORPORAL, *and* LOOKOUT, *who has just entered.)*

DERRICK: *(To* LOOKOUT*)* And what does the Sergeant say?

LOOKOUT: They are routed, sir, like mice from their hole.

DERRICK: Dead?

LOOKOUT: Two, sir. One by us, and one without our help.

DERRICK: Any familiar faces?

LOOKOUT: They're Canucks, sir. We don't know any Canucks.

DERRICK: Of course. *(Distant gun shot)* Are we still firing?

LOOKOUT: That's not us. There's still one of 'em who fights or rather sort of fights, that is—he shoots, but not at us—only at the works.

DERRICK: The works?

LOOKOUT: He shoots once and then moves quickly. We've found blood so we think he's hit.

DERRICK: He moves where?

LOOKOUT: Toward us now. The Sergeant's behind him, pushing him in this direction, just as you'd stalk a wounded deer.

DERRICK: Tell the Sergeant to hold his ground, we'll deal with this one ourselves. Go. Hurry.

*(*LOOKOUT *leaves.)*

DERRICK: Corporal.

CORPORAL: Sir.

DERRICK: Take the men to the ridge and block any retreats.

CORPORAL: *(Starts to leave.)* And you, Colonel?

DERRICK: I'll be with you soon enough.

*(*CORPORAL *leaves. Gun shot, closer)*

DERRICK: Closer. Come to me, nephew. Sit on my lap, boy. I may still save your face. *(Leaves)*

Scene Five (d)

(Another part of the woods)

*(*COCKLES*, wounded, sits aiming rifle toward the works.)*

COCKLES: *(Shaking)* Steady. Steady. No! *(Grimaces)* Don't hurt. Wipe off face. *(Wipes off blood)* No blood. That's sweat, Cockles. Don't hurt. Steady. *(He shoots.)* Oh. Again. Again. *(Grabs powder horn)* Fill. *(Drops horn)* Don't spill! *(Scoops up powder)* Not wet. Steady. Fill. Eyes burn. Steady. Now hit the barrel. Which barrel? I see two. Pick one, Cockles. You picked one? *(Shakes his head)* Aim. Aim. Don't shake!!!! There. *(Pulls trigger—nothing)* No? Wet? Try again. Aim. *(Pulls trigger—nothing)* No? No! ! !! Oh, forgot to load. *(Laughs)* Dumb. Here. Here. I load. *(Puts in a bullet)* I load. Ha ha. Aim. Aim. *(Cries)* What's this? I got sweat in my eyes. Don't sweat. I'm shaking!!!! Aim. Two barrels. Aim. *(Shoots)* No blast. Load! Load! Load!

(Stops, breaks down crying. DERRICK *enters.* COCKLES *feels his presence and quickly turns around.)*

COCKLES: Oh, load! Load!

DERRICK: *(Slaps his face)* Fly. Got him.

(Pause)

COCKLES: *(Turns towards the works)* Blast. Blast.

DERRICK: Get up, boy. They don't know you're a part of all this. And you think I want them to find out? Wouldn't look good, boy. Get up. Up.

*(*COCKLES *cries.)*

DERRICK: I have pity for you. No one will ever know.

(Slowly COCKLES *gets up.)*

COCKLES: *(Holding up his hands)* Shaking.

DERRICK: Yes. I know. I know.

*(*DERRICK *stabs* COCKLES *in the chest. He falls and dies.* DERRICK *takes off* COCKLES'*s jacket, bunches it up and throws it in the woods.* RIP *enters without being seen. He watches.* DERRICK *takes his knife and carves off* COCKLES'*s face. Blood.* RIP *stares.)*

DERRICK: *(To the body)* I'll say you went to Europe. No one will know. *(He drags the body out.)*

*(*RIP *watches them off. Pause)*

RIP: Wrong. Wrong.

Scene Six

(The Garden. Early evening. Chairs, etc. as in Scene Two. MEENIE *and the* SCHOOLTEACHER *enter from the house.)*

SCHOOLTEACHER: October.

MEENIE: But that's three months away!

SCHOOLTEACHER: September then.

MEENIE: I mean, that's too soon. June. Maybe early June.

SCHOOLTEACHER: But why should we wait so long? Late October then.

MEENIE: What if you changed your mind? I want to give you time to change your mind.

SCHOOLTEACHER: It won't change. Late October.

MEENIE: But I've so much to learn. You'll be bored with me in a week. I'll guarantee you that.

SCHOOLTEACHER: I won't be bored. Middle of October.

MEENIE: You're going backward!

SCHOOLTEACHER: November then.

MEENIE: April. Very, very late April. Maybe father will send me to New York and I'll see things there and I won't be so boring. It'll take you at least two weeks to get sick of me if I've been to New York.

SCHOOLTEACHER: The middle of November. November's a good month for a wedding.

MEENIE: March.

SCHOOLTEACHER: December and we can go to New York together.

MEENIE: February. And I'll read a hundred books between now and then.

SCHOOLTEACHER: January because there's only eighty books worth reading.

MEENIE: No. Too cold. Too cold. We'd be stuck inside then, and you'd really see how boring I am.

SCHOOLTEACHER: I can see that there's no point in talking to you today. I'll go get the books you want. You want to come?

MEENIE: No, I'll wait.

SCHOOLTEACHER: I won't be long.

*(*GRETCHEN *enters from the house.)*

SCHOOLTEACHER: Mrs Derrick.

GRETCHEN: James.

MEENIE: Let's go, James.

SCHOOLTEACHER: I thought you weren't coming.

MEENIE: I'll walk with you as far as the blacksmith's. I feel like getting out of the house.

(HOUSEKEEPER *has entered from behind* GRETCHEN.)

HOUSEKEEPER: Wait 'til she has children of her own.

(GRETCHEN *nods, obviously hurt.* SECRETARY *runs in from the path.)*

SECRETARY: They're back! They've just come back!

GRETCHEN: My husband?!

SECRETARY: It'll take more than the Canucks to bring down the colonel.

GRETCHEN: Hans! *(Starts to go, stops)* And...and Cockles???

SECRETARY: Gone.

HOUSEKEEPER: Gone?

SECRETARY: The colonel said he booked a seat on the morning coach. Told somebody he was going abroad.

GRETCHEN: Who?

SECRETARY: Somebody. I guess the engagement hurt him more than we thought. I mean, to run away like that.

GRETCHEN: Yes... Thank God they're back. Hans...! *(She runs off.)*

SECRETARY: They've got prisoners too.

HOUSEKEEPER: Canucks?

SECRETARY: No, Baptists. Of course Canucks! Three. And a boy.

HOUSEKEEPER: A boy? They brought a boy with them?

SECRETARY: Killed three more. One of the bodies, I saw it myself. It had no face.

HOUSEKEEPER: What do you mean, no face?

SECRETARY: What do you think? He had no face. They carved off his face. That's what Canucks do, you know. They're very superstitious. They carve off the face and then they think it's all right.

(Servant GIRL *runs in from the house.)*

HOUSEKEEPER: *(Stopping her)* Where are you going?

GIRL: To the square. I just saw from the window, Mr Derrick's giving a speech! Most of the town's there already!

HOUSEKEEPER: *(To* GIRL*)* You stay here.

GIRL: What? Why?

HOUSEKEEPER: Someone has to. Hurry.

*(*HOUSEKEEPER *and* SECRETARY *hurry out.)*

GIRL: It's not fair!

(Sulking, she starts to walk back to the house. GUARD *enters with* HEINRICH, HENRY, BOY, *and* RIP, *as prisoners, their hands tied, all tied to one piece of rope.* RIP *is the only one gagged.)*

HEINRICH: *(Quietly)* I saw her!

GUARD: Shut up!

GIRL: Oh! Oh! *(She is frightened, stands behind a chair.)*

GUARD: If it was up to me, I'd be dragging all of you along by your throats. So don't tempt me. Get! *(He pushes them through the gate.)* Excuse us, miss, but it's the colonel's orders. I'll see to it that these gentlemen mind their manners.

GIRL: Are they...?

GUARD: Canucks? *(She nods.)* That they are, miss. Beasts in human flesh. *(To prisoners)* Let me see. *(Tests the wind)* Yeh, this is a good place. Down wind. Now sit! *(He pushes them down.) (To* GIRL, *rubbing his hands.)* A dirty business, isn't it?

GIRL: Can I get you something to drink?

GUARD: Cold. Anything cold.

*(*GIRL *leaves.)*

GUARD: *(Looking after her)* Good buns. Now you boys watch yourselves, I see you getting it up and I'll lop it off. *(He goes to the fence, looks down the path.)*

HEINRICH: *(Whispers)* She's here! I saw her!

HENRY: Who?

HEINRICH: Meenie!

HENRY: *(To* BOY*)* I guess we're supposed to know who Meenie is. Do you, boy?

BOY: *(Shakes his head)* Good rope. Could have used this to fix the shovel.

*(*RIP *tries to talk through the gag.)*

HENRY: What's he saying, boy?

BOY: *(Listens)* He's saying, he's been here.

HENRY: Ah, is that good or bad?

(GIRL enters with drink.)

GIRL: Can you see Mr Derrick speaking?

GUARD: Just backs of heads. *(Takes drink)* Thank you, miss.

GIRL: Should I get something cold for... *(Points to prisoners)*

GUARD: If you have blood, miss.

GIRL: Blood??! Is that what they drink?

GUARD: I wouldn't be surprised.

GIRL: Think of it.

GUARD: It's a strange world, miss.

GIRL: And the old man, is he their leader? Is that why he's gagged?

GUARD: If the one who talks the most is their leader then he's the leader all right.

GIRL: What does he talk about?

GUARD: Mostly nonsense, miss. I think he's mad.

GIRL: Their leader's mad?

GUARD: Seems logical to me, miss.

GIRL: Do you think I could hear him say something?

GUARD: I'm not sure if....

GIRL: Oh please! Nobody ever lets me see anything I want to see!

GUARD: Well, I guess there's no harm in it.... As long as you stay back. Remember—beasts.

GIRL: Yes. Yes.

(GUARD goes to RIP takes off his gag. RIP just looks at him.)

GUARD: Come on old man, don't embarrass me. *(Short pause)* Say something mad. *(Short pause)* Speak! *(Kicks him)*

RIP: Wrong. Wrong.

GUARD: There. Here it comes.

GIRL: Oooh!

RIP: Tear it down. I've seen hell and it is blood on a head. Bury. Bury. Where is my shovel? I want to dig. Get away. Hurry. The world has been carved faceless. Run and get away. Die once and be happy. Do not go asleep. Do not dream. Do not lie in wet grass even for one night. Tear it down. I know. And the fields will grow and have a face again and I will know where I am. Look. Look. I have eyes and I see bad. Bad and wrong. I don't know anything but I know it is wrong. Gut and level and drive to the dogs, that would be a start. I can see and I say stop. Stop! Wrong and not right and not good. Bad, I say, and awful. Put away all knives. Put them into your chests. I have moss on my chin. It grows. Do not shave my face, but let the weeds grow. Where is my shovel so I can dig and have moles in my stomach and worms for my fingers and let ants scratch my itch. Ants, they were not meant to have faces. They are the lucky ones. Have I convinced you? I must. I must. Because we must all band together and kill each other. Her too. Her too. Because she is young. And him. *(The* GUARD*)* Kill him.

GUARD: That's enough, old man.

RIP: Kill him so he may feed the sun. I have dug the shit hole. Take me there and let me jump. I want to help a tree. Plant. Plant. And then lie down and feed the seed. Breath. Let's have breath and let it be the wind. The sun has eyes and the moon a mouth, that is face enough. Let them live, let us die.

GUARD: I said, that's enough. *(He is getting worried.)*

RIP: You're right. That is enough. We are too much. So let's tear us down! *(Screams)* Where is my shovel?!!!!

GUARD: Take it easy.

RIP: Take me home!!!! Take me home!!!!

GUARD: *(Trying to gag him)* Shut up!

RIP: Wrong. Wrong. Wrong.

GUARD: Don't bite!

RIP: Wrong!!!!!

*(*GUARD *beats him across the head.* RIP *collapses—knocked out. Pause.* GUARD *rubs his bit hand.)*

GIRL: He gives you the chills.... Let me see. Bleeding. Come inside. We'll clean it out.

*(*GUARD *hesitates, then starts to go, turns back and forces a laugh. They leave.)*

HEINRICH: *(To* BOY*)* Pull. Pull you rope. Tight. Come on. Hurry.

HENRY: Do as he says, boy.

HEINRICH: Good. Not that tight! There. Like that. Keep it like that. *(Tries to untie knot with his teeth.)* It's coming. It's... No loosen. Just a bit. Little more. There. *(He unties the knot, begins to free his hand, hears someone coming.)* Relax! Relax! *(He hides his hand and face—pretends to be asleep.)*

*(*SECRETARY *and* HOUSEKEEPER *enter, talking.)*

HOUSEKEEPER: A party! That's easy enough for him to say. But who's going to cook?

SECRETARY: Victory deserves its celebration.

HOUSEKEEPER: I haven't even shopped today.

SECRETARY: Relax. The girl will help.

HOUSEKEEPER: She'll help me to my grave. *(Passing by the prisoners)* Look at them.

SECRETARY: Animals.

(They exit into the house. HEINRICH *waits for them to go, then quickly stands up.)*

HEINRICH: Sh-sh. *(He sneaks off.)*

HENRY: *(Trying to bite his rope)* How did he do that boy? Pull, boy. *(The rope gets tighter.)* That hurts. Don't pull like that, boy, pull like you did for him. *(Gets tighter.)* Is that how you pulled when he said pull? Try again, boy. Oh, it hurts, boy. *(His hands have been pulled tight together in front of his face.)* That man must have teeth like a dog. This isn't going to work, boy.

BOY: *(Shakes his head)* No.

HENRY: *(Looks at* BOY*)* You're a good boy.

*(*SGT JONES *and* GRETCHEN *enter, they are followed at a distance, by* MEENIE *and* DERRICK. GRETCHEN *keeps turning back to glance at* MEENIE *and* DERRICK.*)*

SGT JONES: *(Entering)* Quite the speaker. That's the colonel for you. You should have seen him at Saratoga. What a speech.

GRETCHEN: *(Turning back)* Hans?

MEENIE: *(Pulling at his sleeve)* Father, I thought you were just wonderfully handsome up there.

(He pats her head.)

MEENIE: So now tell me just one reason why I can't.

DERRICK: Why you can't what?

MEENIE: Go to New York!

DERRICK: I don't know why you can't, Meenie.

MEENIE: Then I can?!

DERRICK: And I don't know why you can go. Meenie, I don't think this is the time.

MEENIE: It's never the time!

DERRICK: Meenie...

GRETCHEN: Hans?

MEENIE: Don't you butt in, he's talking to me!

DERRICK: Don't shout at your mother.

GRETCHEN: Hans, don't...

SGT JONES: I never heard anything like it.

*(*HEINRICH *has returned—unnoticed. He stares at* MEENIE.*)*

SGT JONES: Then you should have heard him at Ridgefield.

DERRICK: *(To* MEENIE*)* I don't know what's the matter with you two.

MEENIE: Ask her!

SGT JONES: The gift of words. Some of us have it, and some of us...well, look at me. *(He sits.)* Is there any sherry?

DERRICK: Meenie, get the sergeant some sherry.

MEENIE: Let her get it! Or maybe you don't trust her.

GRETCHEN: I'll go.

*(*GIRL *and* HOUSEKEEPER *enter with some plates.)*

GIRL: *(Entering)* I wasn't holding his hand, he has a cut!

DERRICK: Gretchen, I don't think you should take orders from your daughter.

GIRL: You don't believe me do you?!

GRETCHEN: I'll go. We'll talk later. *(She starts to leave.)*

SGT JONES: Talk. Talk. Talk. That man's got the gift from God.

HOUSEKEEPER: Then he could have talked to me and found out we didn't have enough food!

GIRL: *(Suddenly drops a plate)* You have a lot of nerve to call me a liar!!

DERRICK: *(Yells)* What is wrong with everybody?!!!!!!

(Pause)

MEENIE: *(Turns, suddenly sees* HEINRICH*)* Heinrich?

HEINRICH: Meenie?

GRETCHEN: Oh God. Oh God. He's alive.

*(*HEINRICH *starts to move toward* MEENIE. SECRETARY *and* GUARD *enter talking.)*

SECRETARY: I think two of 'em are the ones I ran off this morning....

MEENIE: I don't believe it! Heinrich!!!

(She holds open her arms. GUARD *turns and sees* HEINRICH, *reaches for his gun.)*

GUARD: Stop!!!!

(He shoots HEINRICH, *who falls.* MEENIE *screams.)*

GRETCHEN: Why did you shoot him?!

(Others run to HEINRICH.*)*

DERRICK: He's breathing. Help me get his shirt off. Otto, get the doctor. We'll bring Heinrich to his office. Run!

*(*SECRETARY *runs out.)*

SGT JONES: *(To* GUARD*)* Take his legs.

GUARD: I thought he was going to hurt her.

SGT JONES: Take his legs!!

*(*SGT JONES *and* GUARD *pick him up.)*

DERRICK: Careful. Keep his head up.

*(*SCHOOLTEACHER *enters with books.)*

SCHOOLTEACHER: What's happened here?

GUARD: *(As they carry him off)* He's a Canuck, isn't he?

DERRICK: Hurry. Hurry!

(They carry him off. DERRICK *follows.)*

SCHOOLTEACHER: Meenie.

MEENIE: Get away! Get away!

SCHOOLTEACHER: Meenie, what is it?

MEENIE: *(Hugging* GRETCHEN*)* Mother, it's Heinrich.

GRETCHEN: I know, dear. Come. Let's hurry.

(They leave.)

SCHOOLTEACHER: *(To* HOUSEKEEPER*)* Who is it?

HOUSEKEEPER: The Vedder boy, Heinrich.

SCHOOLTEACHER: Meenie's Heinrich?

*(*GIRL *nods.)*

SCHOOLTEACHER: But he was dead.

HOUSEKEEPER: Maybe is, but he wasn't.

*(*HOUSEKEEPER *and* GIRL *hurry off.)*

SCHOOLTEACHER: *(Nods to himself)* Oh. *(Sits on the fence, facing upstage. He nods to himself again. Pause)*

HENRY: Don't pull, boy. I think I'll stay put right here.

(RIP *groans, begins to wake up.)*

RIP: Hurt. Hurt. My head. Feels like someone's been playing drums on my head. Ow!... What a dream I had. No, Rip, that weren't a dream, that was a nightmare. *(Tries to move his hands)* What's this? Now who would do something like that? Must be somebody's joke. Maybe little Heinrich. I used to do the same thing to my Grandpa when he was sleeping, I'd tie his shoes.... Ow, I do hurt.... *(Turns)* Where????... No, no, that was a dream. You've been sleeping, Rip. Wait a minute, now I remember—there was that queer fellow with the keg. This must be his valley. *(Finally notices* BOY *and* HENRY*)* Who????... Must be friends of that queer fellow. *(Looks around.)* You see my rifle? I had it with me when I come up the hill. What a rain that was. Never seen it rain like that. *(To* BOY*)* You look sort of familiar. But you boys all look alike at your age. I guess, that's it. Or maybe I've seen you playing with little Heinrich. *(Pause, then pats his chest)* Let me see. I got it here.... Be easier if somebody'd untie my hands. *(Struggles as he reaches into his pocket, pulls out the paper)* ...look here. All yellow. Must be the dampness. Here, boy, read this to me. I'd like to hear it said once again.

(BOY *shakes his head.)*

RIP: No? Why not, boy? Read it like Heinrich reads it.

(BOY *shakes his head.)*

RIP: Can't you read, boy?

(BOY *shakes his head.)*

RIP: Oh, I'm sorry for you, boy.

(Looks at HENRY, *shakes his head, and turns to* SCHOOLTEACHER. HENRY *shakes his head.)*

RIP: Hey you! You over there on the fence!

(SCHOOLTEACHER *turns around.)*

RIP: That's right—you! Can you read?

SCHOOLTEACHER: I'm a schoolteacher.

RIP: A schoolteacher! That's even better than Heinrich. Come here come here come here...

(SCHOOLTEACHER *hesitates.)*

RIP: I said, come here.

(SCHOOLTEACHER *approaches.)*

RIP: This. Read this. *(Hands him the paper)* Now we're going to hear a schoolteacher read it. No—out loud. So I can hear it too.

SCHOOLTEACHER: "Know all men by these presents that I, Rip Van Winkle, in consideration for sums received do hereby sell and convey to Mr Hans Derrick all my estate, houses, lands whatsoever whereof he now holds possession by mortgaged deeds from time to time executed by me." Where did you get this?

RIP: Where? Derrick and my whore they try to get me to sign it. But I don't.

SCHOOLTEACHER: *(Starts to run out)* Mr Derrick! Mr Derrick!

RIP: Where you going with my paper?!

*(*DERRICK *and* GRETCHEN *enter; talking.)*

DERRICK: *(Entering)* ...it's lodged in the chest. So there's still a chance....

SCHOOLTEACHER: Mr Derrick, read this!

DERRICK: What is it?

SCHOOLTEACHER: Read it!

DERRICK: *(Reads)* Where did you get this?

*(*SCHOOLTEACHER *nods toward* RIP.*)*

GRETCHEN: What is it, Hans? Give it to me. Give it!

*(*DERRICK *stares at* RIP, GRETCHEN *reads.)*

DERRICK: *(Approaching* RIP*)* Who are you?

RIP: Me? Everybody knows me...I'm Rip Van Winkle.

*(*GRETCHEN *screams and faints.)*

DERRICK: Water! Water!

RIP: I'd like some water.

BOY: Who's Rip Van Winkle?

HENRY: Hell if I know.

Scene Seven

(The Garden. Evening. BOY *is curled up asleep—untied.* HENRY *is passed out in a chair. Remnants of food and drink around. Pause.* HOUSEKEEPER, GIRL, *and* SECRETARY *enter.)*

HOUSEKEEPER: Hurry. Going to rain.

(They start to clean up.)

SECRETARY: And then?

GIRL: Nosey, aren't you?

SECRETARY: Can I help it if I had to stay at the doctor's?! So what happened then?!!!

GIRL: Mr Van Winkle—well, you could tell he was a little....

SECRETARY: A little what?

GIRL: *(To* HOUSEKEEPER*)* Confused?

HOUSEKEEPER: That he was.

GIRL: Confused. He just stood there....

SECRETARY: Where?

GIRL: There by the fence. He just stood there and Mr Derrick, he says "Rip?" and Mr Van Winkle says: "Derrick?", and Mrs Derrick or Mrs Van Winkle she's drinking water now and she says: "Rip?" and he says, he says....

SECRETARY: What?!

GIRL: He says: "Whore".

SECRETARY: Really? Why?

GIRL: *(Shrugs)* And Meenie, she's here by now, and she says, "Father?" and Derrick, he says, "What?" and Mr Van Winkle says, "Meenie?" and it goes on like that for quite a while.

*(*SECRETARY *nods.)*

HOUSEKEEPER: Did you see his face?

SECRETARY: Whose face?

HOUSEKEEPER: Derrick's face.

GIRL: *(Nods)* Chalk.

SECRETARY: No.

GIRL: Yes. And later, after Mr Van Winkle was told where he was and everything that had happened, then he cried.

SECRETARY: Mr Van Winkle?

GIRL: No, Mr Derrick. And so did Mrs Derrick or Mrs Van Winkle. They both cried. That was after Mr Van Winkle said he was going to pull down the works and farm his land.

SECRETARY: Pull down the works?!!!

GIRL: And farm his land. That's when he cried, because he said those works, that was his life, and that was the life of this whole valley, but he just said if what I've seen today, you call a life, then we'd all be better off being dead, so I'm going to start all over and pull them down.

SECRETARY: *(To* HOUSEKEEPER*)* He said that?

HOUSEKEEPER: He's saying that, yes. And he's saying, we're going to be farmers from now on, and we're not going to hurry 'cause you can't hurry a harvest, you got to learn to wait, so there'll be no hurrying anymore....

GIRL: And Mr Derrick says, "You can't destroy it"; he says, "It won't work", and he holds his face.

HOUSEKEEPER: And Mr Van Winkle says, "It will work with me as the boss". You should have been there.

GIRL: I wouldn't have missed it for anything. My favorite was when Mr Van Winkle, he looks at Meenie and he says, "How much you've grown in one night".

SECRETARY: In one night?!

GIRL: Yes. And that's what Meenie and Derrick and Mrs Van Winkle or Mrs Derrick said too, "one night?" Just like you said it, they say, "One night?!" And then the Schoolteacher, he was there though no one was paying much attention to him he was there and he says, "But you've been away fifteen years". And Mr Van Winkle he says: "fifteen years?" And then he looks up at the sky.

HOUSEKEEPER: He looks up at the mountains.

GIRL: No, it was the sky.

HOUSEKEEPER: The mountains.

GIRL: The sky and he just shakes his head.

SECRETARY: Seems like everybody was shaking their heads.

GIRL: Me too. You couldn't help it. It was miracle after miracle. You should have been there.

HOUSEKEEPER: Yes.

GIRL: Now tell us about Heinrich.

SECRETARY: He'll live. *(SECRETARY leaves.)*

HOUSEKEEPER: Hurry. Going to rain.

(They start to leave with the plates, etc. RIP enters from the house, passing them. They nod. RIP is clean shaven, wearing clean clothes. He strolls along, picks up a bottle. Pause. Then he suddenly smashes the bottle.)

RIP: *(Softly)* Enough.

(Thunder and lightning)

RIP: Enough.

(Thunder and lightning)

END OF PART TWO

PART THREE
"SOBER"

Scene One

(A section of a field, near a road. Fifteen years later)

(Farmers work the field: JUDITH *and* DUTCH *upstage with hoes;* RICHARD *and* JONATHAN *down left with picks;* CLYDE *and* EDWARD *center with a plow—* CLYDE *pulls;* EDWARD *guides. Very hot. They are exhausted. The earth is dust.)*

CLYDE: Push! Just push, can you do that?!

EDWARD: What do you think I'm doing?!

CLYDE: Well, I don't think you're pushing! Push! Push!

EDWARD: I am! I am!

RICHARD: You getting anywhere? All I'm doing is making cracks.

JONATHAN: Could plop the seeds in the cracks, then spit in the cracks. Might seem like rain to a seed.

RICHARD: I think these cracks go to China. Think the whole earth's suddenly become rock.

JONATHAN: Got to rain sooner or later.

RICHARD: Who says?

JONATHAN: Always has. These fields fed us good up to now.

RICHARD: Last year's not this year.

JONATHAN: Have to learn to eat dust then.

RICHARD: Or learn not to eat.

CLYDE: You pushing? I ask you, if you're pushing?!

EDWARD: I'm not talking.

CLYDE: Then you better be pushing.

EDWARD: I'm having a cup of tea. What do you think I'm doing?!!! I'm pushing!!!

CLYDE: Must be a stone then.

EDWARD: No stone, that's the ground.

CLYDE: I said, it must be a stone then! Look! Look!!

EDWARD: Don't go blaming me. What I do?

CLYDE: It's what you're not doing. Look!

EDWARD: I'm looking!!! *(Checks for a rock under the plow)* I don't know what you're yelling at me for.

CLYDE: It's hot.

EDWARD: It's hot for me too.

JUDITH: Hot.

DUTCH: *(Hoe breaks in his hands.)* No. Broke.

JUDITH: Dutch?

*(*DUTCH *drops the hoe, falls to his knees.)*

JUDITH: Dutch?!

DUTCH: Broke.

EDWARD: No stone. No stone.

CLYDE: There is! There is!!

RICHARD: *(Looking off)* Fight. Fight!

JONATHAN: Who?

RICHARD: Can't see.

EDWARD: Fight?

RICHARD: In the next field. Can't see who.

CLYDE: Fight?

JUDITH: Fight?

RICHARD: Three of them.

CLYDE: Three fights?

RICHARD: Men. Men.

DUTCH: Fight?

JUDITH: Yes. Yes.

RICHARD: *(Shouting:)* Fight! Fight! Fight!

*(*RIP *runs in; he uses a cane now.)*

RIP: What's happening? What are you shouting about? Why aren't you working?

RICHARD: There's a fight, Rip.

RIP: *(Looks off)* A fight? What about?

RICHARD: The heat must have got them.

RIP: The devil's what's got them! Stop them! *(Turns back)* Keep working. Work! We got a crop to plant! *(Runs off)* Stop them!

GEORGE: *(Running in)* Rip! Rip!

*(*RIP *runs back in.)*

RIP: What is it?! Look—they're fighting.

GEORGE: *(Points behind him)* And they're quitting.

RIP: What?

GEORGE: They're just leaving their plows and walking away.

RIP: Why? Why?

GEORGE: They just are.

RIP: I'll talk to them. I'll talk. Quick.

*(*GEORGE *and* RIP *run off.)*

JONATHAN: To join Derrick, is why they're quitting.

RICHARD: You think?

CLYDE: Derrick????

JONATHAN: Don't you know?

CLYDE: What? What?

JONATHAN: One dollar a week.

CLYDE: What's one dollar a week?

JONATHAN: That's what they're going to pay. One dollar a week.

CLYDE: Who?

RICHARD: I heard two dollars a week.

JONATHAN: Two dollars a week?

RICHARD: At least.

EDWARD: You think they're going to pay two dollars a week?

CLYDE: Who?!

RICHARD: How much you make now?

CLYDE: Thirty cents a week.

RICHARD: Make that in one morning at the works.

CLYDE: The works? What works?

EDWARD: Don't you know?

CLYDE: What? What?

RICHARD: Derrick's going to start up the old works.

CLYDE: No.

EDWARD: He didn't know.

CLYDE: When?

JONATHAN: As soon as Rip decides to sell it to him.

CLYDE: Why won't he?

EDWARD: He will.

JONATHAN: He will?

EDWARD: For ten thousand dollars.

CLYDE: For ten thousand dollars?!!

JONATHAN: Where did you hear that?

RICHARD: He wants to move to Paris.

EDWARD: To London.

RICHARD: To London? I thought it was Paris.

EDWARD: To London.

RICHARD: To London? Really? Where did you hear that?

CLYDE: And what about us, while he's spending his ten thousand dollars in London? What are we supposed to do?

JONATHAN: I've heard a rumor.

RICHARD: A rumor? A rumor about what?

JONATHAN: You haven't heard?

RICHARD: What? What?

JONATHAN: That Derrick just might take the works by force.

RICHARD: Where did you hear that?

EDWARD: So that's why they went to see him.

RICHARD: Who went to see who?

EDWARD: The postmaster and a couple of others. They must have gone to Derrick to plead with him not to use force.

JONATHAN: They'll never convince him. The real question is—can he control his men.

RICHARD: Men? He has men?

JONATHAN: If you're going to take a works by force then you've got to have men. Don't be stupid.

CLYDE: How many men does he have?

RICHARD: I'd say a hundred would be a reasonable estimate, unless one of you knows something I don't.

JONATHAN: No, no, a hundred sounds about right.

CLYDE: No, we don't know anything you don't know.

*(*RIP *returns, upset, shouting to all the fields.)*

RIP: Get back! Get back into the fields! This is no time to run! Come back and work. God gave us the strength to work! This drought is our test! It will rain! It will!

*(*CLYDE *makes a move to leave.)*

RIP: Where are you going?! *(Grabs* CLYDE*)* We are farmers, we belong in the fields! *(Throws him down)* Look up! Look up and pray! This is our trial! *(Falls onto his knees. Sings:)*

We gather together
To ask the Lord's blessing.
He chastens and hastens, His will to make known.

Sing!

So from the beginning,
The fight we are winning,
Sing praises to His Name, He forgets not His....

*(*RIP *collapses. Pause.* GEORGE *runs in.)*

GEORGE: Rip! Rip! Wake up! Wake up!!!... Somebody help me. *(No one moves.)* We'll take him to the nearest house. It's just the heat. Help me! Help!!!!!!

*(*EDWARD *slowly moves to help.)*

GEORGE: Take his shoulders. And watch his head. Keep it up. I said, watch his head! It'll be all right, Rip. It's the heat. It's hot. It's hot.

(They carry RIP *off. Pause)*

JONATHAN: You think he'll come?

RICHARD: Derrick?

*(*JONATHAN *nods.)*

RICHARD: I don't think it's a question of if, but when. And I'd say, the sooner the better.

JONATHAN: Well you won't find me standing in the middle of the road trying to stop him.

RICHARD: With a hundred men on horseback charging down from the hills, you'd have to be crazy not to stay locked in your own house.

CLYDE: They have horses?

RICHARD: I wouldn't be surprised.

(Throws down his pick. They start to leave.)

CLYDE: It's a shame.

JONATHAN: *What is?*

CLYDE: After all Rip's done for this valley.

JONATHAN: Last year's not this year.

(They go.)

JUDITH: Did you hear that, Dutch? Maybe we should get our gun out.

*(*DUTCH *pours out a little bottle onto the ground.)*

JUDITH: What are you doing, Dutch?

DUTCH: Making the ground soft.

JONATHAN: But there's only so much water. You're supposed to save it, so you can drink it, Dutch.

DUTCH: It's not water.

JUDITH: No?

DUTCH: It's piss.

Scene Two

(Outside DERRICK*'s shack in the hills. Bench. Stool. Table. Dogs bark.)*

*(*DERRICK *sits at a table, writing. He is dressed as a goat shepherd.)*

(Pause)

(Mad SHEPHERD *enters with his* BROTHER.*)*

SHEPHERD: No wolf. Looked here and there, but no wolf. Found another goat with its neck gone, but no wolf. I don't like it.

DERRICK: *(Writing)* Keep looking.

SHEPHERD: But where? I looked there and here and there and here and nothing. Didn't I, brother?

BROTHER: He did.

SHEPHERD: He comes out at night, is what I think. He sleeps now then doesn't sleep at night. That's what I think. I've never heard him. Just find dead goats. He comes out at night. Stupid to look for him now. Stupid. Isn't it, brother?

BROTHER: Stupid.

SHEPHERD: I'll look again at night 'cause that's when he will come out.

DERRICK: *(Writing)* Do that.

SHEPHERD: I don't have to look more now?

DERRICK: Look tonight.

SHEPHERD: That's a good idea. I'll do that. See the eyes at night, they sparkle. I'll go lie down now, so I can look tonight.... You have visitors. I've seen 'em.

*(*DERRICK *looks up.)*

SHEPHERD: I saw 'em on the path. Don't like that. They walk stupid. Don't know how to walk on a path, 'cause they're so stupid, is what I think. Shouldn't come here. Is what I think too... One of 'em was here before. Twice before. I remember.

*(*DERRICK *writes.)*

SHEPHERD: Shouldn't come up here. No. Scare the goats. Scare the sheep. Scare me. I don't like it.

BROTHER: Scare me too.

SHEPHERD: See? See?

*(*DERRICK *gets up, goes inside.)*

SHEPHERD: What they come up here for?

*(*BROTHER *shrugs.)*

SHEPHERD: Do I go down there?

*(*BROTHER *shakes his head.)*

SHEPHERD: Stupid. Is what I think.

*(*BROTHER *nods.)*

SHEPHERD: I'll kick 'em out. Kick 'em on their pants so they roll back down. I will. I will for sure. Watch... Here they come. Hide! Hide!

(They run and hide. POSTMASTER *and two men enter; they are tired from their climb.)*

LAWYER: This it?

POSTMASTER: He raises sheep and goats.

PAUL: Who was that? Somebody just ran back into those trees.

LAWYER: What does one do up here?

POSTMASTER: Raise sheep and goats.

PAUL: Trees. Animals. Quiet. I guess everyone needs to get away. Sometime.

LAWYER: Fifteen years is a bit long for a vacation. His shack?

(POSTMASTER *nods.)*

PAUL: I guess I expected something a little more....

POSTMASTER: A little more what?

PAUL: I don't know. Long fall for a man like Mr Derrick.

LAWYER: Read. Relax. Collect one's thoughts. I've had the urge myself. Though selfishness is not an urge I find worth encouraging.

POSTMASTER: After a couple of visits, I'm convinced he thinks he's found paradise.

PAUL: His paradise. Not mine.

LAWYER: Here he comes. Remember he can't think we are in this for ourselves. He must see the need. As we have.

POSTMASTER: Don't push.

LAWYER: You don't have to push a responsible man, they push themselves.

PAUL: He should jump at the chance. I'd be flattered if I were him.

POSTMASTER: And I'd be satisfied if we just got his signature.

*(*DERRICK *enters with another piece of paper, he goes to the table, begins to write.)*

POSTMASTER: Hello Hans. *(No response)* Third visit in a week. Hope you don't think me a pest. *(No response)* Thought you'd like some company. Must get pretty lonely. From time to time. *(No response)* Saw the animals. They're getting fat. Congratulations. Must be a lot of work.

DERRICK: No work getting animals to eat.

POSTMASTER: I guess not. I guess that was a pretty stupid thing to say. Why is it that I always feel stupid talking to you? *(No response)* How's the arm? Did I tell you my arm started to ache? After our last talk? Sympathy pains. That's a joke. The humidity's been awful. Hard to roll out of bed. You ever have that trouble? You lie there thinking about all the things you have to do. Then you sweat. I get this pain in my stomach. Weak stomach. That's what gets me up—it's easier to go do what I have to do than it is to lie there and think about it.... I've thought about what you told me about goat's milk. Fascinating. My wife was a little skeptical. Told her if she'd tasted yours... I promised I'd bring some back....

(Silence; DERRICK *writes.)*

POSTMASTER: Is this a bad time for you?

DERRICK: For what?

POSTMASTER: I brought some friends.

(DERRICK *looks up, then returns to his writing.)*

POSTMASTER: They'd like to talk, Hans. *(Pause)* Go ahead.

LAWYER: Mr Derrick...

DERRICK: Who's he?

POSTMASTER: Bill Hamilton. A lawyer, Hans.

DERRICK: He looks like one of my goats. *(Returns to his letter)*

LAWYER: Mr Derrick, the first thing that I think we must make perfectly clear is that we are not in this for our own gain. Not to understand that would be to misinterpret everything we wish to propose. Do you follow me?

POSTMASTER: Don't push.

LAWYER: I am sure that you are aware of the drought, Mr Derrick. Though, I expect, you may not be totally aware of its severity.

PAUL: It's the worst in memory. The chances of any kind of harvest are basically nil. People will starve.

LAWYER: Those who stay.

PAUL: A third of the valley has already left. What businesses remain survive on credit. The entire valley's a bowl for dust.... He's not listening.

POSTMASTER: Keep going.

LAWYER: Simply put, Mr Derrick, we need the works. And these gentlemen and myself are a committee formed for the purpose of convincing you to reclaim the works.

(They look at each other; DERRICK *continues to write.)*

PAUL: Mr Derrick, Bill here believes that you have an excellent chance with a suit. Given that you built the works and given our present crisis, he thinks certain laws would be bent and what's been boarded up these fifteen years can be unboarded up and given back to you.

LAWYER: All you'd need do, Mr Derrick, is appear at one public meeting, scheduled for this afternoon, and publicly claim what I believe you already own.

PAUL: And we, as a committee, will stand behind you one thousand percent, and will accept responsibility for starting the works up again.

LAWYER: And for running it. Your participation can be as great or as small as you yourself desire. *(Pause)*

PAUL: Mr Derrick?... You have to understand that we, as a committee, could initiate our own legal action.

LAWYER: And in due course I am completely convinced we would succeed in gaining control of the works. But that, Mr Derrick, could take months or even years. A wait that might mean not only the lives of a great number of people, but the life of our valley itself. I don't understand this. I've never been treated like this.

POSTMASTER: Hans, have you heard what we've been saying? Do you understand why we want you to come with us? Do you know what's at stake?! People will starve, don't you care?

PAUL: I don't know what we were thinking of. The man's been up in the hills for fifteen years! Look at him!

LAWYER: If it were his goats starving, he'd care.

POSTMASTER: *(Grabs* DERRICK*)* Hans, if you won't appear, then sign an agreement that'll give us the right to act on your behalf. Bill thinks that might really be all we need. *(Takes out the agreement)* Here. Just your signature... Look at me!!!!

(DERRICK *looks up.)*

POSTMASTER: Keep your goats. Watch the sky. We won't bother you again. But sign. Hans, is that too much to ask?

PAUL: Forget it, he's mad.

POSTMASTER: Madmen have responsibilities too!!! *(Turns back to* DERRICK*)* Sign. We ask only this. Please.

(Long pause. DERRICK *slowly gets up. Looks at all three of them)*

DERRICK: Once a man had a beast inside his breast, his ribs were its cage.

LAWYER: What's he talking about?

POSTMASTER: Sh-sh! Sh-sh!

DERRICK: The beast was mighty and had teeth like a saw and was forever hungry. The man was weak and tired and had not the strength to brush a fly away from his face. All the strength the man had came from his beast, which prowled his chest and growled like a stomach. Everything great this man accomplished in his life was due to the muscle of his beast; and everything terrible was due to this beast as well. One morning the man noticed a dog caught in a rabbit trap clear across the meadow. The man loved dogs and took great pleasure in the way they would curl their necks when they were patted. But the man had not the strength to go and save the dog. So he turns to his beast and says—"beast, give me the strength to pull myself across the meadow." And the beast pushed at the man's ribs and gave him the strength. When the man reached the dog and moved to free it from the trap, the beast stuck out its head from the man's breast and ate the dog. The birds in the treetops watched in horror, but the man shouted—"What did I do? Blame the beast." And the birds replied—but then why didn't you keep the beast locked in your breast? The man sat down and thought and after a half hour he answered—"Without the beast I would not have had the strength to pull myself across the meadow, so can you blame me for wanting to help a wounded dog?" *(Pause)* Well—can you blame him? *(Long pause)*

LAWYER: *(To* POSTMASTER*)* What is this?

PAUL: One of his goats would make more sense.

POSTMASTER: Hans??

SHEPHERD: *(From his hiding place)* Growl. Growl. Growl. I'm a wolf. Better run. I'll bite your neck off. Growl! Growl! I'm going to scare you and get your neck! Growl!

LAWYER: What's going on?

PAUL: They're all mad up here.

POSTMASTER: Hans?????

PAUL: Don't waste your breath.

LAWYER: Let's go. I don't like it here. *(Starts to go)*

PAUL: I'm coming.

LAWYER: Hurry. Hurry. Come on.

(They go.)

SHEPHERD: Growl. Growl.

POSTMASTER: I'm sorry. For you. *(He hurries off.)*

SHEPHERD: Growl. Growl. *(He appears.)* How was I? You think they guessed? I think I was a good wolf. Growl. Got them to run off. Scared them. I was going to kick them if I couldn't scare them. But I scared them. Good wolf. Fun. Growl.

*(*DERRICK *folds the letter; puts it in an envelope, hands it to* SHEPHERD.*)*

DERRICK: Here, put this with the rest of them.

SHEPHERD: Another letter to Cockles?

DERRICK: Yes.

*(*DERRICK *goes inside;* BROTHER *reappears.) (Pause)*

SHEPHERD: Pa always said trouble comes in all colors. First it was the wolf then them. Watch it. Watch out. I didn't like 'em.

*(*BROTHER *shakes his head)*

SHEPHERD: So I scare 'em.

(BROTHER nods.)

SHEPHERD: Growl. Growl.

BROTHER: Growl.

Scene Three

(GRETCHEN's garden. Fence. Path. House Off Right. Chairs. Afternoon)

(GRETCHEN, down on her knees, gardening—downstage left. MEENIE, with a broom, throwing out a MAN)

MEENIE: Get out! Out! You've got no business here! I'll stick this through your head! Out! Leave him sleep!!

(MAN hurries off. HEINRICH enters from down the path, from the opposite direction. He stutters.)

HEINRICH: What was thththat about?

MEENIE: Third one in an hour. Looking to talk to father. Rumors everywhere.

HEINRICH: I heard. Ddddon't know what to think.

MEENIE: I think it's rumors is what I think.

HEINRICH: Lot of people say it's true.

MEENIE: Well I'll believe it when I see it. Let 'em come with their army or whatever they're coming with. Father's going to keep farming like he has.

HEINRICH: People llleaving.

MEENIE: Let 'em.

HEINRICH: Say they're just throwing seed onto rock. Only thing they'll grow is more rrrrrrock. Can't eat rock.

MEENIE: Is that what you say?

HEINRICH: I don't know. No rain. That I do know. Why'd they bring Rip here? Sort of strange.

MEENIE: Closest house. Nothing strange about that.

HEINRICH: Then sort of funny. It beeeeeing Gretchen's house. Is he sick?

MEENIE: Fainted.

HEINRICH: The heat. They fiiight yet?

MEENIE: Who says they'll fight?

HEINRICH: They haven't talked in years. Though when they do talk—and I guess they're going to have to with Rip here—then they'd fiiight.

MEENIE: *(Gestures toward* GRETCHEN*)* Sh-sh.

HEINRICH: She doesn't hear anything when she's gardening. You could scream in her ear and she'd swat you thinking you were a fly. He awake?

MEENIE: The boy?

HEINRICH: Not Nick. Rip. He awake?

MEENIE: Not when I looked in. Neither was Nick, though I better check him what with the noise.

HEINRICH: Meenie...?

MEENIE: What? I'll be right back.

HEINRICH: I wrote a note, Meenie.

MEENIE: No, Heinrich, I don't even want to talk about it.

HEINRICH: Look, if you won't tell your Mother, then let her reeeeead about it. After we're gone.

MEENIE: I haven't said I'm going yet.

HEINRICH: You've said ten times you're going, then when you can't tell your Mother, you change your mind.... I'm going if you're nooooot.

MEENIE: I haven't said I wasn't going either. Just not now.

HEINRICH: When?

MEENIE: Soon. Someday soon. Ohio isn't going to be swallowed up by the earth. It'll still be there when we decide to go.

HEINRICH: I've decided.

MEENIE: Then go!

(Pause)

HEINRICH: And I'm taking Nick with me. After all what's the point in going west, if it's not ffffor your kid.

MEENIE: I got to go check on the boy.

HEINRICH: Boy'll be a man one day. Better to be a man in the west than here. That's all I'm saying. If it were just us, then we could wait. But there's a bbbboy to think about.

MEENIE: You know I can't leave her.

HEINRICH: I know you won't. I don't know why you can't. She's happy. Look at her. She's got her gardening. What she need us for?

MEENIE: It'd kill her.

HEINRICH: But aren't we killing ourselves staying here? And what if the ruuuumors aren't rumors? What if they start up the works? You think they're going to give me a job? People don't forget who you are. The son-in-law of Rip Van Winkle isn't going to be too welcome in those works.

MEENIE: If we take the boy away from her I swear to you she'd die.

HEINRICH: Well how 'bout me?! I'm dying here!

MEENIE: I don't feel like talking about it anymore.

HEINRICH: I'm not asking you to talk about it, I'm sayyyyng, get ourselves packed. I bought a wagon.

(Pause)

MEENIE: You bought a wagon?

HEINRICH: Nice wagon. I gave it a name. I call it "Ohio". One wheel was busted, but I got it fixed. Worked all morning. That's where I've been. Look, Meenie. You know and I know I'm not going without you. And I know I'm going, so that means you're going too. 'Course I wouldn't make you if I thought you didn't want to be made. You've talked about going pretty much as often as I have. Haven't you?!

MEENIE: That was night time talk.

(Long pause)

HEINRICH: Oh. I see. I thought...but never mind.

MEENIE: Heinrich, I didn't mean....

HEINRICH: No. You said what you mean. I didididn't know. That's all.... Then you want me to sell back the wagon? I would, you know.

MEENIE: I know you would, Heinrich. That's why I'm not angry with you cause you bought it, 'cause I know you'd sell it if I asked you.

HEINRICH: You asking me?

(Pause)

MEENIE: I'll go see the boy.

HEINRICH: I said, are you asking me?

MEENIE: I haven't said anything.

HEINRICH: No?

MEENIE: No... Give me your note.

HEINRICH: You want it?

MEENIE: I want to read it. I haven't said anything.

HEINRICH: No... Should I go pack some goods in the wagon in case you do say something?

MEENIE: You want to go today?!!

HEINRICH: We have the wagon.

MEENIE: I might change my mind. I might.

HEINRICH: *I know.*

MEENIE: As long as you know—then go ahead.

(Pause. He looks at her, smiles then hurries off. MEENIE *starts to go inside, reading the note. She stops, turns to* GRETCHEN, *goes to her and hugs her. Then runs inside.* GRETCHEN *looks up.* PAUL *enters from the path. He looks around.)*

PAUL: *(To* GRETCHEN*)* Excuse me, I understand Mr Van Winkle was brought here. Could you tell me if he's awake?

*(*RIP *appears from the house.)*

RIP: What do you want?

PAUL: Don't be hostile, Rip. No one sent me. I came to help.

RIP: Offer me no help. Help yourself. Get out. *(Turns away)*

PAUL: There's talk, Rip.

RIP: The Lord says: whether he be friend or foe, talk not of other's lives. Goodbye.

PAUL: He also says something about heeding warnings. What I've heard, I think you ought to listen to.

RIP: My daughter's inside. She's already thrown three of you out. Strong girl. I watched from the window. She can use a broom like you or I can use a fork, I'll call her.

PAUL: One minute is all, Rip. I'm not in this for myself. It's for the valley.

RIP: The biggest thief's the first to deny he is one. He doesn't even wait to be asked.

PAUL: And the biggest fool is the one who hears what the blind see. There is a drought. Do you understand? Do you care? Starving people aren't plants that will sprout again in the spring.

RIP: Affliction does not come from the dust, nor does trouble sprout from the ground; but man is born to trouble as the sparks fly upward. So says the Lord. *(Turns)*

PAUL: You're a fool. I'll take the abuse and your pompous attitude. But I'll be the first in line to see your face when Derrick arrives.

RIP: Derrick?

PAUL: Suddenly an interest? Like magic. I've found the magical name.

RIP: What do you mean—Derrick?

PAUL: There's talk, that he's come to reclaim his works.

RIP: He has no works.

PAUL: Not as yet.

RIP: What he had he'd stolen.

PAUL: True.

RIP: Anyway, he raises goats in the hills.

PAUL: Did. Some of your friends—your farmer friends—have been calling on Derrick. It appears they have little faith in a harvest. A works would mean jobs.

RIP: I don't believe it.

PAUL: The flesh is weak, Rip.

RIP: A rumor.

PAUL: Which everyone now believes. There's a petition going around which demands that you turn over the works.

RIP: To Derrick?

PAUL: To a committee of businessmen.

RIP: Who's on this committee?

PAUL: I don't know. It's been kept secret.

RIP: And the committee will turn over the works to Derrick, when he arrives?

PAUL: That hasn't been decided yet.... A third of the valley has already left.

RIP: Not to join Derrick.

PAUL: That is the talk, Rip.

(Pause; RIP obviously upset)

RIP: *(More to himself)* I don't understand. How can they turn? We have moved this earth like it was our own muscle. We've flexed the ground, thumbed in the seeds, sweated a rain, nursed the stalk, slapped the harvest 'til it cried. It's been my body. It's been me. *(Short pause)* No. I will not sell it, barter it, share it, or give it away. We've had harvests that would choke a horn of plenty. How can they run? We are farmers. We plow the land, furrow the brow of the earth and make it think it's richer than it is. When the ground breathes, it's because we are its lungs! No! I don't understand. No. They can't take it away! No!!!! Not now, not tomorrow—never!!!!!
(Pause)

PAUL: Are you going to tear down the works?

RIP: Why would I do that?

PAUL: There'd be nothing to take from you then.

RIP: I don't know. Why rip down something that you've forgotten about?

PAUL: But you might? Because others haven't forgotten?

RIP: I said, I don't know. Now get out. Go away. But if you find out who's on this committee, I'd pay to know. Go. Go.

(PAUL *leaves.)*

RIP: Cowards. Thieves. Gutless dogs. They get a sliver in their finger and they scream like they are dying. Their faith's as tangible as a hot breeze. If they can't plow a field with the toe of their boot, then they cry and whine that the ground's too hard, and they give up and whip up the dust as they flee, instead of whipping themselves to keep at their work. They'd rather eat promises of better things to come than drink that sweat off their lips which comes from making things better.... There must be a million wrinkles on God's Face, each one lining His disappointment in us. *(Pause)*

GRETCHEN: I'm afraid I've given Him a wrinkle or two myself.

(RIP *turns to her.)*

GRETCHEN: Hello. I heard. I'm sorry.

RIP: What are you sorry for? Derrick's coming. You'll have him back in your bed.

(She turns away.)

RIP: Forgive me. I didn't mean it.... Not a very tactful way to begin a conversation after fifteen years. How are you?

(She nods.)

RIP: I am sorry. I know you left Derrick. His coming will be as hard on you as it will on me.... That was stupid. Thank you for putting me up.

GRETCHEN: No one asked me.

RIP: And if they had? *(Silence)* I'd better go. *(Starts to go, stops)* Hot. I'd never fainted before. Meenie's been after me to drop by for years. I used to say I'd have to be dragged. I guess I almost was. What are you planting? Peas?

GRETCHEN: Flowers.

RIP: Can't eat flowers.

GRETCHEN: That's why I grow them.

(Long pause)

RIP: I'll go.... What will you do? If he comes, I mean.

GRETCHEN: Why should I do anything?

RIP: I just thought that.... It's not important. I suspect he'll have the works to occupy himself.

GRETCHEN: Then you'll let him take it?

RIP: If it's God's will.

GRETCHEN: Is it?

RIP: I'll pray. Then I'll see. *(Pause)*

GRETCHEN: I have my garden.

RIP: Yes. It'll be lovely.

GRETCHEN: And there's Meenie. And Heinrich.

RIP: Yes.

GRETCHEN: And the boy. Between him and the garden I have my hands full.

RIP: I peeked in on him a moment ago. Handsome child. The way children sleep—I'd like to sleep like that again. Meenie's brought him over a couple of times. I've found I enjoy playing Grandfather. I think I'm a good horse—or my knee is. She's hinted that you didn't know, but I always assumed that you did. *(Pause)* What kind of flowers?

GRETCHEN: Roses.

RIP: From seeds? But that'll take years.

(She turns away. Pause)

RIP: Right. What's the.... What is the hurry? Why do I feel like an idiot right now? *(Long pause)* Have you ever tried to hold onto a rope as it was being pulled through your fingers? You concentrate on every inch, and every inch as it's pulled through seems at the time like a tremendous loss. A catastrophe. Then as feet and yards pass through your clenched hands, a panic almost sets in. Your heart pounds faster. Your breathing gets quicker. It's a very desperate feeling. But it's desperate only because you think that at any moment the end of the rope will pass through your fingers. It could come in five minutes. Tomorrow. Next year. If only you could convince yourself that the rope had no end, then there would be no reason to panic. You could still struggle 'til your muscles broke, the effort needn't be any less. Without an end, without something to struggle for or to struggle to prevent, that I believe would be a wonderful way to live. Then I think I could say to myself, "what is the hurry?" and be convinced. *(Silence)* I'm babbling. I don't know why I'm talking like this. *(Long pause. He turns to leave.)*

GRETCHEN: Because I didn't interrupt you...because I'm your wife. *(Pause)*

RIP: My...? What?

GRETCHEN: Sh-sh. Let us just keep that one thought simple. If we can. *(She gets up to leave.)*

RIP: Gretchen...?

GRETCHEN: Do we have to suffer over everything?

RIP: But...

GRETCHEN: Don't ask. *(Pause)*

RIP: Gretchen...I didn't know.

GRETCHEN: Neither did I, Rip. *(She turns to go inside.)*

RIP: But why didn't you...?

GRETCHEN: Don't ask! *(Pause)* I guess I've been wanting to see you. Because when they brought you here this morning and I thought you'd died, I heard myself think—my luck, when he comes he's dead. Then when they told me you'd fainted in the heat, I almost ran away. Don't ask me why, Rip. *(Turns again to go inside)*

RIP: I don't understand. *(Short pause)* I would have come, but you didn't ask.

(Pause)

GRETCHEN: I'd have asked, but you wouldn't have come.

(Pause. Noise of a crowd off. HEINRICH *enters.)*

GRETCHEN: Heinrich, what's going on?

HEINRICH: The inn. Must be most of the town outside the inn. There's a meeting.

GRETCHEN: Maybe Derrick's come.

*(*RIP *just looks at her.)*

GRETCHEN: You'd better go, Rip. *(Short pause)* Go.

RIP: Gretchen...

GRETCHEN: Hurry. Hurry.

*(*RIP *hesitates.* GRETCHEN *goes inside.* RIP *hurries off.* MEENIE *comes out with a pile of laundry.)*

HEINRICH: The supplies are in the wagon.

MEENIE: How'd you do it so fast?

HEINRICH: I dididid it this morning.

MEENIE: Heinrich...

HEINRICH: You've changed your mind. *(He turns to leave.)*

MEENIE: The letter, Heinrich.

HEINRICH: Yes?

MEENIE: It's on her dresser.

Scene Four

(An Inn. Table. Three chairs. Door to the street POSTMASTER *stands in the doorway, looking out.* LAWYER *and* PAUL *sit behind the table listening to the noise of the large angry crowd outside. Pause)*

POSTMASTER: They've picked three to do their talking.

LAWYER: Show them in.

*(*POSTMASTER *goes out, closing the door behind him. Crowd noise becomes distant.)*

PAUL: What are we going to tell them?

LAWYER: The truth. Of course.

PAUL: Of course. I'll get some chairs.

(Goes Off. Door opens. Noise again, loud. FIRST FARMER, SECOND FARMER, *and* DUTCH *enter with the* POSTMASTER. *They close the door. Noise becomes distant again. Long pause)*

LAWYER: Hello, Sam. How's the missus?

FIRST FARMER: Hungry

LAWYER: She's a good woman.

FIRST FARMER: Not when she don't eat.

(Short pause. PAUL *enters with chairs.)*

LAWYER: Sit.

SECOND FARMER: Where's Rip? It's him we wanted to talk to.

LAWYER: We didn't feel that was necessary.

SECOND FARMER: Then it's true, what everybody's sayin'.

LAWYER: Sit.

(Short pause. The FARMERS *sit.)*

LAWYER: *(To* PAUL*)* Should I start?

*(*PAUL *nods.)*

LAWYER: Gentlemen, believe me when I say that we can appreciate your anxieties. And it is with the hope of relieving some of them that we have called this meeting this afternoon.

DUTCH: You ain't called nothing, it just happened.

FIRST FARMER: Let the man talk, Dutch.

DUTCH: You don't eat talk.

FIRST FARMER: Go 'head.

LAWYER: Gentlemen, a great number of rumors have gripped our town....

DUTCH: What does he mean "rumors"?!

LAWYER: I repeat—rumors have gripped our town these past few weeks, and some of us have felt the need to form a committee whose purpose would be to dispel such rumors as best we can. But before we go on, let me just add that we are all aware of the crisis our valley is going through. And after what we've been up against, one begins to wonder if plague and pestilence are to be next.

(He smiles and chuckles. PAUL *chuckles as well. The* FARMERS *just stare at him.)*

LAWYER: Yes. I think we should all be quite proud of ourselves, our response and resilience has been admirable.

SECOND FARMER: We don't need to hear no speech. You just tell us how you're planning to stop Rip.

LAWYER: Please, let me just finish by saying....

DUTCH: More talk.

LAWYER: ...by saying how proud we are of each and every one of you and how pleased to know you all as friends.

DUTCH: There are friends and there are friends.

FIRST FARMER: Just tell us Mr Hamilton. And tell us simple. What are you going to do about stoppin' Rip?

PAUL: Stopping him from what, Sam?

SECOND FARMER: Where you been? He's raisin' an army. *(To* FIRST FARMER:*)* If he don't even know that I don't know why we're talkin' to them, Sam.

LAWYER: Paul...?

PAUL: Gentlemen, Mr Van Winkle has no intention of raising an army.

SECOND FARMER: See, he knows nothin'. We're wasting our time, we should be talkin' to Rip.

FIRST FARMER: Mr Hamilton, Dutch has seen some letters.

DUTCH: I didn't say I really saw them, Sam.

FIRST FARMER: Dutch, you told me you saw letters.

PAUL: I think our postmaster would know if any such letters went out. Have there been?

POSTMASTER: *(Standing by the door)* No. *(Pause)*

SECOND FARMER: If there's no army, then who's gonna fight Derrick? Us? Like hell we will.

LAWYER: Mr Derrick has raised no army. Is raising no army. And has no plans to raise an army.

SECOND FARMER: I don't believe that.

LAWYER: We visited with him only this afternoon.

SECOND FARMER: Today?

PAUL: We felt compelled to find the truth.

LAWYER: And though I will admit Mr Derrick showed some curiosity in our situation, I'd have to say, his interest was rather minimal. Wouldn't you agree, Paul?

PAUL: Definitely.

SECOND FARMER: So he's not coming?

(LAWYER shakes his head.)

FIRST FARMER: Wait. Then he's buying the works. That's what he's doing. Somebody told me that and I didn't believe him.

LAWYER: Sam, I can say categorically, that no sale of the works has ever been proposed and no potential buyer has ever been approached by Van Winkle or by anyone acting in his behalf.

SECOND FARMER: He's not sellin', Sam.

DUTCH: What about the wagon he bought? Where's he running off to with a wagon?

LAWYER: Paul, you can answer that better than I can.

PAUL: I'm the one who sold the wagon. Though not to Rip, but to his son-in-law, Heinrich. I'm sure you know that Heinrich's been talking for quite some time now about moving to Ohio. I guess he finally decided to stop talking and do it.

POSTMASTER: Or he finally got his wife to go with him!

(The FARMERS turn to the POSTMASTER and smile and chuckle.)

SECOND FARMER: How'd he get her to do that? I'd like to know his secret.

DUTCH: Wish he could persuade my wife to go with him. *(Laughs)*

FIRST FARMER: Need a bigger wagon than that for your wife.

SECOND FARMER: He could tie her to the back and let her roll. *(Laughs)*

LAWYER: Gentlemen, if that's everything... *(Stands)*

FIRST FARMER: *(Looks at the other two* FARMERS*)* I guess it is.

DUTCH: What are we going to tell 'em?

FIRST FARMER: Go home. Gotta rain sometime.

(They start to leave.)

PAUL: Just one second.

(They stop and turn.)

PAUL: I feel sort of foolish bringing this up.

LAWYER: Go ahead, Paul.

PAUL: And please don't misunderstand me. It is only in this spirit of wiping the slate completely clean that I even talk about this. And please, I am not suggesting that this be the case, it's only something I've heard. But in all fairness to Rip, I feel we must clear the air.

DUTCH: What are you talking about? What've you heard?

PAUL: Please understand how much I admire Rip, and to me at least such an action would be completely out of his character.

POSTMASTER: Paul, maybe this could wait.

SECOND FARMER: No, let him talk.

PAUL: So with all this in mind, I visited Rip just a half hour ago and asked him to his face to either confirm or deny.

POSTMASTER: Confirm or deny what?

PAUL: And all I can say is that he did not deny it.

DUTCH: Deny what?!!

PAUL: That he was going to tear down the works.

FIRST FARMER: He's going to tear down the works?

SECOND FARMER: Why would he do that?

PAUL: I don't know. *(Pause)*

DUTCH: It's true. Damn it, it's true!!!!

SECOND FARMER: What is?

THIRD FARMER: Everything!!!!

(He goes to the door and flings it open. Loud crowd noise)

POSTMASTER: Gentlemen, please! I'm sure there's an explanation!

(The FARMER *stop at the doorway, look out. The crowd slowly gets quiet. Silence.* RIP *enters, having walked through the crowds.)*

RIP: I'm confused. What's going on here? I don't believe what I've just heard out there.... Sam, your boy just threw a rock at me.

(SAM *turns away.)*

RIP: I don't understand. *(To* FIRST FARMER:*)* Close the door.

(Hesitates, and then does)

RIP: Why aren't you in the fields? There's work to be done. *(Short pause)*

LAWYER: Rip...

RIP: I'm not talking to you! *(Looks at the* FARMERS*)* We are friends. And 'til now that was the source of tremendous pride for me. We have worked together. And whereas no single man grows a crop, each one of us shares in its glory. Dutch, what did they mean by calling me a traitor?

(Short pause. DUTCH *starts to leave,* RIP *grabs him.)*

RIP: What is happening here?!!!! *(Short pause)* When I first took over the fields, fifteen years ago, my urge was not to build a mecca of wonder. I wanted no Babylon. My urge was more conservative—I envisioned a simple valley, a valley where one lives at peace and hard work; one where neighbors care for each other, share with each other, live for each other. Where one's tasks were simply defined and where all that separated one from a successful completion of one's task was hard laborious work. I know things have been hard, but work is still the heart beat of this valley, without it, it will die. I believe in nothing, if I do not believe in hard work. Fantasy and dreams have no home in the breast of a hard working man. And when one fails, failure is not measured by the lack of the growth of a crop, or by the absence of rain, it is measured only be the lack of faith in one's ability to work!

(SECOND FARMER *moves away.)*

RIP: Please. Listen. Our valley is young. There shall be droughts again. There shall be storms that will drown the tops of corn stalks. There shall be disease and death and hatred and sin. And this shall be as we, our valley, grow old. As a boat in a storm we can't abandon ship, but must weather the winds and the rocks and the tides of the moon, we must work our masts, scoop the seawater out of our hulls, we must work until our hands are stubs. This work may not save our harvest, but it will show what kind of men we are. Look for hope only here! *(Raises his hand)* Hope is a calloused hand! *(Short pause)* It is easy to complain, it is hard to work hard. God gave us sleep as our reward for work. If we do not sleep well, if we wake up tearful, lamenting, and complaining, it is only because we have not worked hard enough. *(Pause)* Try to run to a greener valley, but where do you run when it too has a drought? We could rebuild a works and hire ourselves as laborers and depend upon other valleys to buy what we make. But as farmers, we can depend upon ourselves. We need no one else. We need but two hands, a neck that aches, legs that crumble from tiredness, and there in our fields, stooped and ready to die, we will have breathed our last breath out of exhaustion and we will know then what it means to work as only men can. And only then shall we die men. God put us here on earth not to dream, not to hope, not to run away and hide, but to sweat and to die.... That is our purpose. *(Pause)* Come, there's work to be—

(Suddenly DUTCH *takes his hoe and smashes it on the table.)*

RIP: Wait. Wait. Wrong!

*(*FARMERS *open the door. Loud, angry crowd grows.)*

Scene Five (a)

(A street. GRETCHEN *enters with the letter. She cries.)*

GRETCHEN: Oh God! Oh God! Meenie!!!! Meenie!!!!

(Sobs. RIP *hobbles in; his face is cut.)*

RIP: There you are. Where's Meenie and the boy? We've got to go. It's madness. They would have killed me. Friends. They call themselves friends. Come on, if we can make it across the hills, we can sit and wait this thing out. I've never seen anything like it. The whole town's spooked. Get up! Get up! What's the matter with you?

GRETCHEN: Look. *(Hands him the letter)*

RIP: Thank God, they must have known. Hurry. Hurry. *(Tries to pull her)*

GRETCHEN: Why didn't they tell me?!! Why'd they have to leave a letter?!!!

RIP: It's the best thing they could have done, Gretchen.

GRETCHEN: I want to see the boy!!!!!

RIP: Come on, if we move fast enough maybe we can catch them as they come through the pass. It's quicker over the hills.

GRETCHEN: Catch them?

RIP: Or just follow 'em to Ohio. I don't know, Gretchen, we can't stay here!!

GRETCHEN: You'll come with me?

RIP: Of course, I'm coming. What do you think I've been saying? I'm not going to stay put and be crucified. Come on, we'll need some sacks from your house. They'll be on their way to my house by now. Expect to see it burning by the time we reach the woods.

GRETCHEN: What's happened? What's happened?

RIP: Come with me.

*(*GRETCHEN *suddenly stops. Looks at* RIP*)*

GRETCHEN: With you? *(Pause)*

RIP: We'll catch 'em. *(Pause)*

GRETCHEN: Look at your face.

RIP: I've seen the devil. Hurry. Hurry.

(They go.)

Scene Five (b)

(The same. Half hour later. LAWYER *and* PAUL*, standing together. Down the road come two* FARMERS.*)*

PAUL: Gone.

LAWYER: Better for us. Could have been messy.

FIRST FARMER: *(To* SECOND FARMER:*)* Half way to New York by now.

SECOND FARMER: We should have known, what with him buying a wagon.

FIRST FARMER: *He must think we're real stupid.*

SECOND FARMER: Not stupid, just weak. Hurry. We might still catch him.

(They run out.)

POSTMASTER: *(Entering)* Gone?

*(*PAUL *nods.)*

PAUL: Would have been easier if he'd just stepped aside on his own. But at least it's done.

POSTMASTER: Better this way—clean break. New beginning. They're ransacking his house.

LAWYER: As long as it's just his house.

POSTMASTER: Poor Rip. What if they catch up with him?

LAWYER: He's got a good head start.

PAUL: Watch that "poor Rip" talk. Don't want a backlash. Folks can turn sentimental as fast as they can turn angry.

LAWYER: We'll have to keep our fingers in the air, seeing how the wind blows.

POSTMASTER: And if it starts blowing at us?

LAWYER: We'll turn and blow with 'em. We could always name the works after him.

PAUL: After who?

LAWYER: After Rip. The Van Winkle Works. If they start getting nervous about what they've done, that should soothe their throbbing consciences.

POSTMASTER: The Van Winkle Works. I like that.

PAUL: Could have a little ceremony. Once things get calmer.

POSTMASTER: It's the least we could do.

LAWYER: The least.

POSTMASTER: Bring the valley together. A fresh start. It's for the good of the valley.

PAUL: And what's the good for the valley, is good for everyone.

LAWYER: Come. Let's go and get down to work.

(They leave.)

Scene Six (a)

(The hills. Evening. Wind. DERRICK *enters.)*

DERRICK: *(Calling)* Ho! Ho! Shepherd, ho! *(To himself:)* I've watched one hundred ants race in circles and dance in lines. They know what's coming. They know what's coming. I've witnessed the sky, with white puffs billowing and dark puffs born from underneath. From these two observations, I know it will rain. Between the lowly ants of the earth and the high clouds of the sky, one needs nothing in between. *(Calls)* Ho! Ho! *(To himself:)* Time tells itself one need not ask a man for the time.

(SHEPHERD *runs in.)*

SHEPHERD: I'm here. I'm here. Though I've left my breath back there.

DERRICK: Then it'll be washed away. I've been calling.

SHEPHERD: And I've been running.

DERRICK: And I've been looking.

SHEPHERD: And I've been running.

DERRICK: And I've been waiting.

SHEPHERD: And I've been running.

DERRICK: Then your feet are as slow as your mind. Look at the sky.

SHEPHERD: Ah.

DERRICK: It's going to rain.

SHEPHERD: Yes.

DERRICK: And there'll be wind.

SHEPHERD: Yes.

DERRICK: And lightning and blasts of thunder.

SHEPHERD: Yes, that too.

DERRICK: So?

SHEPHERD: So?

DERRICK: Are you a shepherd or not?

SHEPHERD: I am a shepherd. Yes, I am a shepherd.

DERRICK: Then are you a good shepherd?

SHEPHERD: A good shepherd? Let me think. What's a good shepherd?

DERRICK: One who knows that sheep and goats run off when it thunders.

SHEPHERD: Oh, I know that. Then I'm a good shepherd.

DERRICK: Then you know that a good shepherd gathers his flock together when it thunders.

SHEPHERD: Oh, I know that too.

DERRICK: Then do it.

SHEPHERD: Done.

DERRICK: What do you mean—done? That's why I've been calling you, to tell you what to do.

SHEPHERD: And that's why I've been running, gathering up the goats. One doesn't have to watch the sky to know it will pour tonight.

DERRICK: No?

SHEPHERD: It always pours tonight. Because of the spirits. Tonight is the night. Even the stupidest men know that. My brother knows that.

DERRICK: You know that there are spirits?

SHEPHERD: I know what I know. And that tonight is the night. Every fifteen years the spirits of a man callèd Hudson and his crew, they light the sky and crack the ears.

DERRICK: How is that?

SHEPHERD: They light their pipes and play tenpins. Tonight's the night. I know.

DERRICK: You head has sweat your brains, shepherd. And I suppose tonight your wolf becomes a prince?

SHEPHERD: A prince? Why would a wolf become a prince? That only happens in fairy stories. I am no child. I don't believe in fairy stories. No. The wolf is still a wolf. And that's next. I will now look for the wolf, but had to gather the goats first. Then the wolf. I'll wait and watch for him. And the spirits.

DERRICK: You might as well look to yourself for a thought as look for spirits

SHEPHERD: No, they are here. I've seen 'em.

DERRICK: Seen what?

SHEPHERD: Two spirits. One an old man and one a woman, that's the shape they've taken for tonight.

DERRICK: What did you say to these spirits?

SHEPHERD: I only watched. I'm scared to talk to spirits.

DERRICK: Then how do you know they're spirits, shepherd?

SHEPHERD: Because they're here tonight! But if you want, I can prove it to you, though proving spirits is like proving the sun will shine. It just is.

DERRICK: How can you prove they are spirits.

SHEPHERD: They don't bleed. It's like knifing smoke or water to knife a spirit. They don't cry out. That is how you prove. I go. I go. *(Runs off)*

DERRICK: Shepherd, wait!... Ah, let him go chase the shadows of trees, that is all that's up here tonight. *(Long pause)* Wind. Blow. *(Pause)* It will rain. And make everything soft. Like a sponge. Or a face. *(He goes.)*

Scene Six (b)

(The hills. Evening. RIP *and* GRETCHEN *enter.)*

GRETCHEN: Rip, are you crying?

RIP: I'm hating. I can't keep the hate down my throat. Every time I take a deep breath it claws its way up my neck. I shouldn't have looked back. Maybe we should sit and rest.

GRETCHEN: Why? I can walk. I can walk.

RIP: Your eyes keep closing. *(He falls.)* Ahhh!

GRETCHEN: What happened?

RIP: I stepped in a hole.

GRETCHEN: Give me your hand.

*(*RIP *turns.)*

GRETCHEN: What is it?

RIP: I thought I heard someone. *(Listens)* No.

GRETCHEN: Who would be up here? You don't think they're following you?

RIP: "The Lord is my shepherd; I shall not want.
He maketh me to lie down in green pastures.
He leadeth me beside the still waters; He restoreth my soul.
He leadeth me in the paths of righteousness for His name's sake.
Yea, though I walk through the valley of the shadow of death,
I will fear no evil: for thou art with me:
Thy rod and they staff they comfort me." *(He looks up.)* Look. Up there.
Past the moon. Clouds. When's the last time we've seen clouds?

GRETCHEN: Could be a night mist. Sh-sh! Listen!

(Distant howl)

GRETCHEN: There. Let's go.

RIP: I think we should rest.

GRETCHEN: We'll have the rest of our lives to rest once we catch up with them. Come on.

RIP: I want to sit for a minute.

GRETCHEN: I'll walk on ahead. You can catch up.

RIP: No. Stay with me. Sit.

(She does.)

RIP: Put your head on my lap. I'd like that.

(She does.)

RIP: Comfortable? Any rocks?

(She shakes her head.)

RIP: Let me get the hair out of your eyes. *(Short pause)* The dark is nice. I like it best like this. With all the blackness you can still dream of light. But in the day, with all the light, all you see is black.

(She has fallen asleep.)

RIP: I've forgotten how much a sleeping woman looks like an angel.

(SHEPHERD enters.)

RIP: Who's there?! Who's there?!

SHEPHERD: Oh. Oh. The spirit's seen me. Hide. Hide. *(Runs off)*

RIP: *(Whispers)* Hello? Hello? *(Short pause)* The wind's really come up.

(Pause; thunder)

RIP: What?

(Thunder)

RIP: Again! Gretchen. *(Shakes her)* Gretchen!!!!!

GRETCHEN: What? What is it?

RIP: Listen!!!!!

GRETCHEN: To what? I don't hear anything. The wagon? You heard the wagon?!

RIP: No. No. Sh-sh. Listen. *(Thunder)* Hear it? Hear it? *(Thunder)*

GRETCHEN: Thunder?

RIP: Yes.

GRETCHEN: Thunder.

RIP: Yes!

GRETCHEN: It's not the wagon. It's thunder.

RIP: Gretchen, it's going to rain.

GRETCHEN: Is it? *(Short pause)*

RIP: Listen... Hear it?

GRETCHEN: Do you know if they bought a covered wagon?

RIP: It's raining, Gretchen.

GRETCHEN: Maybe we should find some cover. We'll get wet.

RIP: Some cover? Gretchen we don't have to look for cover. It's raining!

GRETCHEN: Yes.

RIP: Don't you know what that means?

GRETCHEN: We'll get wet.

RIP: Get up. Come on, get up. It's raining!!! *(Laughs)* Dear God—"I have heard of thee by the hearing of the ear, but now my eyes see Thee!" Hurry, we can be back by dawn. Gretchen, feel it! Rain!!!!

GRETCHEN: So?

RIP: We'll let them see who has not flinched, who has not wavered, but has stood the ground. Let this be their lesson and let them be the better for it. We'll plow and plant by the moon if we have to. But there will be a harvest!! Get up. Hurry. Let's go.

GRETCHEN: I'm not going.

RIP: What do you mean, you're not going? It's raining. Feel it. It rains!!!

GRETCHEN: I'm not going.

RIP: What's the matter with you? Don't you understand? The drought's over, Gretchen. There will be no reason to start up the works. Because it rains!!! We have struggled and suffered and God has said—enough. Enough. There's no reason anymore to keep running.

GRETCHEN: There is for me. Rain or no rain.

RIP: Look, we'll call back Meenie. I'll send a wagon. Ten wagons! They'll come back.

GRETCHEN: I'm not going, Rip.

(Long pause. RIP *backs away from* GRETCHEN.*)*

RIP: *(Suddenly screams)* Gretchen, don't destroy this for me!!!!!!!

GRETCHEN: I don't wish to destroy anything.

RIP: My life and work's down there. God in His great compassion has given me it all back. I can't deny Him!!!!

GRETCHEN: Then go.

RIP: They'll come back!

GRETCHEN: Leave me.

RIP: Don't be stupid. I can't leave you up here.

GRETCHEN: Go. Go.

RIP: Do you hate me so much?!

GRETCHEN: *(Screams:)* No!!!!!!!!!!!!

RIP: I don't understand how you can do this to me!!!

GRETCHEN: *(Crying)* I'm not doing anything to you!

RIP: Has nothing changed? From the beginning, you've done your best to keep me crawling. Keep me on my knees and begging!!!! *(Erupts)* What did Derrick do, pay you to keep me up here so the two of you can steal my land again?!!!!

GRETCHEN: That's not fair, Rip. Meenie!!!! She's all I have.

RIP: Maybe I'm her father and maybe I'm not.

GRETCHEN: How can you!!!! Leave me!!!!

RIP: It'd serve you right if I did.

GRETCHEN: I've been alone up here before!

RIP: Doing what? Whoring with Derrick?!!!!!!!

(She slaps him.)

RIP: Still scratching like a rabid dog. *(Short pause. He hits her.)*

(She screams.)

GRETCHEN: I was up here looking for you!

RIP: What?

GRETCHEN: For you!!!!!

RIP: Right. Don't weight your soul with any more lies, or it'll be so heavy it won't be able to fly a foot!

GRETCHEN: *(Sobbing)* For five years I looked. I'm up here every day. Every day. First, I'm looking for the body of my husband. Then just the bones. Until mad or half-crazed, I don't know, and one day my legs seem to break and my head, it goes dark and I wake up months later in a bed.

RIP: I don't know what you're talking about!

GRETCHEN: And while I was ill, they told me later how they'd dug my grave. And Derrick, he's taken Meenie as a ward, and so still in bed, I married him, because of being so kind.

RIP: Have you no shame? Why do I want to hear this?

GRETCHEN: No!!!! You have to listen!!!!! All the time I'm married to Derrick, I don't know what that paper said that he wanted you to sign. I think it's just what they'd told me—a promise to stay sober.

RIP: You're lying. You knew! You knew!!!

GRETCHEN: I knew when you came back, and so I leave Derrick, because I hate him. I leave him not because he lost the works, but because I hate him!!!! And I hate me, for marrying the man who wished to destroy my husband.

(RIP turns away.)

GRETCHEN: Wait!!!! Listen!!!

(He turns back.)

GRETCHEN: And since you've come back, I've done all I could do to do my duty, and be your wife.

RIP: Gretchen, please.

GRETCHEN: I've tried to be a good wife, Rip. God knows how I've tried; He knows how many years I've been sending Meenie to see you.

RIP: You?... I don't understand.

GRETCHEN: No. I not only knew, but I sent her. I wanted you to see your child. Watch her grow. Be her father. And I used her visits to learn about you—I know what you eat. How you dress. In my mind, I've nursed you when you've been sick. I've watched you for hours through her words; and heard your voice speak in her mouth.

RIP: No. No. Gretchen...?

GRETCHEN: No. Don't say anything!... Haven't you ever noticed flowers on your table? Shirts in your dresser that have been washed? A polished floor? Hot bread in your kitchen and wondered how did this all happen?

RIP: I thought Meenie....

GRETCHEN: It happened while you were in the field and I've come into your home and worked like a wife in the only way I could. I was determined to be your wife, Rip, though without ever seeing you until today.

RIP: I don't understand. Why didn't Meenie ever tell me?

GRETCHEN: Because I wouldn't let her. I was afraid then I'd have to see you. It seemed better like this.

RIP: Then come with me now. Be my wife.

GRETCHEN: *(Crying)* No.

RIP: *(Erupts)* Why not?!!!!!

GRETCHEN: I've lived without you and can again, but the thought of life without Meenie and her boy, is a thought I couldn't live. Go. Leave me! Please, Rip. I've hurt you, don't let me hurt you more. Meenie and the boy are all I have; they're what I am. I have not hurt them—yet. Go. I won't ask you to come with me, because I understand: it rains, it rains. Go. Go... Bye. *(She hurries off.)*

RIP: Gretchen! Gretchen!

(He hesitates looks up at the rain. Thunder and lightning)

RIP: Gretchen, wait!!!!... Wait!!!!... Stop, Stop!!!!!!!

(Thunder and lightning. He starts to go in her direction. The SHEPHERD *hurries in and stabs* RIP *in the back.* RIP *groans and falls. Thunder and lightning)*

SHEPHERD: *(Looks at his knife)* Blood. Blood. Must be only part spirit. Because he groans too. Yes, he groans. But does he hurt? I think no, 'cause spirits don't hurt. I better tell Derrick that I have caught us a spirit. And a spirit's even better than a wolf. Ho! Ho!

(Runs out. Storm. DERRICK *enters.)*

DERRICK: Shepherd! Shepherd! With this thunder I've seen two goats already run from the herd. And if this rain keeps up this will be a hill of mud and it'll be hell to unstuck them. Shepherd! *(Sees* RIP.*)* What's this? A man. A curious place for a man in a rainstorm. In a rain a tree can sprout new limbs, though I think a man should not have such hopes. Hello? Hello?

Are you asleep?... He doesn't answer. He may be asleep or maybe not. Hello? Are you dead?

(RIP *groans.)*

DERRICK: He groans so he's not dead. I'll get closer. *(Looks at* RIP. *Long pause)* This face. I think I know it. *(Short pause)* And if there's one thing I know it's that I know faces. I see them all the time. When I close my eyes I see them too. I think this is one that I have seen with my eyes closed. *(Pause. Looks at Rip:)* Wait. He's saying something....

RIP: Gretchen...

DERRICK: Gretchen? He says "Gretchen". Now there's a name I know very well. My answer's yes. Yes. If the question is if I have heard of a Gretchen. It is yes. Wait. He's speaking again

RIP: Gretchen. Gretchen.

DERRICK: Oh. Gretchen Gretchen. Now that is a name I do not know. I once knew a Benjamin Benjamin, but I have never known a Gretchen Gretchen. I am sorry. But come, this is no place to get acquainted. Let's get out of this rain before the mud rises like a tide.... I know your face...and we both know a Gretchen, though you know both a Gretchen and a Gretchen Gretchen. But still we have much in common. Come, I'll sit you down in a chair and talk to you and if you die I'll keep the bugs off you 'til you rot. Come. Come. You look sleepy. Here put this on. *(Puts his coat on him)* It rains. Come.

(DERRICK *carries* RIP *off.)*

Scene Six (c)

(The hills. Rain. Wind. SHEPHERD *runs in.)*

SHEPHERD: Ahh! Ahh! Oh Lord, I have been looking for Derrick, but the Spirit has found him first. It lives. It lives. It bleeds but it lives. And it has killed Derrick. I know him by his coat. It drags him here. Poor Derrick. It must have been a terrible struggle. Poor me. It comes for me. I'm next. It has been roused and a spirit roused must be nothing nice. I'll fight back. I'll fight. Kill. Kill. Kill. Kill. I know what to do. Surprise. Surprise. Here it comes. My skin wants to hide in my bones.

(Hides. DERRICK *carries in* RIP.)

DERRICK: You are heavier than a goat because a goat I can carry far. I have to set you down for a while. Though here is not where I'd like to be. *(Sets him down)* So tell me—are you alive? I think you breathe but that maybe is the rain bouncing on your chest. I have a nice shack, when we get there you will be dry. Talk to me, I'd like some hot breath against my face.

SHEPHERD: *(From his hiding place)* Oh clever. Clever. The spirit has taken Derrick's voice. I know that voice, it has been stolen from him. It is a trick to get me. But I can play the trick too.

DERRICK: No? Then I will talk to you and that might loosen your tongue. Soon we will know everything about each other. It's nice to have a face in front of me even when I don't close my eyes.

SHEPHERD: *(Coming out of hiding)* Ho! Ho!

DERRICK: There you are, shepherd. I'd been calling. Two goats are loose in this rain.

SHEPHERD: They won't get far. I've been watching for the wolf. Remember the wolf?

DERRICK: Yes, I remember the wolf.

SHEPHERD: That body wears a nice coat. Just like Derrick's.

DERRICK: It is mine.

SHEPHERD: Of course. Of course. What one wins one keeps.

DERRICK: I found him down the way.

SHEPHERD: I know—you find them where you find them. It must have been a struggle. He was a strong man.

DERRICK: What are you talking about? There was no struggle. Though he moans, he doesn't move. I was about to tell him a story while we rested.

SHEPHERD: Is that your code to take off his head? When you say tell him a story, do you really mean take off his head? I've heard it said that instead of balls you people bowl heads.

DERRICK: Why are you talking like this?

SHEPHERD: You look like him too. How you people change shape.

DERRICK: Look, go find the goats. Go! go!

SHEPHERD: Can you breathe fire too? Or will I just drop dead because of your invisible hands?

DERRICK: Didn't you hear me? I told you to go! Go!

SHEPHERD: I'm going. I know that. I have no hope. As soon as I knew you were after me, I knew I must go.

DERRICK: Idiot, go! Get away from me. Why are you looking at me like that? Go!!

SHEPHERD: I'm going. But I will go like Derrick did. I will go screaming.

(Screams. He stabs DERRICK, *who collapses.)*

SHEPHERD: He bleeds. He bleeds. I did not expect this. I expected smoke to come out of his eyes and choke me. What do I do? What do I do? I'll get my brother, he'll know what to do.

(SHEPHERD *runs out.* DERRICK *gasps. Long pause)*

DERRICK: *(To* RIP*)* There is this story I wanted to tell you. Because I saw it in your face. There are stories in people's faces, Rip. See, I know who you are. I know who you are. We have much in common. Listen. *(Cringes in pain)* Once there were two brothers; the first was strong, handsome and wise; the second weak, ugly and stupid. One day the stupid brother was slicing an apple with his penknife and as his mind was not on what he was doing, his hand slipped and he cut off his finger. His wise brother used all of his wisdom trying to put the finger back on, but it just kept falling off. The stupid brother just cried and cried. Then something amazing happened, out of this finger grew first a whole hand, then an arm, then a chest, a body with legs, and finally a head and a face. So now the wise brother had two brothers, both weak, ugly and stupid. And he worked very hard to feed them both.

Months went by, until one day the three brothers were cutting wheat with a scythe. It was a hot day and one of the stupid brothers was not paying attention to what he was doing and his hand slipped and he cut off a finger. The wise brother felt terrible and used all of his wisdom trying to put the finger back on but it just kept falling off. Then suddenly from this finger grew another whole brother who was weak, ugly, and stupid.

This happened many more times until the wise brother had one hundred weak and ugly and stupid brothers all of which he had to feed. He worked and worked trying to feed his brothers, until he could not work anymore. Then the wise brother in his great wisdom got an idea. In the middle of the night he snuck away to the woods, took out his penknife and cut off his finger and set it on the ground and waited for it to grow a new body, one that would be handsome, strong and wise. He waited and waited. He became weak because of the blood rushing from his hand. And then he died. When the other brothers found him and saw the finger, they were amazed. And they said to each other: "Here all the time we thought our brother was very wise, but only a stupid man would cut off his own finger."

(He laughs. He becomes quiet. He sits. Leans over. He dies. Silence. Rain. The earth has become mud. RIP *stirs. Slowly sits up.)*

RIP: Hurt. Hurt. The back. Like something's been biting the back. Ahhh! Hurt... Where am...? How long have I been here? What's this? *(To* DERRICK:*)* Get up! Get up! *(He struggles to get up.)* We got work. Got a crop to plant. Get up! *(Kicks* DERRICK*)* You. Get back into the fields. This is not time to... God, He gave us the strength to... *(Suddenly stares at* DERRICK.*)* You. You. No. No. I dream. Hurt. Gretchen. Gretchen!!!!!!!! *(Stumbles and falls. To* DERRICK*)* Fade. You are smoke. *(Pause. He looks around, unable to get up.)*

BROADWAY PLAY PUBLISHING INC

TOP TEN BEST SELLING FULL-LENGTH PLAYS AND FULL-LENGTH PLAY COLLECTIONS

AVEN'U BOYS

THE BROTHERS KARAMAZOV

THE IMMIGRANT

ONE FLEA SPARE

ON THE VERGE

PLAYS BY TONY KUSHNER
(CONTAINING A BRIGHT ROOM CALLED DAY
& THE ILLUSION)

PLAYS BY AISHAH RAHMAN
(CONTAINING THE MOJO AND THE SAYSO,
UNFINISHED WOMEN...,
& ONLY IN AMERICA)

PRELUDE TO A KISS

TALES OF THE LOST FORMICANS

TO GILLIAN ON HER 37TH BIRTHDAY

BROADWAY PLAY PUBLISHING INC

PLAYWRIGHTS' COLLECTIONS

PLAYS BY NEAL BELL

MCTEAGUE: A TALE OF SAN FRANCISCO
RAGGED DICK
THÉRÈSE RAQUIN

PLAYS BY ALAN BOWNE

BEIRUT
FORTY-DEUCE
SHARON AND BILLY

PLAYS BY LONNIE CARTER

LEMUEL
GULLIVER
GULLIVER REDUX

PLAYS BY STEVE CARTER

DAME LORRAINE
HOUSE OF SHADOWS
MIRAGE
ONE LAST LOOK
TEA ON INAUGURATION DAY

PLAYS BY ANTHONY CLARVOE

LET'S PLAY TWO
THE LIVING
SHOW AND TELL

PLAYS BY DONALD FREED

ALFRED AND VICTORIA: A LIFE
CHILD OF LUCK
IS HE STILL DEAD?

PLAYS BY ALLAN HAVIS

HOSPITALITY
MINK SONATA
MOROCCO

PLAYS BY ALLAN HAVIS, VOLUME TWO

A DARING BRIDE
THE LADIES OF FISHER COVE
SAINTE SIMONE

PLAYS BY TONY KUSHNER

A BRIGHT ROOM CALLED DAY
THE ILLUSION

PLAYS BY RICHARD NELSON EARLY PLAYS VOLUME ONE

CONJURING AN EVENT
JUNGLE COUP
THE KILLING OF YABLONSKI
SCOOPING

PLAYS BY RICHARD NELSON EARLY PLAYS VOLUME TWO

BAL
THE RETURN OF PINOCCHIO
THE VIENNA NOTES

PLAYS BY RICHARD NELSON EARLY PLAYS VOLUME THREE

AN AMERICAN COMEDY
JITTERBUGGING: SCENES OF SEX IN A NEW SOCIETY
RIP VAN WINKLE, OR "THE WORKS"

PLAYS BY LOUIS PHILLIPS

BONE THE SPEED
CARWASH
CONRAD ON THE VINE
ETHIOPIA
THE MAN WHO ATE EINSTEIN'S BRAIN
PRECISION MACHINES

PLAYS BY AISHAH RAHMAN

THE MOJO AND THE SAYSO
ONLY IN AMERICA
UNFINISHED WOMEN CRY IN NO MAN'S LAND WHILE A BIRD DIES IN A GILDED CAGE

PLAYS BY EDWIN SÁNCHEZ

CLEAN
FLOOR SHOW: DOÑA SOL AND HER TRAINED DOG
TRAFFICKING IN BROKEN HEARTS

PLAYS BY NAOMI WALLACE

IN THE HEART OF AMERICA
SLAUGHTER CITY
THE WAR BOYS

BROADWAY PLAY PUBLISHING INC

ADAPTATIONS OF THE CLASSICS

ALKI (PEER GYNT)

ANYTHING TO DECLARE?

THE BROTHERS KARAMAZOV

A CHRISTMAS CAROL

DEAD SOULS

DON JUAN

DON QUIXOTE DE LA JOLLA

THE FATHER

FIGARO/FIGARO

FRANK LANGELLA'S CYRANO

IL CAMPIELO

THE ILLUSION

JITTERBUGGING: SCENES OF SEX FROM A NEW SOCIETY (LA RONDE)

MAN OF THE FLESH (DON JUAN)

THE MARRIAGE OF FIGARO

MCTEAGUE: A TALE OF SAN FRANCISCO

PLAYBOY OF THE WEST INDIES

THE PROMISE (THE DYBBUK)

THÉRÈSE RAQUIN

THREE SISTERS